## Child Soldiers
### Sierra Leone's Revolutionary United Front

Tragically, violence and armed conflict have become commonplace in the lives of many children around the world. Not only have millions of children been forced to witness war and its atrocities, but many are drawn into conflict as active participants. Nowhere has this been more evident than in Sierra Leone during its 11-year civil war. Drawing upon in-depth interviews and focus groups with former child soldiers of Sierra Leone's rebel Revolutionary United Front, Myriam Denov compassionately examines how child soldiers are initiated into the complex world of violence and armed conflict. She also explores the ways in which the children leave this world of violence and the challenges they face when trying to renegotiate their lives and self-concepts in the aftermath of war. The narratives of the Sierra Leonean youth demonstrate that their life histories defy the narrow and limiting portrayals presented by the media and popular discourse.

MYRIAM DENOV is an Associate Professor at McGill University. She holds a Ph.D. from the University of Cambridge where she was a Commonwealth Scholar.

D1091977

# Child Soldiers

## Sierra Leone's Revolutionary United Front

MYRIAM DENOV
*McGill University*

CAMBRIDGE
UNIVERSITY PRESS

CAMBRIDGE UNIVERSITY PRESS
Cambridge, New York, Melbourne, Madrid, Cape Town, Singapore, São Paulo, Delhi

Cambridge University Press
The Edinburgh Building, Cambridge CB2 8RU, UK

Published in the United States of America by Cambridge University Press, New York

www.cambridge.org
Information on this title: www.cambridge.org/9780521693219

First published 2010

Printed in the United Kingdom at the University Press, Cambridge

*A catalogue record for this publication is available from the British Library*

*Library of Congress Cataloguing in Publication data*
Denov, Myriam S.
The making and unmaking of child soldiers in Sierra Leone / by Myriam Denov.
   p.   cm.
Includes bibliographical references.
ISBN 978-0-521-87224-9 – ISBN 978-0-521-69321-9 (pbk.)
1. Child soldiers – Sierra Leone – Interviews.   2. Revolutionary United Front –
Biography.   3. Sierra Leone – History – Civil War, 1991–2002 – Personal
narratives.   4. Sierra Leone – History – Civil War, 1991–2002 – Participation,
Juvenile.   5. Life change events – Sierra Leone – Case studies.   6. Self-perception –
Sierra Leone – Case studies.   7. Sierra Leone – Biography.   8. Sierra Leone – Social
conditions – 1961–   9. Children and war – Case studies.   I. Title.
DT516.827.D46 2010
966.404–dc22

                                                              2009054028

ISBN 978-0-521-87224-9 Hardback
ISBN 978-0-521-69321-9 Paperback

*À ma petite Léoni*

# Contents

# Acknowledgements

First and foremost, my deepest thanks, admiration and gratitude go to the young men and women whose lives and experiences are highlighted in this book, as well as the youth focus group leaders. These extraordinary young people offered their time and insights, and were unwavering in their commitment to this project. They opened their lives to complete strangers and, in doing so, enriched our own. I was constantly moved and humbled by their strength, candour and unbounded intelligence. I owe them all a debt of gratitude and can only hope that this work does justice to their trust, generosity, power and resilience.

For their generous financial support during the course of this research, I would like to thank the Social Science and Humanities Research Council of Canada, and the Child Rights and Protection Unit at the Canadian International Development Agency (CIDA). At CIDA, I was fortunate to work with individuals whose commitment to issues of children's rights and to this project was unmatched. In particular, I would like to thank Micheál Montgomery for his steadfast support, his dedication and assistance during the course of the research. Micheál, your friendship has meant the world to me.

In 2005, I presented a paper at Columbia University for the Research Initiative on Small Arms entitled 'The Making and Unmaking of Child Soldiers in Sierra Leone'. It was the helpful commentary and feedback that I received from conference participants that encouraged me to embark on this much larger book-writing project.

I owe a profound debt of gratitude to my dear friend and colleague Abdul Manaff Kemokai. Over the years, Manaff has generously offered his insight and wisdom, introduced me to groups of war-affected young people, and patiently and enthusiastically taken the time to show me the beauty and complexities of Sierra Leone. Heartfelt thanks also go to Tom Beah, John Caulker, Pa Momo Fofanah, John Kamara, Ansumana Konneh, Momo Turay and Moses Zombo for their guidance during the research process, their kindness and, most especially, their friendship.

Two people deserve special mention. They have been my mentors, challenging me intellectually and providing me with numerous forms of professional and personal support. Richard Maclure played a key role in the project upon which this book is based. He travelled with me to Sierra Leone and experienced alongside me the highs and lows of field-work. It has been my good fortune to work with such a brilliant and committed scholar, and such a kind person. Susan McKay's ground-breaking work on war-affected girls has been essential to informing my own. Far more than that, however, Susan has been a constant source of support and insight, and a much-needed sounding board for the many issues that arose during the course of this research, as well as the book-writing process. Richard and Susan, thank you for your friend-ship and your guidance.

I am grateful to Alusine Bah, Simon Atem, Deng Majok and Ken Sango – each of you has provided me with great insights and kindness and it is truly a gift to have you in my life. I would also like to thank Jennifer Brown, Kathryn Campbell, Vera Chrobok, Jessica Rich and Christina Yeung. Despite great distance, and my frequent lapses in communication due to a new baby and the realities of writing, these exceptional women have been an unvarying source of friendship and encouragement.

I am very fortunate to have wonderful colleagues at McGill University who make going into work a pleasure. Special thanks go to Sharon Bond, Shari Brotman, Sydney Duder, Estelle Hopmeyer, Nicole Ives, Julia Krane, Tamara Sussman and Jim Torczyner for their support, laughter and encouragement. Thanks are also due to Alana Bonner, Arlene Cohen, Lydia El-Cherif, Lillian Iannone, Elizabeth Ierfino, Marilena Orsini and Maria Pacheco, whose daily support and cheer has made my time at McGill so enriching.

I am enormously grateful to my editors, John Haslam, Tom O'Reilly and Carrie Parkinson at Cambridge University Press, who patiently and supportively awaited the final delivery of the manuscript. Their assis-tance and tenacity have been greatly appreciated. I am also thankful to the anonymous reviewers for their thorough and insightful reading of the text, and their helpful suggestions.

Many other individuals, from near and from far, have offered invalu-able help along the way. I am deeply indebted to Catherine Bryan, Tamsyn Farr, Sofia Gutierrez-Isaza, Lindsay Jones and Inbal Solomon not only for their practical assistance, but also for their kindness, commitment, patience and support. Special thanks also go to Mike Acton, Ron Crelinsten, Peter de Jong and Maria Los.

My family has been an important part of this journey. My late father, Al Denov, inspired creativity and conscience. My parents, Celia Denov and Robert Bell, have supported me every step of the way, and provided boundless encouragement. Myna Denov, Josh Holowach and Nancy Zboch have been a constant source of love, encouragement and laughter, and to them I owe a huge debt of thanks. Leah Richards read early drafts of the text and, despite illness, provided me with helpful feedback. To André, who endured the long and sometimes arduous writing marathon alongside me. Your wit, support and patience sustained me throughout this work, and your keen intellect, critical eye and editorial comments helped to ensure that I did not go too astray. Without you, there truly would be no book. Finally – à ma petite Léoni – who has brought hope, light and laughter. Ce livre est pour toi, ma puce.

# Introduction: Child soldiers, iconography and the (il)logic of extremes

OVER the past decade, images of child soldiers have inundated the popular media. Whether adorning the pages of popular magazines or newspapers, or flashing briefly before us in the form of video clips and news reports, images of boys armed with AK-47s appear ubiquitous, providing a cautionary tale not only of the reality of innocent childhood gone awry, but also of children as profoundly vulnerable, dangerous, victimized, disturbed and sometimes heroic. These images turn commonly held assumptions of protected and innocuous childhood on its head. They may simultaneously evoke collective shock, fear, revulsion, intrigue, pride, horror and sympathy. Such imagery harnesses our attention and compels us to look and perhaps read on momentarily. However, as captivating as these images are, what they obscure and conceal is equally illuminating. We, of course, learn little about the child behind the gun – how he ('he' because rarely are girls portrayed or included in such images) came to pose menacingly with a weapon – the gun essentially defining him. Moreover, we have no sense of what might have happened to the child in the years since the image was captured. What happened to the boy? Did he, as many would predict, grow up to be part of a terrorist organization? A mercenary? A warlord? Did he, seemingly against conventional wisdom and great odds, manage to overcome his violent past and embrace a 'civilian' identity? What about the many war-affected girls who are notably absent from such media depictions? What became of them? Indeed, in the shadows and dimness of such powerful yet formulaic imagery lie profound silences and cavernous empty spaces.

This book explores the lives and realities of a group of former child soldiers in Sierra Leone, both boys and girls, and traces what happened to these children during and following the 11-year civil war. It attempts to fill these silences and empty spaces with children's personal stories and narratives and to put human accounts to the often dehumanizing

1

and pathologizing wartime imagery that we are so accustomed to con-
suming through the media.

What will become evident through the narratives of these Sierra
Leonean youth is that their life histories intensely defy the limiting portrayals offered by media and popular discourse. While these children are
frequently constructed through the logic of extremes (as either extreme
victims, extreme perpetrators or extreme heroes), in reality, the lives,
experiences and identities of these children fall within the messy, ambiguous and paradoxical zones of all three, which proves to be one of the
most challenging aspects to contend with in their post-conflict lives.

## Definitions and ambiguities: Defining 'child soldiers'

Several terms have been used to represent the realities of children
actively implicated and engaged in armed conflict. These terms, which
are often used interchangeably, range from 'child soldiers', to 'children
associated with fighting forces'. It must be said, however, that neither of
these terms adequately captures the realities of children implicated in
war and both terms are inherently problematic. While the term 'child
soldier' encapsulates the paradox of children's involvement in wartime
violence, particularly the blurring of constructed notions of childhood
'innocence' with the brutality and violence of war, defining what is
considered a 'child' is invariably problematic. The United Nations
(UN) Convention on the Rights of the Child defines a child as 'every
human being below eighteen years' (Article 1). However, 'childhood' is
indeed a contested concept and a social construction that varies in form
and content across cultures and social groups, and is defined by loca-
lized understandings and values. Defining a childhood based solely
upon age not only reflects a bias towards western notions of childhood
which are rooted in biomedical theory (Kemper 2005), but also may
overlook other salient cultural, social, economic, gendered, class and
other status determinants that extend well beyond the notion of age. As
Boyden and Levinson (2000) note:

Many different kinds of criteria – although seldom age – are used to demarcate childhood. These criteria include the commencement of work, end of
schooling, onset of menarche, betrothal, and marriage amongst others ...
Further, children in different social classes within the same society may
reach adulthood at different stages, depending on their social and economic
roles. (Boyden and Levinson 2000, p. 28)

Contexts of war render the position of children even more complex because children may acquire the status of an adult as they become sole caretakers of younger children or take on active roles in combat.

To complicate matters further, constructed and formalized definitions of 'child', 'youth', 'adolescent' or 'young people' differ between international organizations and, in some cases, overlap. While the UN Convention on the Rights of the Child considers a child to be anyone under the age of 18, the UN's World Programme of Action for Youth identifies 'youth' as 15–24 years old (United Nations 2005). Moreover, the World Health Organization and the United Nations Children's Fund (UNICEF) differentiate between 'adolescents' (15–19 years old), 'youth' (15–24 years old), and 'young people' (10–24 years old) (World Bank 2007b). Within Sierra Leone, the context to be explored in this book, the Sierra Leone National Youth Policy defines 'youth' as 15–35 years of age (Government of Sierra Leone 2003).[1] Ultimately, defining who is a child is in fact 'a process of negotiations between individuals, family members, peer groups and the wider community in the context of life events and rites of passage' (Mawson 2004, p. 226).

Age is certainly not the only difficulty when considering the concept of 'child soldier'. The term 'soldier' tends to conjure up archetypal symbols of uniformed men with extensive military training in active combat. This image counters the realities of most of the inadequately trained and outfitted child soldiers who fill the ranks of rebel groups in post-colonial wars (Honwana 2006). Moreover, the stereotypical conceptualization of 'soldier' conceals the realities of women and girls' participation in war, as well as the many supporting roles that children take on during conflict as messengers, bodyguards, cooks, spies or porters.

Recognizing the varied roles that children take on in war which extend far beyond combat, the term 'children associated with fighting forces' has been recently introduced into the vernacular. Yet, this term is also problematic as it fails to adequately connote children's active contributions to contemporary war, implying that they remain at the periphery. Also, the use of such a term may deny children who have served in wartime-supporting roles access to programmes provided to those labelled as 'combatants' in the period of disarmament, demobilization and reintegration.

---

[1]  It should be noted, however, that in 2007, the Government of Sierra Leone passed a Child Rights Act that defines children as individuals under 18 years of age.

Importantly, the globalized use and broad encompassing nature of both terms, whether 'child soldiers' or 'children associated with fighting forces', also fail to capture the diversity and nuances of children's wartime realities. While there may be similar experiences, implications and consequences for all children who are exposed to hostilities, regardless of whether they are in the developing or industrialized world, the experiences of a 12-year-old associated with an armed guerilla group in sub-Saharan Africa may be significantly different from a 17-year-old associated with an armed force in the United Kingdom, although both may be perceived as 'child soldiers'. Moreover, although broad definitions are helpful in capturing the global realities of children's involvement in armed conflict, they simultaneously hinder complex understandings of the individualized experiences and realities of war. However, at the same time, when such nuanced and individualized understandings are introduced, further complexity and debate are revealed. As an example, should children involved in armed violence around the world, such as armed children in the Brazilian favelas, Palestinian children involved in stone throwing, and armed gang members in North America who have organized command structures, be considered 'child soldiers'?

While acknowledging its obvious imperfections and contradictions, this book will employ the term 'child soldier' and rely upon the definition provided in 'The Paris Principles',[2] a set of guidelines on children in armed conflict established in 2007 at an international conference in Paris.[3] The conference, organized by the French government and supported by UNICEF, introduced the following designation, which represents the most current internationally recognized definition of the child soldier phenomenon:

[2] These Principles were developed by 'States, human rights actors, humanitarian actors, development actors, military and security actors (state and non-state), associated organisations including UN organisations, other inter-governmental actors, national and international organisations and community-based organisations ... [The Principles] were designed to guide interventions for the protection and well-being of ... children and to assist in making policy and programming decisions ... [T]he principles aim to prevent unlawful recruitment or use of children[,] ... facilitate the release of children associated with armed forces and armed groups[,] ... facilitate the reintegration of all children associated with armed forces and armed groups [and] to ensure the most protective environment for all children' (UNICEF 2007, p. 6).

[3] Similarly despite the earlier-noted imperfections, in this book the definition of a child will coincide with the definition set out in the United Nations Convention on the Rights of the Child (see p. 2). 'Children' refers to both boys and girls.

Any person below 18 years of age who is or who has been recruited or used by an armed force or armed group in any capacity, including but not limited to children, boys and girls, used as fighters, cooks, porters, messengers, spies or for sexual purposes. It does not only refer to a child who is taking or has taken a direct part in hostilities. (UNICEF 2007, p. 7)

According to 'The Paris Principles', the concept of an 'armed force' as noted in the above definition, refers to an armed force of a state, whereas an 'armed group' refers to groups distinct from armed forces as defined by Article 4 of the Optional Protocol to the Convention on the Rights of the Child on the Involvement of Children in Armed Conflict.[4] Noting the distinct differences between the two designations, this book will adhere to these terms throughout.

Definitions and conceptualizations of childhood and child soldiers obviously reflect current knowledge, and are thus continuing to alter and transform over time. Just as the notion of childhood as a social category constitutes a relatively recent concept (Ariès 1962; James and Prout 1990), prior to the induction of international legal instruments, protocols and protections, the recruitment of children into armed conflict was not banned or prohibited. This book aims to contribute to the transformative and changing conceptualizations of child soldiers by attempting to shift the boundaries and limits of our understanding of these young people. By revealing the multi-faceted and paradoxical lives of a group of child soldiers from Sierra Leone, I hope to bring forth a complex image of these children that contradicts the conventional and popular representations, which are highlighted below.

## (Mis)understanding militarized children: Portrayals and representations

The past decade has seen burgeoning popular interest, advocacy and growing scholarly attention to the topic of child soldiers. Yet representing the (il)logic of extremes, children caught up in the cycle of war and

---

[4] The Optional Protocol raised the minimum age for direct participation to 18 for state forces and prohibited the compulsory recruitment of under 18s into national armed forces. The Optional Protocol explicitly prohibits non-state armed groups from both recruiting and using persons until 18. State parties are also obliged to criminalize such activities.

violence have tended to be portrayed by the world's media (whether through written, verbal or visual representation) and by policy discourse in largely contrastive ways as dangerous and disorderly, hapless victims and, most recently, as redeemed heroes. Notably absent from such imagery are girl soldiers, whose invisibility defines them. This powerful iconography and its implications are explored further below.

## Dangerous and disorderly

As noted by several authors including Honwana (2006), Macmillan (2009), Rosen (2009) and Skinner (1999), child soldiers have tended to be stigmatized as dangerous and evil sociopaths – as 'bandits', 'vermin', 'barbarians' and 'monsters' – often fully aware of their actions. In newspaper reports, child soldiers have been described as 'chillingly efficient killing machines' (Schuler 1999), who hold little remorse for their victims: 'Drug crazed child soldiers kill like unfeeling robots' (*The Montreal Gazette* 1999). Particularly apparent when examining discussions of Africa, media reports and discourses suggest that not only is the continent falling prey to a 'new barbarism' (Kaplan 1994), but also that a myriad of interrelated circumstances have created a dangerous new class of armed thugs: 'Ugandan child soldiers have been warped by war' (Wasswa 1997); 'Liberian boy soldiers leave a swathe of ruin' (*The Independent* 1993). Highly racialized and imbued with stereotypes, these child soldiers act as fodder for those 'who seek to present African warfare as inexplicable, brutal and disconnected from the "civilised" world order' (Aning and McIntyre 2004, p. 77).

Moreover, according to such reports, the violence and disarray embodying the actions of child soldiers during conflict are said to be destined to continue in the war's aftermath. Perceived to be lost in a cycle of unrelenting violence, irrationality and iniquity, children who have participated in armed conflict have generally been assumed to be permanently damaged: 'fluent in the language of violence, but ignorant to the rudiments of living in a civil society ... it's often too late to salvage their lives' (*Newsweek* 1995). 'When they do return to civilian life, they are walking ghosts – damaged, uneducated pariahs' (*New York Times* 2006).

Sensational media portrayals of child soldiers as dangerous and disorderly have also influenced the language and thought of policymakers. In a statement to the UN Security Council in January 1996,

Madeleine Albright, the US Ambassador to the UN, expressed outrage at the situation of child soldiers in Liberia who were 'toting automatic weapons, slaughtering innocent civilians, and ignoring the rule of law'. Child soldiers, Albright said, 'have no identity other than through the weapons they carry' (cited in Cain 1999, p. 296). More recently in 2007, the French foreign minister, who was a keynote speaker at a conference on children and armed conflict, warned that child soldiers 'are a time bomb that threatens stability and growth' (BBC News 2007).

By portraying child soldiers as largely threatening and uncivilized, the bulk of international news reporting, and indeed much of academic and policy-oriented discourse, has tended to 'pathologize' children who have been caught up in armed conflict. The images of child soldiers have been used to convey the horror of childhood perverted from its 'natural' course of innocence, fragility and purity.

An example of a child soldier depicted by US authorities as potentially dangerous, pathological and threatening is Omar Khadr, a young Canadian currently being held in Guantanamo Bay, Cuba. Khadr has been held for the past 8 years for allegedly throwing a grenade that killed a US soldier in Afghanistan in 2002, when he was 15 years old. Khadr is the first child in US history to be tried for war crimes including murder, attempted murder, conspiring with Al Qaeda, providing material support for terrorism and spying on US military convoys in Afghanistan. Describing Khadr to the media in 2006, the former US chief military prosecutor Col. Morris Davis declared: 'We'll see evidence when we get into the courtroom of the smiling face Khadr as he builds bombs to kill Americans' (Alberts 2006).

Similar threatening portrayals were given to Johnny and Luther Htoo, the (in)famous twins who in 2001, at the age of 12, were the leaders of a band of Karen rebels known as God's Army against the government of Myanmar. The media referred to the pair as the 'Terror twins' (*Newsweek* 2000) and 'Little lords of the jungle' (Horn 2001) and photos were circulated globally of them smoking cigars – the epitome of dangerous youngsters whose age and pathology appeared to define them.

## The hapless victim

In stark contrast to the construction of child soldiers as dangerous is their portrayal as hapless victims (Macmillan 2009; Rosen 2005;

Shepler 2005). Within this construction, children associated with fighting forces have been depicted as the pawns of deceitful yet powerful warlords, as well as broader undemocratic regimes and social forces. Such children are constructed as 'traumatized children', 'permanently scarred' (*The Ottawa Citizen* 1998), 'lost young souls' (*The Los Angeles Times* 1999), generally evoking deep compassion. Such imagery draws from some of our most fundamental and romanticized contemporary western conceptions of childhood and its association with innocence, vulnerability and the need for protection. Children are cast as wholly dependent, helpless and victimized – ultimately deserving of our sympathy.

Several authors have noted that representations of child soldiers as quintessential victims have been strategically propagated by some non-government organizations (NGOs) in order to capture world attention to the issue (McIntyre 2003; Rosen 2005). While not all NGOs propagate the image of child soldiers as victims, Machel (cited in McIntyre 2003) has nonetheless maintained that 'in an effort to publicise a relief programme or organisation, or even make a political point, ex-child soldiers have been asked to pose with guns [and] ... humanitarian organisations have been known to comply with requests from film makers and journalists to talk to ... children with "more traumatic" stories' (p. 9). Acting as visual indices of vulnerability and need that transcend culture and politics (Burman 1994), children's innocent faces, particularly those offset by a menacing AK-47, demand responses. Positioned alone and out of place in a situation that is not of their making, child soldiers come to represent a compelling illustration of adult wrongdoing. As Brocklehurst (2006) notes: 'particular images of children seem to symbolize or concretize at least the horror of a situation in the mind of the observer' (p. 17). Moreover, framed within the context of victimhood, the propagation of such imagery may, in some contexts, work to promote donor support for the issue, increase public outrage and response and, in the aftermath of war, facilitate child soldier demobilization, community acceptance, reintegration and even compensation, thus propelling some NGO agendas.

While such imagery may help to garner international attention and advocacy for child soldiers, it nonetheless has important implications. Burman (1994, p. 246) has named the imagery of children used in Third World emergencies as 'the iconography of emergencies', or 'disaster pornography' – a term that describes the gruesome fascination with depicting and commercially benefiting from people's suffering and degradation. Burman (1994) warns that while the imagery of children in Third World disasters may evoke sympathy, sympathy is a double-edged tool as 'its evocation can threaten to be patronising and render recipients as "other"' (p. 249). Children in such contexts become signifiers of distress and are dehumanized, as are their families and their cultures. They are rendered as passive objects of a western gaze that 'seeks to confirm its own agency and omnipotence to ward off its own insecurities' (Burman 1994, p. 238). Ultimately, such imagery maintains prevailing colonial and paternalistic relations.

## The hero

The image of child soldiers as heroic figures is not particularly new. During the American Civil War, hundreds of boys who served as musicians and drummer boys in the Union and Confederate armies became associated with valour and heroism. Biographies and descriptions of young soldiers' lives became staples in children's literature. Newspapers, books and magazines featured stories and tales of drummer boys who were depicted as heroic adventurers (Marten 2004). Moreover, in many contexts around the world, children's participation in war may bring unique social and cultural rewards of heroism through participation in a liberation struggle (Wessells 2006). Nonetheless, it is only quite recently that the portrayal of child soldiers as heroes has entered into western media discourses, often assigning celebrity status and even stardom to former child soldiers, particularly those living in the west. Unlike the Omar Khadrs of the world, these youth have been portrayed as brave survivors of extreme violence who have overcome great adversity and ultimately, despite their participation in violence, have been redeemed. An obvious example of this construction is the media's early portrayal of author Ishmael Beah, whose memoir on his life as a child soldier in Sierra Leone gained him international attention. While Beah's book has not been viewed as a simple, heroic tale, Beah's journey in and out of armed violence was documented by some journalists as a heroic transformation from violence to redemption: 'Once a drugged child soldier, Beah reclaims his soul' (*The San Francisco Chronicle* 2007); 'From child soldier to poster boy' (*The Independent* 2007).

Symbolizing this powerful transformation, Beah was featured in *Playboy* magazine donning an Armani jacket and holding school books. Signifying his past, an AK-47 is seen on the floor in the background, jutting out of a camouflage bag.[5] The media's depiction of Beah and his constructed transformation from unknown African child soldier to global hero and fashion model is not entirely unique. There have been other examples of child soldiers who have captured the public's attention and gained heroic stature as a result of their journeys out of wartime violence. A case in point is, Eritrean-born pop singer Senait Mehari whose story as a former child soldier is outlined in a 2004 autobiography entitled *Heart of Fire* (2006). Embodying her heroic passage from violence to civilian life and later to stardom, her book's cover reads: 'One girl's extraordinary journey from child soldier to soul singer'. Luscombe (2007) wrote in *Time Magazine* that western society currently holds 'a cultural sweet spot for the African child soldier' and that 'the kid-at-arms has become a pop-cultural trope of late. He's in novels, movies, magazines and on TV, flaunting his Uzi like a giant foam hand at a baseball game.'

While youth such as Beah and Mehari have undoubtedly been instrumental in increasing public knowledge and awareness of the realities of child soldiers, there are inevitably implications to such portrayals. One former child soldier who is now living in the west has told me of his very conscious decision to avoid the media, despite constant solicitation for interviews, public appearances and offers of large amounts of money to feature his story in book form, as well as through film. For him, the western media's seeming fascination with child soldiers, and especially the assigned hero status, brings forth profound discomfort and ambivalence. First, he does not want to be known solely and unidimensionally as a former child soldier. Perhaps most importantly for him, such celebrity comes at a price and with a heavy burden. How can he reconcile having committed horrible wartime atrocities and then is ultimately being rewarded, both implicitly and explicitly, with attention, status and celebrity as a result?

---

[5] To view this image go to www.playboy.com/style/fashion/bookjackets/ishmael-beah.html

## Invisible girls, emblematic victims

When exploring current representations of child soldiers and the seemingly ever-present images of boys carrying guns, one would assume that girls have no presence in contemporary armed groups. Scholarly literature shows similar patterns of gender (in)visibility. While there is growing descriptive evidence of the conditions and factors underlying the phenomenon of child soldiery in the developing world, much of the scholarly and policy literature has portrayed child soldiery as a uniquely male phenomenon and failed to include gender perspectives on armed conflict. Informed largely by traditional perceptions of armed conflict as a phenomenon occurring between males, girls have been frequently deemed peripheral and rendered invisible within armed forces or armed groups (McKay 2004, 2005, 2006).

Mazurana et al. (2002) suggest that girls have long been used militarily, although they have been largely overlooked and under-studied. Among the few historically documented cases of girls' mobilization are the examples of Joan of Arc, the female combat unit of the Dahomey Kingdom in West Africa and German girls within the Nazi regime. At the age of 16 Joan of Arc led an army of 4,000 against the English, successfully expelling them from Orléans in 1429. According to Mazurana et al. (2002), using her ability to motivate soldiers with religious fervour, Joan led the army to a series of victories, culminating in the coronation of Charles VII at Reims with Joan by his side. Captured by Burgundian soldiers a year later and sold to the English, Joan died a martyr at the stake.

In the Dahomey Kingdom of West Africa (present-day Benin) was a large-scale female combat unit that functioned over a long period as a part of a standing army. The female 'Amazon corps' appears to have originated in 1727 when Dahomey faced a grave military situation. The king armed a regiment of females at the rear to make it appear that his forces were larger, and inadvertently discovered that the females fought exceedingly well. The king organized the Amazon corps to guard the palace and eventually the corps grew in size from about 800 females in the early nineteenth century to over 5,000 at mid-century, several thousand being combat forces (Goldstein 2001). Girls who trained to be warriors followed a strict code of celibacy to free them of emotional ties and the possibility of pregnancy. To maintain the female force, fathers were to report every 3 years with daughters between the ages of 9 and 15, with the fittest selected for military duty (Mazurana et al. 2002).

More recently, within the Nazi regime, German girls and young women were deemed eugenically valuable because of their biological complement to men, and their role in perpetuating the German 'master race'. Within Nazi ideology, girls were officially 'spared' from shouldering industrial and agricultural responsibilities and it was declared that girls would never have to bear arms. Nonetheless, in 1930, the Hitler Youth instituted a female section called the *Bund Deutscher Madel* (League of German Girls), which emphasized girls' secondary status, but propagated Nazi ideals and 'was based on physical training, discipline, rationality and efficiency' (Reese, cited in Brocklehurst 2006, p. 79). At the height of the war, tens of thousands of young women were involved in farming, industry and served in semi-military positions. Moreover, largely hidden from the German public, in 1944 girls were employed as anti-aircraft gunners, and were instructed how to fire cannons, machine guns, grenades and firearms. Kater (2004) notes that there was a 'death squad' of young girls commanded by the Waffen-SS who 'had painted red lips and fought with abandon' (p. 238).

In current discussions and analyses of armed conflict, the invisibility of girls has remained firmly intact. Girls' experiences of war have accounted for 'the smallest percentage of scholarly and popular work on social and political violence' (Nordstrom 1997, p. 5) and the diverse roles girls play both during and following war have only recently been acknowledged (Coulter 2008; Denov and Maclure 2006; Fox 2004; Keairns 2003; McKay and Mazurana 2004; Park 2006; Schroven 2008; Veale 2003). Indeed, officials, governments and national and international bodies frequently cover up, overlook or refuse to recognize girls' presence, needs and rights during and following armed conflict (McKay and Mazurana 2004).

Despite their relative invisibility, girls are currently used in fighting forces far more widely than is reported. Between 1990 and 2003, girls were associated with fighting forces in 55 countries and were active participants in conflict in 38 countries around the globe (McKay and Mazurana, 2004).[6] Girls appear to be most often present in armed

---

[6] These international and civil conflicts include Angola, Burundi, Colombia, Democratic Republic of the Congo, El Salvador, Eritrea, Ethiopia, Guatemala, Lebanon, Liberia, Macedonia, Nepal, Peru, Philippines, Sierra Leone, Sri Lanka, Sudan and Zimbabwe (Mazurana et al. 2002).

opposition groups, paramilitaries and militias, yet they are also present in government forces. Girls continue to be involved in fighting forces in Central African Republic, Chad, Colombia, Côte d'Ivoire, Democratic Republic of the Congo, Nepal, Philippines, Sri Lanka and Uganda (Coalition to Stop the Use of Child Soldiers 2008). While the proportion of females in armed groups and forces varies according to geographic region, it generally ranges from 10% to 30% of all combatants (Bouta 2005). In recent conflicts in Africa, girls are said to have comprised 30–40% of all child combatants (Mazurana et al. 2002, p. 105).

Importantly, when girls within armed groups *are* discussed, whether within the realms of academia, policy or the media, there has been a tendency for them to be portrayed predominantly as silent victims particularly as 'wives', in tangential supporting roles, and as victims of sexual slavery (Coulter 2008; Denov 2007). While these gendered portrayals undoubtedly represent the experiences of some war-affected girls, to characterize girls *solely* as victims of sexual violence and/or 'wives' presents a skewed picture of their lived realities. Moreover, although highlighting girls' victimization is critical to advancing our understanding of girls' experiences of war and the profound insecurities, human rights abuses, as well as the challenges they face both during and following armed conflict, a danger is that girls become personified as voiceless victims, often devoid of agency, moral conscience and economic potential.

The iconography of child soldiers is highly revealing. The images and discourses surrounding (male) child soldiers as dangerous or as hapless victims come to stand for some of our most paradoxical 'common-sense' ideas about children more generally: that, on the one hand, to be a child is to be passive, innocent and deserving of sympathy; while, on the other, they are to be feared and dreaded, and their 'deviant' actions must be explained by reference to their inherent duplicity, their taintedness. We can see how the logic of opposite extremes and ideological norms of childhood behaviour combine either to deny children agency, and make them the 'innocent victim', or to cast them as essentially wicked.

Moreover, the three depictions – the dangerous youngster, the hapless victim, and the hero – have important elements in common. In each portrayal, child soldiers are exoticized, decontextualized and essentialized. The complexity of their wartime and post-war situations and lives is lost. Such representations, whether used to strategically prevent the recruitment of child soldiers or to draw public attention to the problem, easily generate archetypal images that eventually form part and parcel of the public's conceptualization of the issues. The representations also reflect and reproduce enduring hierarchies between the global North and South, cementing notions of race, perversity and barbarism, alongside the dehumanization of child soldiers and their societies. The imagery and discourses on child soldiers present a site where colonial themes can be played out (Macmillan 2009).

Ultimately, the one-sided, gendered and largely unidimensional depictions highlight our uncertainty and ambivalence in dealing with girl and boy soldiers. The reliance on formulaic imagery reveals, above all, that we do not have a language to adequately represent the complexity of girls' and boys' involvement in armed conflict.

## The making and unmaking of child soldiers

The contrastive iconographic and gendered images of child soldiers are exceedingly significant not only for what they convey, but, also, for what they obscure. The typical representations of pre-pubescent boys armed with guns are finite and cursory – they offer no attempt at capturing or understanding what occurred to bring children into the fold of violence and armed conflict, and what may be needed to bring them out again.

### Understanding militarization and reintegration

The narrow depictions offer little insight into militarization and reintegration processes that are key to understanding the depth of children's experiences of war. Militarization, defined by Geyer (1989, p. 79) as 'the contradictory and tense social process in which civil society organizes itself for the production of violence', constitutes a blurring of the boundaries between what is regarded as military life and civilian life with few distinctions between the frontlines and the rear, between civilians and combatants (Adelman 2003; Feldman 2002).

Militarization involves the political use of symbols, the glorification of force and social manipulation through pro-military themes, and results in the quiet acquiescence in the transfer of power from civil society to a military regime (Regan 1994). In relation to the militarization process and children, how are child soldiers 'made'? In what ways are the reconfiguration of children's identities as soldiers and members of a military regime realized? How do children become armed fighters capable of committing acts of brutality? Rarely do descriptive accounts of child soldiers adequately explain how they undergo fundamental changes from lives of relative tranquillity to the perpetration of destruction and violence, sometimes on defenceless civilians. It is critical to begin to unpack the militarization process and children's initiation into the complex world of violence and armed conflict.

Just as the process of militarization is essential to understanding children's transition into armed violence, the process of demilitarization and children's post-conflict reintegration is equally crucial to ascertain their long-term realities and prospects. The UN defines reintegration as follows:

the process by which ex-combatants acquire civilian status and gain sustainable employment and income. Reintegration is essentially a social and economic process with an open timeframe, primarily taking place in communities at the local level. It is part of the general development of a country and a national responsibility, and often necessitates long-term external assistance. (United Nations 2006, p. 19)

Although reintegration may be highly challenging, for individuals and communities, the frequent assumption that former child soldiers are destined to pathology and deviance post-conflict is both immoderate and premature. In reality, research has only recently begun to explore the process of 'demilitarization'– the ways in which these children leave a world of systemic violence, as well as their efforts to adapt to civilian life (Annan and Blattman 2006; Betancourt *et al.* 2008; Boothby 2006). The 'unmaking' of child soldiers and their attempts to renegotiate their lives and self-concepts following demobilization merits further exploration.

This book thus seeks to examine the 'making' and 'unmaking' of a sample of children formerly associated with Sierra Leone's Revolutionary United Front (RUF). Drawing from in-depth interviews and focus groups conducted over a 2-year period with a sample of 76 Sierra Leonean children (36 boys and 40 girls), the book aims to uncover how these child soldiers were 'made' and the ways in which the militarization and reconfiguration of their identities as soldiers and warriors was achieved. It also explores the process of demilitarization and reintegration and traces the challenges associated with carving out one's identity and self-concept in the aftermath of war.

The book employs several sets of conceptual tools to trace the lives of these children both during and following armed conflict. First, the concepts of 'making' and 'unmaking' provide tools to map out the chronological process of children's wartime and post-war lives – that is the process of 'becoming' a child soldier, what it meant to 'be' a child soldier during the heart of the war, as well as how children left the world of violence at the conflict's end. Second, Anthony Giddens' theoretical concepts of 'structure', 'agency' and 'duality of structure', to be discussed further in Chapter 1, are used as a lens through which to examine the lives of the children, both during and following the war. These conceptual tools provide a means to frame the empirical data collected in Sierra Leone, as well as helping to improve our understanding of the lives of these children.

## Approach to the book: Giving voice to the marginalized

Despite being protagonists in contemporary war, children's views on armed conflict, its causes and its impact, are seldom considered. Indeed, reflecting conventional notions of power, and what is regarded as 'expert' knowledge, children are often *talked about* by scholars, rather than *talked to*. Boyden (2004) has noted that information on war and its impact is largely drawn from adult informants, which has significant implications:

It implies that children's insights have no relevance or scientific validity as compared with the expert knowledge and interpretive skills of the researcher. It suggests that children's testimony is unreliable and that children do not have the capacity to give a proper account of their lives ... Children are thought to lack the maturity to hold and articulate valid views. (Boyden 2004, p. 248)

Girls and boys who have been caught up in circumstances of severe disadvantage and prolonged violence rarely have opportunities to publicly articulate their own perspectives, knowledge, concerns and needs. As Downe (2001) has observed:

Despite the undeniable visibility of children in ... academic and popular representations of despair, rarely are the experiences, thoughts, actions and opinions of the children explored analytically in a way that gives voice to these marginalized social actors or that elucidates what it means to be a child under such conditions. In effect, the children are seen, but not heard. (Downe 2001, p. 165)

In light of the linear portrayals of child soldiers and their marginalized perspectives, there is a compelling rationale to develop alternative visions of child soldiers that are grounded in the perspectives of the children themselves. A reasonable first step, as Rudd and Evans (1998) have argued in relation to marginalized youth, is to 'map out young people's attitudes and beliefs' (p. 41). By engaging former child soldiers, both boys and girls, to talk about their own personal experiences and to reflect on the forces that led to their involvement in war, as well as their post-conflict realities, researchers and those desirous of facilitating processes of reconciliation and reconstruction should come closer to 'depathologizing' children who were involved in armed conflict (Ungar and Teram 2000).

In addition, however, it is essential to account for diversity among young people and to acknowledge how factors such as gender, race and class shape and constrain children's realities (Caputo 2001). This is particularly significant in relation to war-affected girls who are often excluded from the realms of social, political and economic power and marginalized in discussions of armed conflict (Coulter, Persson and Utas 2008; Denov 2007; Human Rights Watch 2003b).

Accordingly, drawing upon interviews and focus groups with girls and boys formerly associated with Sierra Leone's rebel RUF, the children's conflict and post-conflict experiences are traced both in terms of their victimization and their active participation. Also explored are children's intrinsic agency and heroism: their strategies for survival, their capacity for independent action and their ingenious modes of resistance within a pervasive culture of violence.

Importantly, the experiences of boys and girls within the RUF cannot be generalized to the experiences of all RUF child soldiers, or those within other fighting factions in Sierra Leone or indeed to child soldiers in other contexts. While similarities and parallels may exist with regard to the making and unmaking experiences, the unique specificities and socio-historical conditions of each context must be taken into account.

## Overview of the book

A significant aspect of this research has been to gain an in-depth look at the mental and experiential world of former child soldiers, and the transitions into and out of violent conflict that have been inherent to this world. In light of this, statistical analyses are not provided on the research data and, instead, the focus is more upon capturing children's complex, ambiguous and shifting wartime and post-war realities and narratives. Throughout the book, direct citations from the interviewed boys and girls are used to highlight their unique perspectives and experiences. As Nordstrom (1997, pp. 5, 36) has commented: 'we need to ask [children] to tell their own stories of war … rather than assuming the right to speak for them'.

Chapter 1 outlines the global phenomenon of child soldiers and reviews the current literature and predominant explanations concerning the involvement of children in contemporary warfare. These explanations centre on two main perspectives – one that sees children's involvement in armed conflict as mainly a derivative of the socio-cultural and economic environments in which they grow up, and the other that argues that children are possessed with agency, frequently acting with an awareness of the meaning and consequences of their actions. Following a review of both perspectives, I address Anthony Giddens' theory of structuration, and particularly his concepts of 'structure', 'agency' and the 'duality of structure' which offers an alternative framework to exploring this issue.

Chapter 2 addresses the history of armed conflict in Sierra Leone. It traces the country's colonial legacy, the gradual militarization of Sierra Leonean society, and its path to political oppression, corruption, state failure and civil war. Given the book's focus on child soldiers in the RUF, the chapter outlines the emergence of the rebel group and its tactics and activities. The chapter then provides a summary of the central events surrounding the war and the multitude of local, national and international actors, groups and institutions implicated.

Chapter 3 outlines the methodological approach of the research – how the data to be presented in subsequent chapters were collected and analysed. Given the multiple ethical and methodological dilemmas that are central to conceptualizing and conducting research on former child soldiers, the chapter highlights the use of a participatory research approach whereby a group of former child soldiers were engaged in the project as researchers and collaborators.

Chapter 4 examines the 'making' of child soldiers in the RUF. It explores how participants were recruited into the RUF and their gradual initiation into the world of armed conflict. In particular, the chapter addresses the physical, technical and ideological training and indoctrination participants underwent. It also highlights the importance of solidarity and cohesion, role allocation, rewards and promotion, and the RUF culture of violence – all of which worked to facilitate the militarization process.

Chapter 5 provides an in-depth look at the daily lives and experiences of participants within the RUF's culture of violence. It highlights the multi-faceted world that girls and boys contended with – one in which the realities of victimization, participation and resistance were experienced by children in a shifting and dialectical fashion. It also explores the degree to which participants embraced an RUF identity, as well as their responses to the culture of violence.

Chapter 6 traces the 'unmaking' of child soldiers – the ways in which these young people left the world of violence and armed conflict and their struggles to redefine themselves and reintegrate into their communities following demobilization. The chapter examines the individual and structural factors that influenced participants' demilitarization experiences immediately following the war, as well as their efforts to carve out a new post-conflict identity.

Chapter 7 summarizes the ways in which both structure and agency infused the process of the making and unmaking of child soldiers in this study. It also discusses the new and figurative battlefields that exist at the war's end – for both the former child soldiers in this study, as well as the governments, organizations and institutions that seek to assist these young people in their long-term rehabilitation and reintegration. The chapter concludes by drawing attention to the lessons that can be heeded in utilizing the framework of structure and agency within the long-term context of the 'unmaking' of child soldiers.

# 1 | *Children's involvement in war: The quandary of structure and agency*

All warfare affects children, but there is mounting evidence that current conflicts are having a greater impact than ever before ... African communities are increasingly ... permeated by forces, relations and pressures ... integrally related to globalization ... Constrained by debt and structural adjustment programmes the economies of many developing countries have undergone restructuring which has involved cutting basic services and reducing the size of the public sector. Inequalities have widened and the effect on the social fabric has been to make livelihoods more insecure. Household and community capacities to nurture and protect are declining and there has been a weakening of the norms to protect children ... This has resulted in the commodification of children ... which is inducing an increase in child labour, including child soldiering.

(Maxted 2003, pp. 51–2, 65)

Many under-age combatants choose to fight with their eyes open and defend their choice, sometimes proudly ... [M]ilitia activity offers young people a chance to make their way in the world ... As rational human actors, they have [a] surprisingly mature understanding of their predicament.

(Peters and Richards 1998, p. 183)

While international concern and scholarly attention has increased about child soldiers and their seeming omnipresence within armed groups and forces, for the most part, children's involvement in armed conflict has tended to be explained by largely contrastive viewpoints. As illustrated in the above quotations, on the one hand, children's participation in conflict has been linked to broader structures and forces that children neither control nor fully comprehend. On the other hand, scholars have challenged this largely structuralist perspective for its overly deterministic portrayal of child soldiers, and instead suggest that child soldiers are possessed with agency and frequently act on the basis of rational choice and deliberation. While both perspectives capture parts of the realities of children's participation in armed conflict, each draws away from the essential connection between society and individuals, between structure and agency. To provide contextual information, this chapter begins by outlining the contemporary reality of child soldiers to offer a picture of the global nature of the phenomenon. Following this, the chapter then reviews the two – largely opposing – perspectives on children's involvement in warfare. In order to offer an alternative to the dualism inherent to the two perspectives, I draw upon Anthony Giddens' theory of structuration and outline its applicability as a framework for examining the complex lives and realities of child soldiers.

## The contemporary reality of child soldiers

Violence and armed conflict are commonplace in the everyday lives of many of the world's children. In countries around the globe, children have been first-hand victims and witnesses of war and the atrocities that invariably accompany armed aggression. In addition, children continue to be drawn into conflict as active participants. Singer (2005b) has declared that children are '*the new faces of war*' and 'a *new feature* of nearly every area at war in our world' (Singer 2005a, p. 28; emphasis added). However, the participation of children in armed conflict is not a new phenomenon. In fact, if one relies upon the definition outlined in 'The Paris Principles' (UNICEF 2007), which includes children's participation in both active and supporting roles within armed groups and forces, it becomes clear that the mobilization of boys and girls for the purposes of armed conflict has occurred – rather consistently – over time.

The Crusades, the Napoleonic Wars, America's War of Independence and its Civil War, and the Fascist wars in the first half of the twentieth century all embroiled children in armed conflict (Marten 2002; Mazurana et al. 2002; Rosen 2005). The Children's Crusade in 1212 recruited an estimated 30,000–50,000 children, both boys and girls, as untrained soldiers under the assumption that divine power would enable them to conquer the enemy. Children set out from France and Germany with the aim of capturing Jerusalem and redeeming the Holy Sepulchre (Shahar 1990). None reached their destination, and few returned home, with most being sold into slavery or drowning in the Mediterranean Sea (Watson 2006).

Whether in Prussia, Britain or Austria, children had long been a part of European armies when the French Revolution broke out in 1789. In 1786 the French army developed a unique system in which children were officially incorporated into their parent's regiment as '*enfants de troupe*'. Representing future soldiers and military personnel, the *enfants de troupe* were viewed as a valuable resource and manpower tool as children could be shaped and trained, eventually becoming experts in their allotted roles before the age of 16 (Cardoza 2002, p. 206). During the same period, young boys, often not older than 8, and referred to as 'powder monkeys', formed part of the crew of British Royal Navy ships. They were responsible for many important tasks including the dangerous job of reloading cannons on ships. When on land, boys were required to relay messages between infantry regiments on the battlefield (Collmer 2004).

During the American Civil War, hundreds of boys as young as 9, served as musicians and drummer boys in the Union and Confederate armies (Marten 2004). Drummers and buglers not only signalled when it was time to wake, sleep, drill and water horses, but also drums and bugles provided the only means of signalling and providing commands on the battlefield. Other duties included digging ditches, assisting surgeons in the field hospital and carrying wounded men from the battlefield. A minority of drummer boys were also involved in combat (Marten 2004).

The Nazi creation of the Hitler Youth in 1922 (Hitler Jugend, HJ) sought to train future soldiers who would fight faithfully for the Third Reich. Between 1933 and 1936, voluntary membership to the HJ increased from one million to five million. In 1936, membership to the HJ became compulsory (Rempel 1989). The hallmark of HJ socialization was militarization, with the goal of territorial expansion and the neutralization and eventual annihilation of Europe's Jews. Physical and military training took precedence over academic and scientific education. Youth in HJ camps learned to use weapons, built up their physical strength, learned war strategies and were indoctrinated in anti-Semitism. According to Kater (2004), after years of military training, some of it initially camouflaged, young people fought and killed in the war. During the battle of Berlin in 1945, they were a major part of the German defences.

These represent only a few of the many historical examples of children's involvement in armed conflict.[1] While children have been part of

---

[1] For further historical examples of children's involvement in armed conflict see Marten (2002).

armed forces and groups throughout history, they have garnered increasing attention over the past decade, and have moved to the forefront of current political, humanitarian and academic agendas (Honwana 2006). The Coalition to Stop the Use of Child Soldiers has produced numerous reports outlining recent estimates of child soldiers around the world. In their *Global Report* published in 2004, the Coalition to Stop the Use of Child Soldiers estimated that 250,000 soldiers under the age of 18 were part of fighting forces in conflicts in forty-one countries around the globe. In 2008, the Coalition to Stop the Use of Child Soldiers reported that the number of child soldiers was fewer than in 2004 as tens of thousands of child soldiers had been released from armed groups and forces following peace agreements and demobilization programmes.[2] However, at the same time conflicts in other countries had broken out, were reignited or intensified and thus child soldier recruitment had, in some regions, increased.[3] While there appears to be a downward trend in the number of conflicts in which children are used as soldiers (from 27 in 2004 to 17 in 2007) this is likely the result of conflicts ending rather than the impact of initiatives to end child soldier recruitment and use (Coalition to Stop the Use of Child Soldiers 2008). Nonetheless, child soldiers are said to exist in all regions of the world and, inevitably, wherever there is conflict (Coalition to Stop the Use of Child Soldiers 2008).

Although the presence of child soldiers in current conflicts is undeniable, garnering precise country-specific figures remains an ongoing challenge. It is not unusual to find that local, national or international organizations provide conflicting statistics on the number of implicated children in a particular country or region. In addition, during the heat of violence, and within the fog of war, it is exceedingly difficult to gather clear-cut numbers of implicated children. Restrictions on media reporting and/or access to conflict-ridden regions complicate matters further and, in some cases, statistics on child recruitment are simply not available. Moreover, given the myriad of protective legal norms, instruments and treaties currently in place that ban and proscribe the recruitment of those under the age of 18,[4] armed groups and forces have a vested

---

[2] Countries include Afghanistan, Burundi, Côte d'Ivoire, Democratic Republic of Congo (DRC), Liberia and Southern Sudan.

[3] Countries include Central African Republic, Chad, Iraq, Somalia and Sudan (Darfur).

[4] This includes the Geneva Conventions and the Additional Protocols (1949, 1977), the United Nations Convention on the Rights of the Child (1989), International

interest in concealing the reality of children within their ranks. Other agendas may also drive estimates of numbers and proportions of child soldiers. While armed groups and forces have a vested interest in obscuring child recruitment, some NGOs may benefit from highlighting the 'grave' and 'growing' nature of the problem, in order to garner public attention, support and advocacy (McIntyre 2003). These realities must be taken into account when considering any estimates of child soldiers.

While this book focuses specifically on the experiences of a sample of boys and girls formerly associated with Sierra Leone's rebel Revolutionary United Front (RUF), the use of child soldiers is certainly not unique to Sierra Leone. To help situate the reality of child soldiers in Sierra Leone within the broader international context, the upcoming sections provide contextual information on the global phenomenon of child soldiers. While not an exhaustive summary, the sections trace the principal regions and countries where child recruitment into armed groups has taken place over the past two decades.[5] Armed groups (as opposed to armed forces) are focused upon in order to offer relevant comparisons to the context of Sierra Leone's rebel RUF. In light of the earlier-noted issues associated with garnering precise data on the incidence of child recruitment, any figures presented below should be heeded with caution.

## Africa

Nearly all armed conflicts in Africa over the past two decades have involved children in armed groups in active and supportive roles. In 2004, the Coalition to Stop the Use of Child Soldiers estimated that there were over 100,000 child soldiers associated with armed groups and forces in Africa, a figure that has fostered the perception of Africa as being the 'epicentre' of the child soldier phenomenon (Singer 2005b). Over the past two decades, children have been recruited into armed

Labour Organization's Convention No. 182 (1999), the African Charter on the Rights and Welfare of the Child (1999), the Optional Protocol of Convention on the Rights of the Child on the Involvement of Children in Armed Conflict (2000), UN Security Council Resolutions 1261, 1314, 1379, 1460, 1539, 1612, 1882, the Rome Statute of the International Criminal Court (1998), 'The Paris Principles' (2007) and the Machel 10-Year Strategic Review (2007 – Part 2 of A/62/228).

[5] It should be noted that in some of the contexts mentioned below, children have also been recruited into armed forces.

groups in the wars in Angola, Côte d'Ivoire, Liberia, Mozambique, Rwanda and Sierra Leone. Many of these countries have experienced protracted conflicts affecting multiple generations of its citizenry. More recently, between 2004 and 2007, children have been recruited as soldiers in Burundi, Central African Republic, Chad, Democratic Republic of Congo, Somalia, Sudan and Uganda. These contexts are addressed below.

During the civil war in Burundi (1993–2005), children were recruited by the primary opposition group the Forces Nationales de Libération (FNL) in their rebellion against the government. Despite the cessation of major hostilities in the country, a small number of school children from Bururi and Ngozi provinces were reportedly recruited between April and May 2007. Many former FNL child soldiers have been recently detained and imprisoned for their association with the armed group (Coalition to Stop the Use of Child Soldiers 2008).

In the Central African Republic, two main armed groups, the Popular Army for the Restoration of the Republic and Democracy (APRD) and the Union of Democratic Forces, have used children since the outbreak of hostilities in 2005. Although statistics are not available, commanders in the APRD have confirmed that children as young as 12 occupy roles in their ranks (Coalition to Stop the Use of Child Soldiers 2008). The cross-border recruitment of children through abductions from Chad and Sudan is also practised.

Two main opposition groups in Chad continue to recruit children including the Front Uni pour le Changement (FUC) and the Socle pour le Changement, l'Unité et la Démocratie. The FUC has reportedly recruited children as young as 12 and more than 25 per cent of its forces are estimated to be children (Coalition to Stop the Use of Child Soldiers 2008). Many children have reportedly been forcibly recruited from refugee camps in the Darfur region. In September 2007, it was estimated that between 7,000 and 10,000 children, who had been forced or press-ganged into fighting, were in need of disarmament, demobilization and reintegration (DDR), from both armed forces and armed groups (Coalition to Stop the Use of Child Soldiers 2008).

The conflict in Côte d'Ivoire began in 2002, with the majority of hostilities ending in 2004. However, reports have suggested that children were recruited by the opposition group Forces Armées des Forces Nouvelles (FAFN) until at least late 2005. In August 2007, the UN reported that there was no evidence to support the claim that children were still being actively recruited by armed groups until October 2006. However, anecdotal reports suggest that children continue to be used by FAFN as servants and that girls are victims of ongoing sexual violence within the group.

The war in the Democratic Republic of Congo (DRC) has claimed the lives of an estimated 5.5 million since 1998 (Coalition to Stop the Use of Child Soldiers 2008). Although the conflict officially ended in 2003 when the Transitional Government of the DRC took power, violence and instability has continued. Within the main opposition armed group in the country – the Rassemblement Congolais pour la Démocratie-Goma – children are said to represent between 20 and 25 per cent of its total force (Human Rights Watch 2003a). Estimates put the total number of children implicated in the war in the DRC at 30,000 for both government and insurgency forces (Warchild UK 2006, p. 3).

In Sierra Leone, thousands of children were recruited into numerous armed groups during its 11-year civil war from 1991 to 2002 including the Revolutionary United Front, the Armed Forces Revolutionary Council and the Civil Defence Forces. The details and historical realities surrounding child recruitment within the context of Sierra Leone will be explored further in upcoming chapters.

Political instability in Somalia since the 1980s has facilitated the military recruitment of thousands of children by all warring parties. The two main armed groups using children in their hostilities include the Union of Islamic Courts and the Alliance for the Restoration of Peace and Counter-Terrorism (Coalition to Stop the Use of Child Soldiers 2008).

Clashes in Sudan's Darfur region led to the recruitment of thousands of children by government-backed militias and armed groups between May and June 2006 alone (Coalition to Stop the Use of Child Soldiers, 2008). The South Sudan Defence Force, Sudan People's Liberation Army and the Janjaweed militia have all engaged in local and cross-border recruitment of children (Coalition to Stop the Use of Child Soldiers 2008). In 2007, the Chadian government alleged that over a thousand children had been abducted from refugee camps along its eastern border with Sudan (Coalition to Stop the Use of Child Soldiers 2008). Children in Sudan are also vulnerable to recruitment by armed groups from the neighbouring conflicts of Chad and Uganda, with those confined to refugee and internally displaced persons camps at the greatest risk (Coalition to Stop the Use of Child Soldiers 2008).

Armed conflict in the northern districts of Uganda has created a steady threat to the security of children since 1986. Over the past two decades, the rebel Lord's Resistance Army (LRA) has forcibly abducted approximately 25,000 children (Coalition to Stop the Use of Child Soldiers 2008). According to Troyer (2005), the group has resorted to the near exclusive recruitment of children into its ranks, as boys and girls are estimated to comprise between 80 and 90 per cent of its total force (Troyer 2005). Abduction peaked between May 2002 and May 2003 wherein 10,000 children were taken from their homes, schools and communities. While there has been an apparent decline in recruitment activities by the LRA in recent years, an estimated 2,000 young women and children remain with the group (Coalition to Stop the Use of Child Soldiers 2008).

## The Americas

Over the past two decades, armed groups in Latin American countries such as Colombia, El Salvador, Guatemala and Peru have involved thousands of children (Coalition to Stop the Use of Child Soldiers 2004).

During Guatemala's civil war between 1960 and 1996, many children were forcibly recruited by armed opposition groups, including the Unidad Revolucionaria Nacional Guatemalteca (Coalition to Stop the Use of Child Soldiers 2004). However, the lack of clear information on the number and ages of implicated children has prevented many from benefiting from post-conflict reparation and reintegration programmes (Coalition to Stop the Use of Child Soldiers 2008).

During the civil war in El Salvador from 1980 to 1992, it has been estimated that 20 per cent of the main opposition group, the Farabundo Martí National Liberation Front, were children (Coalition to Stop the Use of Child Soldiers 2001). According to the Coalition to Stop the Use of Child Soldiers (2001), many children were forcibly recruited from poor suburbs and rural areas of the country.

In 1980, the Sendero Luminoso, or Shining Path, movement in Peru was reported to have forcibly recruited thousands of children from indigenous communities in waging its war against the government (Coalition to Stop the Use of Child Soldiers 2001). Also in the 1980s, the Comités de autodefensa (CAD), or self-defence committees, began to recruit children as young as 12. In November 2005, a human rights NGO found children as young as 15 participating in CADs in

indigenous communities in Ayacucho. Interviews with community leaders in these areas revealed that there was an expectation for all those
between the ages of 12 and 60 to defend their villages from external
threats (Coalition to Stop the Use of Child Soldiers 2008).

Although the number of conflicts in Latin America appears to have
declined in recent years, there continue to be thousands of children
recruited as soldiers on the continent, with the vast majority of children
fighting in the protracted civil war in Colombia. Currently, child soldiers
are fighting within two main armed opposition groups in Colombia:
Fuerzas Armadas Revolucionarias de Colombia and Ejército de
Liberación Nacional. Over the course of the country's 40-year civil war,
it has been estimated that between 11,000 and 17,000 children have served
within these armed groups (Schmidt 2007). It is believed that one in every
four irregular combatants is under the age of 18 (Human Rights Watch
2003a, p. 4).

## Europe

Although not a part of the world typically associated with the phenomenon of child soldiery, Europe has not been exempt from the practice of
child recruitment. Over the past 20 years, children have been used
as spies, messengers, porters of weapons and ammunition, and active
fighters in armed groups in Bosnia-Herzegovina, Chechnya, Nagorno-
Karabakh, Turkey, Kosovo and the Former Yugoslav Republic of
Macedonia (Coalition to Stop the Use of Child Soldiers 2001).

During the ethnic civil conflict in Bosnia-Herzegovina, an estimated
3,000–4,000 children as young as 10 were recruited by armed groups
between 1992 and 1995 (Coalition to Stop the Use of Child Soldiers 2001).

During the crisis in Kosovo which lasted from 1998 to 1999, paramilitary and armed groups were reported to have recruited children
within their ranks (Coalition to Stop the Use of Child Soldiers 2001). In
October 2000, approximately 10 per cent of the 16,024 registered
soldiers with the Kosovo Liberation Army (KLA) were reportedly children, the majority of whom were between the ages of 16 and 17
(Coalition to Stop the Use of Child Soldiers 2001). Journalistic sources
offer anecdotal evidence that children as young as 14 were associated
with the KLA (Coalition to Stop the Use of Child Soldiers 2001).

Children under the age of 18, and as young as 12, have reportedly been
recruited into opposition separatist forces in the Chechen Republic and

other parts of the north Caucasus. The Coalition to Stop the Use of Child Soldiers (2004) has indicated that Chechen boys have participated in a number of armed political groups including the main Chechen armed opposition, Islamist groups and village-based defence units. Boys are also believed to be involved in criminal gangs of under-18s which were often attached to local fighters seeking to profit from the war economy.

## Middle East and Asia

Over the past two decades, the Middle East and Asia have been considered increasingly problematic in relation to the recruitment of children into armed groups. While the majority of the contexts have experienced protracted conflicts, the involvement of children has been particularly apparent over the past 5 years. Between 2004 and 2007, child soldiers have been recruited into armed groups in Afghanistan, India, Indonesia, Iraq, Myanmar (Burma), Nepal, occupied Palestinian territory, the Philippines, Sri Lanka and Thailand. Interestingly, child soldiers have been reportedly used in suicide attacks – a practice that is not commonly seen in other regions – in the conflicts in Afghanistan, Iraq, occupied Palestinian territory and Sri Lanka.

Afghanistan's fighting forces have a long history of recruiting children. In a survey of over 3,000 Afghans, Becker (2004) notes that up to 30 per cent had participated in military activities as children. A rapid assessment undertaken by UNICEF between March and June 2003 found an estimated 8,010 child soldiers in fighting forces across Afghanistan (cited in Chrobok 2005).

In India, a range of left-wing revolutionary groups in the Jammu and Kashmir regions of the country have reportedly used children as young as 10 in a variety of their activities. A sharp amplification of violence by Maoist groups in 2005 led to an overall increase in child recruitment (Coalition to Stop the Use of Child Soldiers 2008).

In Indonesia, Jemaah Islamiyah, an Islamist armed group whose long-term objective has been to establish an Islamic state in the country, is reported to have created an elaborate indoctrination process, involving early training and schooling for children who are later recruited as soldiers (Coalition to Stop the Use of Child Soldiers 2008). Children have also been used in active and supportive roles in the Gerakan Aceh Merdeka, a separatist group seeking independence for the northern territory of Aceh (Coalition to Stop the Use of Child Soldiers 2008).

In Iraq in the 1990s, Saddam Hussein created Ashbal Saddam (Saddam's Lions Cubs), a paramilitary force of boys between the ages of 10 and 15 that was formed after the first Gulf War and whose members received training in small arms and light infantry tactics. This youth paramilitary force was, according to Singer (2006), the feeder organization to the paramilitary Saddam Fedayeen force that was apparently of greater concern to US forces than the Iraqi army. More recently, after discovering videos of young boys being trained in kidnapping and assassination, American forces in Baghdad have warned of a 'disturbing trend in the use and exploitation of children by al-Quaida [sic]' (Howard 2008). Moreover, children have been reportedly sold to or abducted by Al Qaeda forces and used for marketplace suicide attacks (Coalition to Stop the Use of Child Soldiers 2008).

In Myanmar (Burma), an estimated 70,000 children have been implicated in the armed conflict, making it the country with the largest estimated number of child soldiers in the world (Twum-Danso 2003, p. 16). Nearly all of the approximately thirty government forces and rebel groups recruit children between the ages of 12 and 18 with children making up some 50–60 per cent of some of these combat units (Coalition to Stop the Use of Child Soldiers 2004; Human Rights Watch 2007a). Many armed groups reportedly purchase and sell child combatants through 'brokers' in order to bolster their forces (Human Rights Watch 2007a, p. 5). According to UN reports, children can be purchased for the equivalent of US$30 and a bag of rice (United Nations Security Council 2007).

In Nepal, the Communist Party of Nepal (Maoist) and its armed wing, the People's Liberation Army, have recruited boys and girls, mostly between the ages of 10 and 16 (Coalition to Stop the Use of Child Soldiers 2008). It has been reported that children over 16 have been involved in active military duties, while children between the ages of 10 and 16 have been used in supportive roles including carrying out propaganda campaigns, delivering messages and providing food for the armed group (Coalition to Stop the Use of Child Soldiers 2008, p. 247).

Children from the age of 7 played an important part in the first Palestinian *intifada* which began in 1988 (Kuttab 1988). Some youth stood guard and notified others when Israeli soldiers and citizens were in proximity, others engaged in stone throwing, while still others secured materials for the uprising and sheltered youth who were wanted by the Israeli military on suspicion of participating in the *intifada* (Rosen 2005;

Usher 1991). During Palestine's second *intifada* (2000–4), youth who had participated in the first *intifada* began to recruit and lead a new group of young people; they became more organized and followed a more formalized military structure, ultimately intensifying levels of violence children were willing to engage in (Rosen 2005; Sirajsait 2004). Some Palestinian children have received military training, and are used as messengers and participate in attacks against civilians and the Israeli army as fighters and suicide bombers (Coalition to Stop the Use of Child Soldiers 2004). Writing in 2007, Sela-Shayovitz (2007) noted that there have been 164 suicide bomb attacks in Israel since the eruption of the second *intifada*, with the mean age of the suicide bombers being 20.

In the Philippines, the Communist Party of the Philippines (CPP) and its armed wing, the New People's Army (NPA), Moro Islamic Liberation Front (MILF), Abu Sayyaf group, the Moro National Liberation Front (MNLF) and the Revolutionary Proletarian Army-Alex Boncayao Brigade (RPA-ABB) are armed groups that have all implicated children (Coalition to Stop the Use of Child Soldiers 2008). Children involved with these groups have reportedly been from rural, impoverished families where economic opportunity is limited (Coalition to Stop the Use of Child Soldiers 2008). Of the 7,500 members of the NPA, approximately one-fifth are estimated to be children and MILF's force of 10,000 is said to contain over 1,000 children (Coalition to Stop the Use of Child Soldiers 2008). Although estimates are less well known for the Abu Sayyaf group, the MNLF and the RPA-ABB, anecdotal reports have confirmed the presence of children within these groups (Coalition to Stop the Use of Child Soldiers 2008).

In Sri Lanka, the Liberation Tigers of Tamil Eelam (LTTE) was notorious for recruiting and using children in its forces from the mid-1980s (Hogg 2006; Kanagaratnam et al. 2005). Children were initially recruited into the LTTE's 'Baby Brigade' but were later integrated into other units where they were involved in combat and suicide missions (Jayamah 2004; Keairns 2003). Despite a rise in the average age of child recruits, from 14 in 2002 to 16 in 2007, thousands of children swelled the ranks of the LTTE, a third of whom were said to be girls (Coalition to Stop the Use of Child Soldiers 2008). UNICEF reported that between January 2002 and December 2007 there were 6,248 cases of child recruitment by the LTTE (Watchlist on Children and Armed Conflict 2008). Writing in 2005, Van de Voorde asserted that 60 per cent of LTTE members killed in combat since 1995 were children

(Van de Voorde 2005). In 2008, the Sri Lankan Permanent Representative to the UN reported that the LTTE did not permit children to pursue and successfully complete secondary education until and unless they had undergone weapons training so that they could be used for combat purposes as and when the need arose (The Hindu News Update Service 2008). More recently, the Karuna group – officially known as the Tamil Makkal Viduthalai Pullikal (TMVP), a breakaway faction of the LTTE – also recruited children into its ranks.

In Thailand, children have been found fighting with armed separatist groups in the southern region of the country. The most dominant group, the Barisan Revolusi Nasional-Koordinasi (BRN-C) currently has a youth wing containing over 7,000 members, which was reportedly responsible for many violent attacks across the countryside, including on government schools (Coalition to Stop the Use of Child Soldiers 2008). The BRN-C is known to have selected children to participate in after-school study groups, where they were later initiated and recruited into the armed group (Coalition to Stop the Use of Child Soldiers 2008). According to the Coalition to Stop the Use of Child Soldiers (2008), precise numbers of children involved with the BRN-C is not known.

The available statistics are helpful in providing an overview of the prevalence of child soldiers in armed groups internationally. However, they also mask an important reality – the involvement of girls. As is evident, available statistics on child soldiers have failed to provide a breakdown by gender and thus the gendered realities of armed conflict are often neglected, rendered invisible and, to a great extent, remain unknown. Far greater attention and care thus needs to be placed on ascertaining the number of girls implicated in conflicts around the world, as well as their implications.

The pervasiveness of child recruitment into armed groups over the past two decades underscores the global nature of the phenomenon. It also highlights that despite ongoing advocacy and noble international efforts, as well as the creation of numerous protective legal instruments, as a global society we have been highly unsuccessful in trying to eradicate or significantly curb the phenomenon. While the reality of child soldiers is irrefutable, how do we begin to understand this seemingly universal practice of warfare? How is the ongoing reality of children's involvement in armed conflict and within armed groups understood and explained by scholars, policy-makers and children's advocates? What factors, elements and realities are said to facilitate or enable the problem? It is vital to answer these questions not only to ensure the protection of children and the prevention of the practice of child recruitment, but also to understand children's pathways into and out of violence, as well as to assure appropriate post-conflict responses and interventions. Over the years, explanations have tended to fall into two main approaches, both of which are addressed next.[6]

## Child soldiers and structural forces

Structural forces are considered critical to understanding the involvement of children in armed conflict, and constitute the bulk of current scholarly discourse on the issue. Scholars have asserted that in contexts of globalization, the changing nature of warfare, the realities of economic stagnation, and widespread poverty and social breakdown, children may be easily drawn into activities that are essentially extensions of the tensions and violence inherent to their own social surroundings (Brett and Specht 2004; Maxted 2003; Murphy 2003). Deeply affected by deteriorating or non-existent social services, violent clashes between weak states and regionally based forces of resistance, the proliferation of small arms and light weapons, and the tyranny of unscrupulous military regimes and warlords, children have been perceived as caught in social forces that are beyond their capacity to control or even comprehend.

### *The changing nature of warfare*

The involvement of children in armed conflict is said to be intimately connected to trends associated with the changing nature of contemporary warfare (Brocklehurst 2006; Honwana 2008). A number of scholars have argued that qualitative changes have occurred in the nature of violent conflict and, as a result, it is now possible to speak of 'contemporary', 'modern' or 'new' war (Duffield 2001; Kaldor 1999; Singer 2005b; Snow 1996). As Kaldor (1999) writes:

During the 1980s and 1990s, a new type of organized violence has developed, especially in Africa and Eastern Europe, which is one aspect of the current globalized era. I describe this type of violence as 'new war'. (Kaldor 1999, pp. 1, 16)

---

[6] While explanations have tended to fall within two main approaches, efforts at synthesis have been encouraged by several scholars, which will be addressed further on in the chapter.

Unlike 'old war', which Kaldor (1999) has argued was motivated by clearly articulated ideologies of social change, 'new war', influenced largely by the forces of globalization, is instead criminal, depoliticized, private and predatory. Lacking clear political or ideological purpose and largely characterized by ethnic and religious conflict, new wars are said to be epitomized by senseless and gratuitous violence and massive violations of human rights, including the direct targeting of civilians, rape, ethnic cleansing and atrocities.

The concept of new war has come under considerable scrutiny, discussion and debate, with many questioning its validity and veracity (Kalyvas 2001; Newman 2004). This debate will be discussed further on in the chapter. Nonetheless, it has been suggested that the trends associated with contemporary war, particularly the increase in civil conflict, state failure and the reality of globalization and transnational networks, are invariably entwined with the participation of children in current armed conflicts.

### The increase in civil conflict

No longer are the majority of wars fought on a clear and distinct battlefield between sovereign opposing armies. Instead, wars between nations have been largely replaced by more local, internecine forms of hostility. From 1990 to 2003, there were fifty-nine different major armed conflicts in forty-eight locations – and only four of these involved war between nations (Harris 2006).

The increase in civil conflicts is important because it ultimately has an impact on who is implicated in the fighting. Civil conflicts are frequently associated with the blurring of boundaries between civilians and combatants, the frontlines and the rear. In fact, wars are increasingly being fought by irregulars – civilians drawn into military roles, in many cases by force. As Olara Otunnu, former UN Special Representative for Children and Armed Conflict, has written in relation to contemporary civil conflicts:

They are fought among those who know each other well – they pit compatriot against compatriot, neighbour against neighbour ... [I]n the intense and intimate setting of today's internecine wars, the village has become the battlefield and civilian populations the primary target. (Otunnu 2000, p. 11)

Within such contexts of where the fighting lines are blurred, and the distinctions between combatants and civilians are few, it is argued that children, who are inevitably caught in the crossfire, have become progressively more implicated in armed conflict as both victims and combatants (Brocklehurst 2006; Singer 2005b).

## State failure

State failure is increasingly viewed as a critical component of contemporary war (Kaldor 1999; Newman 2004). As Kaldor (1999) writes: 'the new wars arise in the context of the erosion of the autonomy of the state and in some extreme cases, the disintegration of the state' (p. 4). Failed states are characterized by conflict, humanitarian crises and economic collapse (Carment et al. 2007). According to Rotberg (2003), nation states fail because they are shaken by internal violence, cannot deliver positive political goods to their inhabitants and become incapable of projecting power and asserting authority within their own borders. Governments lose legitimacy and the nation-state itself becomes illegitimate in the eyes of its citizens. Failed states have come to be feared as 'breeding grounds of instability, mass migration and murder' (Rotberg 2002, p. 127). Rotberg (2002) characterizes failed states in the following manner:

[F]ailed states are tense, conflicted, and dangerous. They generally share the following characteristics: a rise in criminal and political violence; a loss of control over their borders; rising ethnic, religious, linguistic and cultural hostilities; civil war; the use of terror against their own citizens; weak institutions; a deteriorated or insufficient infrastructure; an inability to collect taxes without undue coercion; high levels of corruption; a collapsed health system; rising levels of infant mortality and declining life expectancy; the end of regular schooling opportunities; declining levels of GDP per capita; escalating inflation; a widespread preference for non-national currencies; basic food shortages, leading to starvation. (Rotberg 2002, p. 130)

The widespread poverty that is associated with failed states inevitably has a profound effect on ordinary citizens, especially children. Not surprisingly, children living in countries that are defined as failed states[7] appear to be among the worst off in terms of access to adequate shelter, safe water, health and social services, nutrition, and education and employment opportunities (UNICEF 2008). Moreover, in contexts of institutional collapse, the breakdown of state and family structures, profound poverty and social and political alienation may create an environment where youth may become ripe for recruitment into armed groups and forces (Brett and Specht 2004; Honwana 2006).

---

[7] These include Afghanistan, Burundi, Côte d'Ivoire, Democratic Republic of the Congo, Iraq, Sierra Leone, Sudan and Uganda (The Fund for Peace 2007).

### Globalization and transnational networks

In her analysis of contemporary warfare, Kaldor (1999) has underscored the impact of global forces and the process of globalization in understanding the context, characteristics and nature of 'new war'. By globalization, Kaldor (1999) means 'the intensification of global interconnectedness – political, economic, military, and cultural … [which is] explained as a consequence of the revolution in information technologies and dramatic improvements in communication and data processing' (p. 3). Kaldor (1999) argues that the impact of globalization is visible in many contemporary wars through the global presence of international reporters, mercenary troops, military advisers, diaspora volunteers, as well as a veritable 'army' of international agencies such as the United Nations and other international NGOs.

Alongside the multitude of global players present in new wars, Kaldor also argues that forms of global military integration, connection and sharing increasingly occur between political and military actors from paramilitary groups, organized criminal groups, warlords who control particular areas, mercenaries and private military companies. These connections and alliances have formed as a result of growing international arms production and trade, various forms of military cooperation and exchanges, and arms control agreements and are facilitated and spread through transnational criminal networks and institutions.

Honwana (2006) has suggested that child soldiering has become part of a broader war strategy that is shared across lines of combat and war zones across the globe. She writes:

Information about tactics and technologies is transmitted from one war to another through soldiers, military advisers, and mercenaries. Media reports and popular films also spread this type of information … In this transnational process, ideas and values about acceptable war practices are established. It is precisely in this context that I consider the spread of the child soldiering phenomenon. (Honwana 2006, p. 45)

Honwana argues that the similarities between what happened to children during the wars in Cambodia, Uganda, Sierra Leone, Mozambique and Angola are of no accident. Instead, they are reflective of broader social and economic crises and transnational networks intimately connected to globalization. Within such contexts, the community's capacity to nurture and protect children is reduced, thus increasing their vulnerability to involvement in armed conflict.

**New and old wars: A valid distinction?**

While helpful in explaining patterns of contemporary conflict, particularly drawing attention to the social and economic aspects of war, scholars have argued that what are deemed 'new' aspects of conflict are, in fact, not new at all (Kalyvas 2001; Newman 2004). Kalyvas has maintained that not only have ideological motivations in 'old' civil wars been greatly overstated by scholars, but also declaring current wars as largely 'purposeless' is erroneous and short-sighted given that rebel motivations are often diverse, highly calculated and go well beyond mere banditry (Kalyvas 2001, p. 104; Keen 1997; Utas and Jorgel 2008). Moreover, it is argued that the senseless and gratuitous violence and massive violation of human rights that are typically associated with new war are not uncharacteristic of wars in the twentieth century, or of past civil wars. In fact, Newman (2004) suggests that such factors have been present in conflicts, to varying degrees, throughout the past hundred years. Newman (2004) writes: 'the actors, objectives, spatial context, human impact, political economy, and social structure of conflict have not changed to the extent argued in the new wars literature' (p. 179). Newman postulates that what *is* different about the current context of war is that academics, policy analysts and politicians are focusing on these factors to a greater degree than in the past, thus artificially inflating their significance. Futhermore, advances in communication and the media have worked to bring the realities of civil war and atrocities to public attention. Ultimately, critics suggest that the shifts in the causes, nature and impact of war are more visible than they are real and the distinction between 'contemporary' forms of conflict and wars of 'earlier' times is overdrawn and does not stand up to scrutiny (Newman 2004).

The new wars debate rages on. Ultimately, however, whether 'new' or not, the prevalence of structural factors such as the increase in civil conflicts, state failure, and globalized social and economic forces and transnational networks are said to play a powerful role in shaping and contributing to children's participation in armed conflict.

## The proliferation of small arms and light weapons

It has been argued that the global proliferation of small arms and light weapons[8] (hereafter referred to as small arms) has had an important

---

[8] 'Small arms' are defined as pistols, rifles, sub-machine guns, assault rifles and light machine guns. 'Light weapons' are defined as heavy machine guns, grenade

impact on the involvement of children in armed conflict (Freedson 2002; MacMullin and Loughry 2004; United Nations News Centre 2008). Following the end of the Cold War, millions of weapons have been declared surplus by their original owners and have since flooded the world market (Klare 1999). The Small Arms Survey (2009) estimates that the documented global authorized trade in firearms reached about US$1.58 billion in 2006. In many regions, small arms are widely available through legal as well as illegal channels. Illegal proliferation is often facilitated by porous and poorly policed borders, inefficient border controls, and corruption – all of which make illicit trafficking difficult to control (Atanga 2003). The undocumented trade, likely to be in the hundreds of millions of dollars, remains significant despite greater reporting on firearms transfers (Small Arms Survey 2009).

Small arms have a number of characteristics that make them the weapon of choice in many contemporary conflicts: they are increasingly lethal, durable, easily portable, inexpensive, lightweight, concealable and require minimal maintenance. These factors increase the prospect of their proliferation, especially to armed groups. Stohl (2002b) argues that the wide availability of small arms 'has meant that more individuals become combatants, conflicts last longer, and more people (especially children) suffer' (p. 281). An estimated 80–90 per cent of all casualties in recent wars have been produced by such weapons (Endleman 2001; Klare 1999).

The proliferation of small arms has been identified as a critical component in the expansion of children's involvement in hostilities across the globe (Freedson 2002; UNICEF 2001; United Nations News Centre 2008). As Maxted (2003) writes: 'the increased reliance on light weapons in new wars is one of the reasons for the increased use of child soldiers' (p. 65). Similarly, Klare (1999) has declared that 'the most deadly combat system of the current epoch [is] the adolescent human male equipped with a Kalashnikov – an AK-47 assault rifle' (p. 19). It is argued that throughout history, weaponry relied upon the brute strength and skilful training of the operator, thereby excluding children from combat roles. However, the development of lightweight weapons, which have been simplified in their use

launchers, portable anti-aircraft, anti-tank and missile launchers, small mortars, and ammunition and explosives (United Nations 1999).

and require only a few hours of training, has brought children from the margins of war to the very heart of conflict.

While the reality of children carrying guns in contemporary conflict is evident, a *direct* link between the proliferation of small arms and the use of child soldiers has also been challenged as children continue to be used as soldiers in areas where arms are in short supply (Stohl 2002a). Also, in many contemporary conflicts, small arms have not necessarily been the weapon of choice. Instead, in many conflicts everyday tools like machetes and fire have been far more prominent in the execution of violence (Shepler 2004). Moreover, Rosen (2005) has noted that weapons like the AK-47, regarded as the most popular weapon for contemporary child soldiers, are actually similar in weight or heavier than many of the rifles used in past conflicts.

## Child soldiers and agency

The aforementioned arguments represent the predominant structural understandings of the participation of children in armed conflict, particularly as it pertains to the developing world. While the structuralist perspective holds great merit, it is not without flaw. A central critique of this perspective is the neglect of individual agency in social and political processes and for ultimately rendering individuals as 'merely passive dupes of the structures we bear' (Hay 1995, p. 195). Detractors point to the reality that social structures such as globalization, state failure and the realities of small arms proliferation do not simply act on people like forces of nature and compel them to behave in a particular way. This, it is argued, ultimately dehumanizes people by robbing them of their essential characteristics as human beings and regards them as mere 'effects' of the encompassing structure (Becker 1970). In a similar vein, structural considerations fail to elucidate why some individuals end up engaging in violence while others do not (Bangura 1997). Set against a background of failed states, globalization, small arms proliferation and limited opportunity, it is inaccurate to assume that young people will inevitably resort to violence. As Argenti (2002) notes, 'despite the disillusionment ... of the young, young people very often do not simply reproduce ... violence but rather find ways of appropriating it and subverting it' (p. 133). Indeed, it is this aspect of individual agency that is said to be missing from structural explanations.

Despite an association between structural factors and the phenomenon of child soldiery in the developing world, some observers and scholars have nonetheless rejected what they feel is an overly deterministic portrayal of child soldiers. Indeed, Machel (1996) has cautioned that to view child soldiers solely as victims of adverse social forces and circumstances is to ignore the capacity of youth, no matter how adversely affected, to exercise a measure of personal autonomy in their decisions and actions. A rather different view is that far from being in thrall to structures and forces that they neither control nor comprehend, children involved in armed conflict are possessed with agency and frequently act with deliberation and awareness of the meaning and consequences of their actions. It is argued that in contexts of poor governance, corruption and resource disparities that work to dispossess a nation's citizenry, youth may *consciously choose* to rebel against dominant political and economic institutions and oppose those deemed to have benefited from or supported an exclusionary status quo. By perpetrating violent actions, asserting power over others and accumulating resources through coercive means, youth often attain a sense of personal empowerment and heightened social status (Green et al. 2000; Pombeni et al. 1990).

Studies of child soldiers in a variety of contexts have highlighted children's capacity for rational choice and agency. During Sierra Leone's civil war, accounts of child soldiers sometimes portrayed young people as committing violence with alacrity, fully aware of the effects of their actions (Human Rights Watch 2003a; Peters and Richards 1998). Peters (2004) asserted that child soldiers are 'for the most part, knowledgeable young people who take rational and active decisions to maximise their situations under difficult circumstances ... It is dangerous to overlook the agency of youth; it has clearly played a critical role in the Sierra Leone conflict' (pp. 30–1). Other analyses of child soldiers in Sierra Leone have referred to such youth as an assortment of misguided revolutionaries and 'lumpen' delinquents who were knowing agents of terror and destruction (Abdullah et al. 1997).

Other important research studies, while not altogether discounting structure, have nonetheless emphasized the importance of agency in understanding the experiences of child soldiers. Veale (2003) conducted a study of female ex-combatants who were recruited between the ages of 5 and 17 into Ethiopia's Tigray People's Liberation Front. Veale's research highlighted that these ex-combatants were highly politically aware and none of the women regarded themselves as having been powerless or victimized.

Moreover, Veale notes that being an ex-fighter was not something that women had relegated to the past, but continued to be an active part of their identities, and part of their experiences that differentiated them from other women in Ethiopian society. The women felt they were changed by their experience as fighters and overwhelmingly saw this as a positive change compared to women who had never been fighters.

West (2004) conducted interviews with adult women in Mozambique who had served as children in FRELIMO's female detachment. Reflecting upon their experiences as child soldiers, these women viewed their participation in combat as both empowering and liberating. Moreover, many of these women perceived their wartime experiences as releasing them from colonial rules and from predominant patriarchal structures of dominance in Mozambican society. West highlights that girls were not simply inducted into mindless violence but acted as central players in the historical drama that defined their times and that, ultimately, young people are not merely the passive receptors of adult ideas or surrounding circumstances.

Drawing upon examples from war-affected youth in Palestine and Afghanistan, Boyden (2004) has emphasized that children are often more aware, more active politically and more developed morally and socially than adults assume. Underscoring the importance of viewing children as playing a transformative role in the production and reproduction of culture, particularly during and following war, she notes that rarely have war-affected young people acted as principal informants: 'seldom have they been considered in their role as carers of younger siblings or incapacitated adults, educators of peers, freedom fighters, community advocates or volunteers, workers or political activists. The young are portrayed, in other words, as the receivers of – rather than contributors to – adult culture' (p. 255).

In a discussion of Jewish child soldiers of World War II, Rosen (2005) notes that these children played a major role in partisan resistance against the Germans. Driven into warfare by a combination of necessity, honour and moral duty, the children and youth imagined themselves as a revolutionary vanguard, turning on its head conventional thinking that child soldiers are victims of their recruiters. Emphasizing their agency, political ideology and capacity for conscious deliberation, Rosen notes that 'they took up arms as individuals, but they also fought as Jews, Zionists, socialists and communists ... [I]n the end, these child soldiers made dignified and honorable choices, and their lives serve as a reminder of the remarkable capability of children and youth to shape their own destinies' (pp. 55–6).

These reports and others present a cumulative picture of young people acting of their own volition, aware of the effects of their actions. Yet one must be cautious about the notion of rational choice, for it may erroneously attribute processes of deliberation and agency to *ex post-facto* human actions. In light of what is known about the deleterious socio-economic circumstances of child soldiers in many parts of the world, it is difficult to interpret acts of brutality perpetrated by children as outcomes of rational decision-making entirely divorced from their social environment. As Mkandawire (2002) has observed, the flaw with the notion of rational choice as a dominant explanation of excessive violence in Africa is that it 'has always been based upon the parsimony of its assumptions and the universality of its conceptualisation of human beings ... Devoid of any historical sense, the rationality assumption cannot explain the differences among the combatants in different times and places' (pp. 189, 191).

Just as a purely structuralist approach has been criticized for its determinism and failure to consider the role of individual actors, agent-oriented accounts have also been criticized for their excessive 'voluntarism' whereby actors are entirely unconstrained and untouched by social structures. An emphasis on individual agency also fails to adequately take into account the effect of structural features like forms of power and domination on the (micro-)interactions of people in their everyday lives. It appears to over-emphasize the freedom that individuals have to construct their social arrangements as if they stood outside of collective forces. Thus, it would appear that at least some attention to structure is ultimately required.

## Child soldiers and the quandary of structure and agency

From this review of the scholarly literature, how are we to understand children's participation in armed conflict? Is children's involvement in war mainly a derivative of the socio-cultural and economic environments in which they grow up? Or are children possessed with agency, frequently acting with deliberation and awareness of the meaning and consequences of their actions? Although both the structuralist and agency-oriented perspectives may capture parts of the truth about what happened to many children during and following armed conflict, they are confounded by the dialectic of trying to explain human behaviour through the divergent analytical frameworks – one that focuses on underlying historical and structural influences, the other that acknowledges the capacity of humans to act on the basis of independent deliberation and choice.

While both the macro- and micro-perspectives hold great merit, they both draw away from the essential connection between society and individuals, structure and agency. Several authors, including Honwana (2006), Honwana and de Boeck (2005), Maclure and Denov (2006), Peters (2004), Richards (1996) and Utas (2005a, b), have emphasized the importance of collapsing the oppositions of structure and agency that typically characterize analyses of children's experiences and coping strategies in war zones. In a similar vein, Boyden (2004) has encouraged the conceptualization of youth as 'political actors' with the capacity to make conscious decisions that are simultaneously informed 'by analysis of personal and collective history and circumstances' (p. 250). Indeed, there is a need to examine more explicitly the dialectic between the capacity of child soldiers to exercise autonomous rational choice and the broader social circumstances that shape as well as constrain their decisions and actions.

One prominent theoretician who tackles the conundrum of structure and agency is British sociologist Anthony Giddens. Giddens has contended that it is essential to move beyond dualities in order to accurately grasp the dynamics of social life (Giddens 1984). He objects to the notion that structural forces 'externally' constrain and determine individual behaviour. Instead, he argues that individuals must be conceptualized as knowledgeable and active agents and not dupes of the social system or mere reflections or 'bearers' of its demands and requirements. In connection with his theory of structuration, Giddens' work over the past several decades has been concerned with breaking down the divisions and entrenched oppositions in social theory and instead concentrating on the convergences and overlaps between them (Giddens 1984). His theory discounts neither the structural and historical underpinnings of human action, nor the individual agency that humans possess, but rather aims to articulate the connection between what are essentially complementary approaches to the analysis of human actions in a specific time and space. His theory refers to an exceedingly wide range of topics: the nature of day-to-day interaction, the development of the nation state and citizenship rights, class analysis, evolutionary theories of society, time geography and the nature of modernity.[9] His

---

[9] For a summary of Giddens' work in these areas, see Cohen (1989), Held and Thompson (1989), Bryant and Jary (1991) and Craib (1992).

work is not concerned with providing a tightly integrated framework which provides an overall theory of society (Layder 1994). Instead, he aims to offer a set of concepts which may prove to be of use in social analysis more generally, and social research in particular. In this sense, structuration theory can be drawn upon in small segments or as a complex whole, depending upon the particular analysis.

In an effort to overcome the duality of structure and agency and to contribute to and expand upon this growing area of study in relation to child soldiers, elements of structuration theory are employed as an analytical framework later on in this book. I draw upon Giddens' work and concepts because they offer a constructive framework that counters the dualism that has embodied much of the commentary and analysis surrounding child soldiers and their pathways in and out of armed violence. In particular, I borrow Giddens' concepts of 'structure', 'agency' and 'duality of structure'. These concepts, outlined below, may provide a useful lens through which to examine in greater depth the process by which girls and boys became soldiers within the rebel movement in Sierra Leone (the 'making'), and then disengaged from the armed group in the aftermath of the conflict (the 'unmaking').

### 'Structure'

In its orthodox usages, 'structure' has tended to refer to the institutional features of society as opposed to the micro-features of face-to-face interaction. However, Giddens (1984) defines 'structure' as the rules and resources that actors draw upon as they produce and reproduce society in their activities. Rules, whether explicit (such as the rules of promotion in a bureaucratic organization) or unwritten (such as proper conversational distance), are formulae which enable us to 'go on' in social situations even if we cannot explicitly state what the formulae are in any detail. Resources refer to material objects (e.g., land) which enable people to get things done (e.g., start a business) or non-material factors (e.g., status) which enable command over other human beings. Taken together, rules and resources enable people to do things to make a difference to their social world. Importantly, structures do not merely 'act on' people like forces of nature to compel them to behave in a particular way: 'structural constraints do not operate independently of the motives and reasons that agents have for what they do' (Giddens

1984, p. 181). Individuals always have some choice and are capable of both resisting and embracing the structures that surround them. In this sense, structures organize social action, but they do not exist outside of social practices, which are 'chronically implicated' in the production and reproduction of structure (Giddens 1984, p. 17). Structure is thus not to be conceptualized as a barrier to action, but as essentially involved in its production (Giddens 1984, p. 70). Giddens believes that this *enabling* aspect of structure has been downplayed by traditional objectivist approaches which have instead focused on their *constraining* nature. Importantly, structure does not have a continuous or tangible (real) existence. Rather it has a virtual existence which can be understood, first, as traces in the memories of the people who draw on the rules and resources that constitute it.

### 'Agency'

According to Giddens, 'agency' should be conceived as a continuous flow of interventions in the world which are initiated by autonomous agents. Not all action is purposeful in the sense of being guided by clear purposes that an individual has in mind; but much action is 'purposive' in the sense that it is monitored by actors who continually survey what they are doing, how others react to what they are doing and the circumstances in which they are doing it. An important aspect of this reflexive monitoring of action is the ability of agents to explain, both to themselves and to others, why they act as they do by giving reasons for their actions. To Giddens, individuals are knowable agents who are never completely helpless when subjected to the power and control of others. Giddens refers to this phenomenon as the 'dialectic of control' and suggests that it is always at work wherever power exists. The dialectic refers to the alterations in the balance of power over time and in changing circumstances as a result of the attempts by subordinate groups to use the (sometimes meagre) resources at their disposal. Giddens ultimately underscores that people are never simply helpless victims of social forces beyond their control.

### 'Duality of structure'

One of the most critical elements of Giddens' structuration theory is his notion of the 'duality of structure'. Giddens suggests that rather than seeing structure (the macro-features of society) and action/agency (the micro-features of society) as oppositional elements of a dualism and mutually exclusive domains, we should regard them as the complementary terms of a *duality* – a 'duality of structure'. 'By the duality of structure', writes Giddens, 'I mean that social structures are both constituted by human agency, and yet at the same time are the very medium of this constitution' (Giddens 1976, p. 121). Human agency and social structures are thus in a relationship with one another: every act of production is at the same time an act of reproduction as people reflexively produce and reproduce their social life (Giddens 1979, pp. 57, 215–16). Structure is believed to be internal to the flow of everyday action; it is both medium and outcome – that is, as actors draw upon structures in order to provide guidance for their own actions, they reproduce them.

In essence, structures are constellations of established and evolving human practices that function as media through which human agency is shaped and articulated. Structures and the ideologies and values that sustain them are not separate from the agency of individuals, but are constantly produced and reproduced, and sometimes contested, through human actions. By the same token, just as structures are the outcomes of action, so in turn is action bounded by structure. Human behaviours, and the motivations that lie behind individual decisions and actions, are inexorably connected to the properties of social structures. Actors produce their social circumstances, but their knowledge and scope for choice are bounded by historical and institutional conditionalities, and by unintended consequences.

The duality of structure is the core of structuration theory and is the basis upon which other dualisms in social theory may be overcome, resolved or somehow brought together (Craib 1992). As Giddens (1976) writes: 'to enquire into the structuration of social practices is to seek to explain how it comes about that structures are constituted through action, and, reciprocally, how action is constituted structurally' (p. 161).

Since child soldiery is a phenomenon that is likely to reflect both structural considerations as well as the flow of action carried out by individuals within the context of daily life, any conceptualization of the problem needs to address the *dynamic* relationship between structure and agency. My intention is to shed more light on this intersection between youthful agency and the influences of socio-economic structures by examining the experiences and perspectives of a group of child soldiers formerly associated with Sierra Leone's RUF. As such, in upcoming chapters I explore, through the voices and perspectives of child soldiers, how the complex militarization and reintegration processes experienced by research participants were infused by the realities of 'structure', 'agency' and the 'duality of structure'. Giddens' notion of structure is particularly salient in relation to the ways in which child soldiers actively shaped and, in turn, were shaped by structures of violence, historical and cultural realities, patronage, gendered oppression, state failure and small arms proliferation both during and following the conflict. Giddens' concept of agency is critical in relation to the deliberate actions, choices, modes of resistance and identity construction carried out by child soldiers in the context of their daily lives within the armed group, as well as in the aftermath of conflict. Most importantly, the concept of duality of structure is key to understanding the making and unmaking experiences of the child soldiers within the RUF: as child soldiers drew upon the broader structures and social interactions that surrounded them, both during and following the civil war, they ultimately reproduced them, albeit in differentiated and individualized ways.

The historical complexities and conditions that shaped, produced and were simultaneously reproduced by child soldiers within the RUF will become clearer following an overview of Sierra Leone's civil war which is addressed in the next chapter.

# 2 | Recipe for rebellion: Civil war in Sierra Leone

Where are our diamonds, Mr. President?
Where is our gold, NPRC?
RUF is hungry to know where they are

RUF is fighting to save Sierra Leone
RUF is fighting to save our people
RUF is fighting to save our country

Go and tell the President, Sierra Leone is my home
Go and tell my parents, they may see me no more
When fighting in the battlefield I'm fighting forever
Every Sierra Leonean is fighting for his land ...

RUF is the saviour we need right now.

> (Excerpt from 'RUF Anthem', *Footpaths to Democracy:*
> *Toward a New Sierra Leone* 1995)

A small country on the West African seaboard, Sierra Leone has a population of 4.9 million with 42% of the population under the age of 15 years and 34% between the ages of 15 and 35 years (Statistics Sierra Leone 2005). Sierra Leone is composed of a multitude of African ethnic groups, all of disparate origins and practices. These include the Fullah, Gola, Kissi, Kono, Koranko, Krim, Krio, Limba, Loko, Mandingo, Mende, Sherbro, Susu, Temne, Vai and Yalunka. The two largest ethnic groups – the Mende, largely found in the south, and the Temne, largely in the north – make up an estimated 60% of the population. The Krio, who are the descendants of freed slaves, were settled in the area of Freetown in the late eighteenth century and make up 10% of the total population. Sierra Leone is a predominantly Muslim country (approximately 60%) with the remainder of the population practising Christianity (30%) and indigenous religions (10%). Literacy rates in Sierra Leone are low, at 49% for males and 29% for females (Statistics Sierra Leone 2005).

Males average less than 4 years of education, and women less than 2 years (World Bank 2007b). Sierra Leone has among the highest poverty rates in the world, with about 70 per cent of the population living below the poverty line and the country ranking last out of 179 countries in the UN Development Programme's (UNDP) Human Development Index (United Nations Development Programme 2008a). The average annual income of US$249 is among the lowest in the world (Women's Commission for Refugee Women and Children 2008). Life expectancy is only 40 years for men and 43 years for women, which is 10 years shorter than the average for countries in Africa and 25 years shorter than the average for the world (World Bank 2007a).

The foundations of such brutal poverty and grim health and social welfare are complex, multi-faceted and are intimately connected to colonization, a weakened and corrupt state, institutional collapse, structural violence, indeed many of the same factors that contributed to the country's 11-year civil war. Over time, the long-standing institutional fragility of what has been referred to as Sierra Leone's oligarchic 'shadow state' (Reno 1995) was undermined by the very corruption that sustained it. With poor governance and mismanagement, Sierra Leone became plagued by chronic economic stagnation, high unemployment and the gradual erosion of civil society. These circumstances led to mounting disillusionment, particularly among the young, and were a recipe for rebellion and an eventual brutal civil war that led to the death of an estimated 70,000 people, the displacement of more than 2 million people, the amputation of more than 10,000 people and the destruction of the country's limited infrastructure (Hanlon 2005). It is also important to note that the events and conflicts in neighbouring countries such as Liberia, Côte d'Ivoire, Guinea and others have had a significant impact on the events and conflict in Sierra Leone, including a complex web of armed forces and groups providing support to factions in neighbouring countries.

Vast numbers of children were recruited into the conflict by force and non-force, although significant discrepancies exist in the reported number of implicated children and appear to vary according to organization (Sierra Leone Truth and Reconciliation Commission 2004).[1]

---

[1] These discrepancies may, in part, be due to how a 'child soldier' is defined. The Sierra Leone Truth and Reconciliation Commission (2004) notes that some organizations defined 'child soldiers' as those who fought in combat, while other organizations defined the term more broadly to include all children associated with an armed group or force, regardless of their role.

For example, the United Nations Mission in Sierra Leone (UNAMSIL) indicates that 10,000 children were associated with the various fighting factions (cited in Sierra Leone Truth and Reconciliation Commission 2004, p. 235). UNICEF estimates that 6,000 children were conscripted into violence (cited in Sierra Leone Truth and Reconciliation Commission 2004, p. 235). McKay and Mazurana (2004) indicate that 48,000 children were recruited into the conflict. Ultimately, the precise numbers of children in armed forces and groups are 'impossible to calculate' (UNICEF 2005, p. ix), as many children likely died during battle or escaped without ever being identified as soldiers. As noted by the Sierra Leone Truth and Reconciliation Commission (2004; TRC), 'while the total number of children associated with fighting forces will in all probability never be completely accurate, the submissions of the various agencies to the Commission attest to the widespread use of children in this conflict' (p. 235).

This chapter first outlines some of the structural antecedents of the civil war, and then traces the escalation of the war and the multitude of players and events involved.

## Understanding war in Sierra Leone

A war not rooted in ethnic rivalry (Bangura 2004), Sierra Leone's descent into terror and armed conflict has been linked to many factors including a patrimonial crisis (Richards 1996), a lumpen and rebellious youth culture (Abdullah 2004; Abdullah et al. 1997), greed (Kpundeh 2004), state complicity, political corruption and oppression (Abraham 2004) and historical and cultural conditionalities. These factors, *taken together*, paint a picture of the diverse and interrelated antecedents to the brutal conflict, which had a powerful impact on the lives and choices of young people in Sierra Leone.

### Colonial oppression and patrimonial order

Warfare and terror in Sierra Leone have deep historical roots, particularly as a result of the Atlantic slave trade. In her book *Memories of the Slave Trade*, Rosalind Shaw (2002) notes that by the 1700s, up to two hundred slaves a day were being sent from Sierra Leone. Such practices brought communities into a state of continuing warfare, and local peoples became both victims and perpetrators in their quest to capture slaves for both the Atlantic and domestic trade. The slave trade had a critical impact on the demography within the region, creating labour shortages in agriculture and deeply affecting the structure and composition of political institutions, ultimately consolidating the power of chiefs and armed merchants. With the total number of slaves estimated to be between 11 million and as high as 20 million (Peters 2006), the legacy of slavery was profound. Shaw (2002) argues that the continuity of the slave trade well into the modern era (it continued in rural Sierra Leone until 1929), and the exploitation, murder and predatory economy that underlay the practice, had a lasting impact on Sierra Leone's cultural patterns, history and daily practices: 'terror had become a taken for granted aspect of the environment in which people's lives unfolded' (p. 41). Moreover, the post-slavery realities of poverty, social dependency and vagrancy replicated themselves across generations, creating 'a rural underclass – ripe for militia recruitment' (Peters 2006, p. 23).

By the 1780s, freed slaves who had served on the side of the British in the American War of Independence and later found themselves in England and Canada (alongside various domestic slaves set free when the courts in Great Britain outlawed slavery on British soil) petitioned the British government to resettle in Africa. They sailed to Sierra Leone where they established the settlement of 'Freetown', intended 'for the happy establishment of blacks and people of colour, to be shipped as freedmen … under the protection of the British government' (Gberie 2005, p. 18). However, the settlement was soon overwhelmed with problems, including the outbreak of disease, food shortages and attacks by Temne landholders who were defrauded of their land to establish the settlement. The British government attempted to resolve the problem by declaring the settlement a Crown colony in 1808 and in 1896 Sierra Leone became a British protectorate. Importantly, the British did not encourage the development of a sense of nation in Sierra Leone, and described the protectorate as 'foreign countries adjoining the colony' (Gberie 2005, p. 19). Keen (2005) notes that there were minimal efforts to sow the seeds of a democratic political culture, as the British ruled through institutions like the army, the police and highly unrepresentative legislative councils where deference and patronage prevailed over representation and rights. Moreover, following a British colonial tradition of indirect rule, the British divided the protectorate into many small 'chiefdoms' which held a council consisting of the paramount chief (the most powerful chief), sub-chiefs and 'men of note elected by the people'

(Jackson 2006, p. 98). Paramount chiefs were accorded increasing power in order to isolate political activity within local administrative sub-divisions and inhibit any colony-wide opposition. Each paramount chief was elected from hereditary families known as 'ruling houses' by an electoral college of councillors. Councillors were elected by twenty 'taxpayers' – a term which systematically excluded women, youth and the poor. The British made the chieftaincy a lifetime and inheritable position which came with economic and social rewards. Both paramount chiefs and their sub-chiefs held the customary rights to extract labour services from their subjects enshrined in colonial law (similar, in fact, to aspects of domestic slavery). It also became a criminal offence for subjects to disobey the lawful orders of a chief or to travel out of a chiefdom without first obtaining the chief's permission. Fanthorpe (2001) notes that British officials collected genealogies, 'identif[ied] "ruling houses" and codif[ied] local "native law" in respect of succession to paramount chiefship' (p. 380). A two-class society was therefore institutionalized, consisting of ruling families whereby children of chiefs were exempted from community labour and sent away for schooling (Richards et al. 2004). As Berman (1998) notes: 'The colonial state allowed chiefs, headmen and elders to define a customary law that asserted and legitimated their power and control over the allocation of resources against the interests of juniors, women and migrants' (p. 321). Discontent at the abuses of chiefs (including forced labour, punishment of dissenters and excessive cash levies) was commonplace. In 1955–6, there were uprisings against the abuses of power of chiefs and their demand for illegal taxes and fees. These 'uprisings' have been described by some as a 'civil war rather than a disturbance' (Fanthorpe, cited in Hanlon 2005, p. 462). On the whole, this system not only lacked democratic foundations, but where it suited the British, they could impose or maintain an autocratic chief. Moreover, all forms of political competition at the local level were ultimately subject to British authority.

Other forms of profound colonial oppression were also apparent. As an example, from 1935 to 1956, a British company known as Sierra Leone Selection Trust (SLST) (eventually connected to De Beers) held exclusive rights to diamond mining in Sierra Leone, making Sierra Leoneans legally prohibited from mining their own diamonds, although illicit mining was prevalent. Towards the end of colonial rule, efforts were made to bring production within the legal sphere and to ensure that proceeds were to be used to develop the country's infrastructure and social services. In 1955, SLST relinquished many of its concessions, confining its operations to Yengema in Kono district and Tongo Field, and in 1956 diamond mining by Sierra Leoneans was legalized (Keen 2005). In the areas ceded by the SLST, the government established the Alluvial Diamond Mining Scheme, which granted mining licences to Sierra Leoneans and Sierra Leonean companies, provided that the local chiefdom agreed. This scheme nonetheless disproportionately benefited the wealthy and powerful, including chiefs, politicians and traders, who could afford the licences and equipment.

These are but a few examples associated with a long period of colonial rule which left a powerful legacy of authoritarianism and deference (Clapham 2003). As Hoshschild (cited in Bundu 2001, p. 34) reveals: 'the major legacy Europe left for Africa was not democracy as it is practised today in countries like England, France and Belgium, it was authoritarian rule and plunder'. With independence, in 1961, the new political leaders were suddenly left with the task of unlearning authoritarianism, deference and patronage and embracing parliamentary democracy and concepts like human rights, tolerance of dissent, public accountability, transparency and a free press. As Bundu (2001) notes, and as will be demonstrated in the upcoming sections: 'this was to prove too much of a tall order' (p. 34).

At independence, the political system was dominated by two major parties – the Sierra Leone People's Party (SLPP) which gained most of its support from the south of the country, and the All People's Congress (APC) which gained the majority of its support from the north. The first prime minister of independent Sierra Leone was Milton Margai of the SLPP. Margai, a British-trained medical doctor, played down the significance of independence, perhaps to diminish expectations, when he noted: 'life must go on all the same, with the same justices in our courts, same taxes and other responsibilities' (Gberie 2005, p. 20). Margai died in 1964 and was succeeded by his brother Albert Margai, also of the SLPP, whose rule from 1964 to 1967 was marred by patronage, authoritarian tactics and corruption.

## Structural violence, militarization and the politics of corruption

Violence, militarization and corruption have plagued Sierra Leone's politics. Sierra Leone was governed by the APC from 1967 to 1991, led by Siaka Stevens (1967–1984) and later by his hand-picked successor Joseph Momoh (1985–1991). Despite their claims to bring accountability and transparency to politics, their governments proved to be systems of oppression and exploitation with corruption and patrimonialism sowing the seeds of popular discontent (Abdullah 2004; Kpundeh 2004). Stevens' long tenure in office was marked by economic decline, growing political authoritarianism, the disenfranchisement of the Sierra Leonean people and the institutionalization of what Reno (1995) has referred to as the 'shadow state'. A shadow state works to control informal markets and clandestine economic operations providing the 'big men' in government with the patronage resources needed for distribution to and control of followers (Murphy 2003). Through a patrimonial system of rationed favours, theft of public funds, illicit payments, as well as bribes from economic distortions (induced by price controls and administrative allocation of basic commodities like rice and fuel), corruption became institutionalized (Aning and McIntyre 2004). This was evident in most of Stevens' conduct and activities including his gross mismanagement of the diamond industry. In 1971, Stevens created the National Diamond Mining Council, which effectively nationalized the industry through control of the Sierra Leone Selection Trust (Smillie et al. 2000). Official diamond production and exports plummeted from 2 million carats in 1970 to 48,000 in 1988 (Smillie et al. 2000). Revenue that should have been invested in the country's social infrastructure instead accumulated in the pockets of corrupt politicians in Freetown and their foreign business associates (Rashid 1997).

The militarization of Sierra Leonean society and politics became an increasing reality. 'Militarization' is regarded as a step-by-step transformative historical process by which a person, society or a phenomenon gradually comes to be controlled by a military regime or comes to depend for its well-being on militaristic ideas (Enloe 2000, p. 3). The notion of militarization, in its most traditional form, often signifies military institutions, combat, soldiering, war-waging, peacekeeping, weaponry and arms availability, and the building up of and daily presence of a military. However, working with a broader conceptualization of the term, Enloe (2000) maintains that 'the military itself is only one part of militarization' (p. xii). Militarization can refer to military rule that has 'become a style of government and a way of life, imposed on the general populace without their consent' (Cervenka 1987, p. 69). Through the militarization process, everyday-life structures become the seminal ground of modern political violence and the routine integration of terror into everyday life means that violence becomes increasingly normalized (Feldman 2002).

Embodying the realities of militarization, Stevens' imposition of a one-party state in 1978 effectively delegitimized political power, alienated the vast majority of Sierra Leonean citizens and sowed the seeds for rebellion and terror. Radical students and academics at Sierra Leone's Fourah Bay College, outspoken critics of the new dictatorship, quickly became targets of state violence and intimidation (Rashid 1997). Kandeh (1999) notes that Stevens was fond of saying that 'force is the only language the ordinary man understands' and that much of what he did as president reflected this self-serving, militarized perception (p. 359). Aptly named locally as 'Siaka Stevens' Dogs', the government sought to suppress civil and political rights and instil fear in the population using government-controlled police forces such as the Cuban trained Internal Security Unit (ISU – or in popular parlance 'I Shoot You'), as well as unemployed youth hired as thugs. Demonstrations and protests were met with violence and bloodshed and members of opposition parties were attacked and imprisoned (Abdullah 2004; Bangura 2004). With politics becoming ever-more violent, traditional institutions were gradually replaced by militarized structures that were sustained by extraordinary violence (Zack-Williams 1999). It was this structurally violent and corrupt political system that shaped the daily lives of Sierra Leoneans.

## Rural isolation, marginalization and the disempowerment of the young

The militarization of politics during the Stevens era occurred in tandem with the mounting economic crisis, rural isolation and youth marginalization. The deliberate concentration of power in the hands of the few in Freetown had many implications. As the personal acquisition of wealth became synonymous with the looting of national resources, funding for social services, health and education became limited and highly centralized, with the rural regions severely mismanaged and marginalized. Local government institutions were weakened, thereby hindering the development of participation at the grass-roots level.

Moreover, in the post-independence period, chiefs became closely associated with the kleptocratic and patrimonial tendencies of the Freetown elite. Within the chieftaincy system, the ruling houses sought the moral and political support of local citizens to win chiefs' elections. In the aftermath of an election, it was regarded as commonplace that these support groups be provided with 'benefits' (Jackson 2006). 'Benefits' ranged from advantageous results in chieftaincy courts, appointments to positions of power or access to land or resources. Moreover, in theory, chiefs are supposed to be loyal to the government, whichever party is in power. In practice, however, rarely apolitical, chiefs have tended to have political patrons at the national level, and are also often part of wider patronage networks, including those extracting diamonds (Jackson 2006).

The chieftaincy system, alongside the patrimonial networks, resulted in large groups of excluded and marginalized citizens, particularly those in the rural areas, with little hope of advancement. The World Bank (2003, p. 44) notes that chiefs' rule led to 'mismanagement, power abuse and failure to ensure the delivery of decentralized services', which was felt particularly harshly by rural youth. As noted earlier, customary law and the patrimonial system enabled elders to exercise strong controls over the younger generations, particularly for youth from weaker lineages, and prevented them access to land, and the right to vote in chieftaincy councillor elections (Keen 2005; World Bank 2007b). It has been suggested that poor governance at the chiefdom level was an important factor in the eventual revolt against authority (Fanthorpe 2001, 2005; Hanlon 2005). As Jackson (2006) has noted: 'Political patronage surrounding chieftaincy has been a defining feature of Sierra Leone over the last 20 years, in that exclusion from patronage networks created the raw material for the violence of the 1990s' (p. 101). As these Sierra Leonean youth reported: '"Most ... young men and women were suffering ... [O]ur chiefs and some elders were doing wrong to our young ...[S]ome preferred to go and join the RUF, either to take revenge or to protect themselves" ... "Nobody was willing to help the young men ... [W]hen ministers or the paramount chief visit any village they ask us to contribute rice and money, instead of bringing development ... That inspired us to fight ... to have justice in the country"' (Richards 2005, p. 578).

Alongside vast forms of exclusion, rural youth were faced with shrinking opportunities as the prices of raw materials dropped and mining was subsumed by the shadow economy.[2] Without sponsorship

---

[2] The reality of 'greed' as an antecedent to the conflict will be briefly addressed later on in the chapter when exploring the RUF.

or protection, young people increasingly found themselves unable to attend school and without income possibilities, which led to widespread despair and feelings of exploitation (World Bank 2007b). Large economic disparities triggered mass migration of mostly unemployed youth to towns and cities in search of a better life. With unmet expectations, due to the deteriorating economy, many resorted to criminal activity, swelling the ranks of socially uprooted and politically alienated 'lumpen' youth (Bangura 2004). Abdullah (1998) refers to lumpens as 'largely unemployed and unemployable youths, mostly male, who live by their wits or who have one foot in what is generally referred to as the informal underground economy. They are prone to criminal behaviour, petty theft, drugs, drunkenness and gross indiscipline' (pp. 207–8). Abdullah (2002) argues that central to the events of the war, the general insecurity and the total collapse of institutions of governance, is the role of youth culture, particularly rebellious youth culture, and the inauguration of a political discourse anchored in violence. For Abdullah (2004), these lumpen and socially excluded youth, their oppositional culture and their search for a radical alternative to the APC regime are pivotal to understanding the later rebellion.[3]

## Traditional structures and young warriors

While all of the above-noted socio-political and economic factors are important contextual realities framing the eventual war in Sierra Leone, traditional practices and cultural imperatives are also of deep relevance. Historically, young soldiers or warriors have been present in many pre-colonial African societies and were, according to Rosen (2005), part of the military in virtually every anti-colonial war of liberation on the African continent. In Sierra Leone, historical cultural practices, including initiation practices, have indeed encouraged the militarization of the young. Initiation marks the ending of childhood and allows for 'rebirth into a world of adult responsibility' (Richards 1996, p. 81). In pre-colonial times, every person, male or female, was initiated at puberty and a non-initiate was not considered as a mature person, whatever their age (Ellis 2003). Initiation societies, such as the Poro (concerned primarily with the initiation of boys), and Sande

---

[3] For an in-depth discussion of Sierra Leone's rebellious youth culture and its relationship to the war, see Abdullah (1998) and Abdullah (2002).

(which focuses on the initiation of girls) are typically groups that require elaborate initiation rites whose details may not be divulged to outsiders (which is why they are sometimes called 'secret societies'). Little (1965) notes that secret societies such as the Poro are responsible for

tribal education, [they] regulate sexual conduct, supervise political and economic affairs, and operate various social services, including entertainment and recreation as well as medical treatment ... The Poro is important not only because it is the men's association *par excellence* into which the boys are initiated on reaching puberty – but because of the part that it has played in community affairs from time immemorial. (Little 1965, p. 349; emphasis in original)

As part of the initiation process, initiates were typically removed from their families, and taken to a ritual village in the bush for a long period of seclusion, at times for years. Ellis (2003) notes that during such long absences, the initiate was sometimes perceived as having 'died' as a child and was reborn as an adult. The rigours of initiation are said to symbolically break the family tie, create bonds among peers, as well as the life-long respect for the expertise of elders, and commitments beyond the web of kinship (Richards 1996). While the knowledge and moral conduct handed down during the process of initiation may vary widely, males generally receive education regarding the expectations of manhood, including the moral conduct of war, and the relationship of a man to his community (Ferme and Hoffman 2004). For women, education and training focuses on child rearing, midwifery, medicine and marriage (Ellis 2003; Shaw 2002).[4]

Historically, militarization and mobilization practices have been an integral part of initiation rites whereby boys are prepared for participation in the armed defence of their communities. As Watkins (1943) describes:

These [secret] societies are of fundamental importance in the local culture, and every youth, male or female, must receive such training before being considered worthy to assume the responsibilities of an adult ... [In] the boys' society ... instruction in warfare is accompanied by actual mock battles and skirmishes. The boys are separated into various 'towns' similar in location

---

[4] Although Poro and Sande still exist, the duration of the period spent by an adolescent in the bush has been dramatically shortened, down to a few weeks or even days. During the twentieth century, much of the educational function of initiation was replaced by western-style schooling (Richards 1996).

and arrangement to those in which the general population is or has been distributed. These towns must be barricaded, defended and attacked. Previous wars in which the tribe has been engaged are re-enacted, the boys of one group playing the role of the people under attack at a certain time, while those of another act the parts of the enemies ... The defenders are informed of the errors in judgment and tactics which were formerly committed in actual combat, and the battle is conducted upon the basis of the previous life-situation. Then the entire war game is replayed, the defenders having learned what the shortcomings were and how to correct them, and the 'enemy' making special effort to succeed in the face of the new improvements in defense. (Watkins 1943, p. 671)

The mobilization of the young is thus not an unfamiliar reality in Sierra Leone and, in many instances, childhood and military life are not necessarily understood as either incompatible or contradictory (Rosen 2005). Moreover, Poro and other societies have played important roles in the coordination of civil defence in Sierra Leone (Ferme and Hoffman 2004; Kandeh 1999; Richards 1996). Demonstrating the link between militarization, warfare and traditional structures such as Poro, Ferme and Hoffman (2004) note that during the war, the early mobilization of males for the Civil Defence Forces (CDF) in Kenema were referred to as *hindo hindo* ('man man'), the words with which Poro members are called together. Ferme and Hoffman (2004) argue that civil defence groups 'drew on the same tenets of masculine responsibilities and punishments for nonparticipation that characterize Poro' (p. 82).

In addition, Ellis (2003) notes the adulation that has historically been accorded to young men involved in military coordination on behalf of the community. As evidence, initiators within Sierra Leone's CDF who mobilized large numbers of children to fight, garnered high degrees of popular legitimacy and support in some areas of the country. While traditional structures can in no way be seen as precursors or causes of the war, these examples highlight the relevance of existing traditional structures in the mobilization of the young and the ways in which such structures may work to influence and shape individual decision-making for participation in warfare.

When examining its colonial history, like much of sub-Saharan Africa Sierra Leone was integrated into the world system in a way that marginalized its traditional social systems and left its economy colonized by international enterprises and a kleptocratic governing elite. Moreover, profound inequalities, and the exclusion of youth from mainstream society, resulted in a growing array of disempowered, disillusioned and marginalized youth. Ultimately, the aforementioned structural realities, whether historical, economic, social, political or cultural, unquestionably shaped and framed the options and prospects of the young.

## The emergence of the Revolutionary United Front

Drawing upon the growing disillusionment and frustration with governance under the APC, particularly among the young, former Sierra Leonean Army corporal Foday Sankoh, backed by Liberian warlord Charles Taylor, formed the rebel Revolutionary United Front (RUF). Relying on the emancipatory rhetoric of 'freedom, justice and democracy to all Sierra Leoneans' (Revolutionary United Front 1995), Sankoh systematically recruited largely uneducated, unemployed and unemployable male youth to join a 'movement' against the government. On 23 March 1991, the RUF entered the town of Bomaru at Kailahun district in Sierra Leone. The RUF was composed of an estimated one hundred fighters – mainly borrowed commandos from the rebel National Patriotic Front of Liberia (NPFL) and Burkinabe mercenaries leading Sierra Leoneans largely recruited in Liberia. The armed militants crossed the Liberian border into Sierra Leone, announcing their intention to liberate the people from the corrupt APC regime. A second small group attacked the Pujehun district, progressing to Pujehun town by mid-April and as far as Sumbuya by early May. At that time, few people took the RUF seriously or realized the senseless and protracted war that was in the making (Abdullah 2004).

The foundations of the RUF are complex and there have been several arguments put forward to explain the RUF's origins, composition and character. Paul Richards (1996) suggested that the RUF was a calculating group of 'excluded intellectuals' that formed in response to the corruption and rural marginalization under APC rule. Abdullah (1998, 2004) has emphasized the rebellious youth culture and lumpen origins of the RUF. Keen (1997, 2005) has pointed to the role and relationship of both greed and grievance in understanding rebel motivations. Gberie (2005) has focused on the mercenary character of the rebels, noting the role of greed, power and the critical function of Charles Taylor in the RUF equation. The following provides a snapshot of the origins and phenomenon that was the RUF.

## The RUF's early history

While radical students were not part of the eventual group that invaded Sierra Leone in 1991, it is nonetheless important to outline the historical place of students in the story of the RUF. Students became increasingly involved in Sierra Leone's national politics in the 1970s and 1980s. They pushed for reform in the political and economic spheres, used the platform of student politics to launch an attack against the government and ultimately created an informal opposition to the APC (Abdullah 2004). In the mid-1980s, a group of radical students at Fourah Bay College began a study group which dedicated itself to propagating the political ideas of Libya's Colonel Muammar Gaddafi as expressed in his *Green Book* (1975–9) – a document calling for humanism, Pan-Africanism, anti-capitalism and charismatic rule.

Following a violent demonstration at Fourah Bay College in 1984, a group of forty-one student leaders associated with the pro-Gaddafi student movement were expelled. In the aftermath of their expulsion, the group flew to Ghana and then to Libya under the patronage of Gaddafi to receive military and 'ideological' training. While the group remained linked together by their common experience of expulsion and commitment to radical change, Abdullah (2004) has emphasized that there was *no agreed upon ideological or political platform* besides acquiring military training. According to Gberie (2005), the group of expelled student leaders eventually recruited mostly urban drifters and secondary school students for their 'revolution' who were taken to Libya for similar training. Importantly, Foday Sankoh, the eventual leader of the RUF, was among the recruits. It was at this point, however, that connections to the student movement or 'intellectuals' appears to have faded. Disputes over finances as well as the commitment level of some members caused friction and divided the group. Realizing that they had no realistic means of launching a revolutionary war, the project eventually dissolved and most of the students resumed their education in Ghana or returned to Sierra Leone.

## The alliance of Sankoh and Taylor

The eventual alliance formed between Foday Sankoh and Liberian warlord Charles Taylor is key to understanding the war in Sierra Leone. Sankoh was born in a small village in the district of Tonkolili in the early 1930s. The son of peasant farmers, Sankoh grew up in poverty. Having only attended primary school, he was functionally literate, and was closely associated with Sierra Leone's 'lumpen' youth culture. Sankoh enlisted in the Sierra Leonean Army in 1956 where he became a corporal and received training in radio and communications operations (Gberie 2005). However, he was cashiered and imprisoned for 7 years for his alleged involvement in a coup d'état against Siaka Stevens in 1971. Released from prison in 1978, the year that the APC enacted a one-party state, Sankoh was embittered and determined to strike back at the APC. Following his incarceration, he worked as a commercial photographer in Bo, where in 1982, as he professed in many later interviews, he began 'organizing his revolutionary movement' (Gberie 2005, p. 45). Sankoh eventually made his way to Ghana and then to Libya for military training. According to Gberie (2005), Sankoh felt let down by the earlier-noted student movement and upon his return to Sierra Leone was determined to resume the so-called 'revolution' and to mobilize disgruntled Sierra Leoneans to overthrow the tyranny of the APC.

Sankoh met Charles Taylor during their mutual military training in 1987 in Ghana, and then again in 1988 in Libya (Gberie 2005). Taylor had recently escaped from a federal prison in the United States while awaiting extradition to Liberia on embezzlement charges, accused of stealing US$900,000 of state funds. Taylor, who was the leader of the NPFL, was not only seeking to extend his control into Sierra Leone, but was also keen to punish Sierra Leone for its role as an air-base for Economic Community of West African States cease-fire Monitoring Group (ECOMOG) forces that were bombing NPFL areas inside Liberia and preventing him from capturing the capital. A rebellion in Sierra Leone may also have appeared useful to Taylor in tying up forces that could otherwise have been deployed against him in Liberia (Keen 2005). Forming a mutually profitable alliance, Sankoh and his troops (largely lumpen youth recruited in the aftermath of his trip to Libya) agreed to lend support to Taylor's NPFL in exchange for Liberian territory on which to strategize and initiate future attacks in Sierra Leone, as well as borrowed troops from the NPFL to fight with Sankoh's rebels (Abdullah 2004). Over time, the partnership evolved and Taylor eventually played the role of banker, trainer and mentor to the RUF by providing them with outlets for diamond exports in return for weapons and military training.

## *Rebels without a cause? Understanding RUF tactics and activities*

The RUF's political rhetoric as outlined in its manifesto, *Footpaths to Democracy: Toward a New Sierra Leone*, called for the 'liberation' of all Sierra Leoneans. However, the RUF's so-called 'democratic revolution' was ultimately fought not through the political realm, but instead through the pillage of rural institutions and industrial assets, the mass looting of village property and, perhaps most disturbingly, brutal violence against the very civilians it was claiming to liberate. Alongside innumerable gross human rights violations against civilians, the RUF used widespread coercion both to secure and retain recruits, particularly among the young. As Bangura (1997, pp. 129–30) notes, young villagers were 'seized and transformed into modern slaves [and] subjected to forced labour on stolen RUF farms'. Mazurana et al. (2002) maintain that up to 80 per cent of RUF forces were made up of children between the ages of 7 and 14. Significantly, the initial recruitment drive by the RUF did not involve children. However, as the rate of attrition among adult RUF combatants increased, with factors such as the prolongation of the war, the horrible conditions of service, the lack of salary (whereby many soldiers augmented their pay through looting or mining), the high death toll and the overall senselessness and brutality of the war, the RUF needed to devise another recruiting strategy. While there is evidence to suggest that some children joined the ranks of the RUF willingly (Peters 2004), particularly in the earliest stages of the conflict, the vast majority of children were abducted from their families and communities and press-ganged into fighting (McKay and Mazurana 2004). Eventually, the increased presence of children became a marked feature of the RUF. McKay and Mazurana (2004) suggest that 22,500 children were associated with the RUF (of which they indicate that 30 per cent were girls).

Alongside forced recruitment, the RUF was also extremely adept at using propaganda and misinformation to instil widespread fear and panic, as well as project an image of control and supremacy. Richards (1996) notes that the rebels used the 'rumour mill' to exert an influence well beyond their numbers or military strength. This had an enormous impact on civilian populations who heard news of horrible atrocities that often led to mass displacement. Moreover, hoping to create widespread panic and amplify its threat, the RUF sent letters announcing its imminent arrival to particular towns and villages. Keen (2005, p. 42) aptly notes that as a former radio and communications officer with the Sierra Leonean Army (SLA), and later a photographer, Sankoh 'seems to have understood how to project an image of power'.

The RUF's campaign of terror included the systematic maiming of civilians. In response to the 1996 Sierra Leonean presidential election campaign, and particularly the campaign slogan of 'The Future is in Your Hands', the RUF embarked on mass amputations to terrorize the population and to punish and prevent them from voting ('Operation Stop Elections'). According to the Women's Commission for Refugee Women and Children (2002), there were special RUF units deployed to cut off hands and their members received a promotion when they returned with a bag of hands.[5] Moreover, throughout the civil war, thousands of women and girls of all ages, ethnic groups and socio-economic classes were subjected to widespread and systematic sexual violence, mostly by rebel forces,[6] breaking a range of powerful cultural taboos including the importance of maintaining virginity until marriage, and community-sanctioned notions of marriage. It has been estimated that as many as 215,000 to 257,000 women and girls were subjected to sexual violence from numerous fighting factions during the conflict (Amowitz et al. 2002).

Further illustrating the apparent commitment to the use of violence against civilians, there is evidence to suggest that Sankoh masterminded the execution of several high-ranking RUF colleagues who opposed the targeting of civilians in the name of 'revolution' (Abdullah 1998).

How do we explain and understand the phenomenon of the RUF and its reliance on abduction, violence and brutality? The uneducated, lumpen background of the RUF leader, as well as his rank and file, have been explored and emphasized by many scholars (Abdullah 2004; Abdullah et al. 1997; Bangura 1997, 2004). Abdullah (1998) has argued that the rebel tactics of civilian murder, rape, forced labour and systematic amputation of limbs reflected the social composition of the RUF and the lack of a concrete plan of social transformation: 'A lumpen social movement bred a lumpen revolution' (p. 223). Moreover, as Abdullah (2004) has noted, the RUF's lack of revolutionary ideology forced it to fall back on

---

[5] According to the TRC (Sierra Leone Truth and Reconciliation Commission 2004, p. 44), the RUF is alleged to have committed 39.8% of the recorded amputations in the TRC's database, with the Armed Forces Revolutionary Council having the next-highest number at 27.1%.

[6] Sexual violence was also committed by the CDF, the SLA and ECOMOG.

its 'natural constituents' – lumpen youth in the cities, mining centres and rural areas of Freetown, Monrovia and the border districts with Liberia.

The RUF's brutal violence has also been linked to its essentially mercenary character (Gberie 2005). The initial presence and collaboration of Burkinabe and Liberian mercenaries 'on loan' from Charles Taylor nullified any potential aim that Sankoh may have originally had of overthrowing the APC and establishing a more just regime. As mercenaries who were indifferent to politics, they forced the RUF 'campaign to devolve into an opportunity to loot and murder at will, creating a cycle of violence from which there was to be no turning back' (Gberie 2005, p. 151).

Many have contended that the RUF had no clear ideology or purpose, and ultimately engaged in senseless, random violence. As Farah (2001) wrote: 'They fought for nothing, and that's what they got.' While the RUF leadership may not have had a clear political or ideological platform, it did, arguably, have a goal: the accumulation of wealth and power through diamond and arms deals. Keen (2000) has suggested that the aim of those carrying out wartime violence may not simply be to 'win' the war, but instead to prolong and deepen the conflict in order to reinforce their status within a government or simply to make money. As an example, he suggested that the RUF's violence against the population was used primarily to force civilian displacement from the diamond fields (Keen 1997). Indeed, in taking control of many of the country's diamond mines, the RUF is reputed to have earned anywhere between US$30 million and US$125 million a year from illicit diamond sales (Smillie et al. 2000).[7] Most of this trade went through Liberia, and was controlled directly by Charles Taylor (Berman 2000). Given the substantial amounts of money that the RUF was gaining through looting and illicit mining, it had a vested interest in assuring that the war became protracted and even collaborative between supposed 'enemy' factions.

However, Keen (2005) has pointed out in more recent writings that economic analyses can go too far, and, for him, the role of greed is only partially convincing. He suggests that a rebellion cannot be understood without also understanding the role of pre-war grievances. He writes:

Whilst greed is part of the explanation for the war, it is only one part, and it is something which itself needs to be explained. The rebels, whilst profoundly

---

[7] As indicated in the TRC report (Sierra Leone Truth and Reconciliation Commission 2004), diamonds were not the cause of the war, but inevitably fuelled it.

abusive and very soon deeply unpopular, nevertheless have fed off a widespread disillusionment (particularly among young people) with corruption, with the long contraction of educational and employment opportunities, and with the long-standing draining away of Sierra Leone's valuable natural resources ... The poverty of many people even with relatively good jobs remains deeply shocking. (Keen 2005, p. 293)

Ultimately, the RUF violence has multiple meanings and cannot be linked to one sole source or cause. Each of the above-noted elements appears to have contributed, to varying degrees, to the overall structure and composition that would ultimately define the culture of the RUF. While the RUF was renowned for its wanton cruelty, the armed forces and armed groups that opposed it – the CDF, ECOMOG and government troops – by no means eschewed similar forms of brutality, particularly against civilians. However, given this book's focus on child soldiers in the RUF, the violence of the RUF is examined in depth.

The remainder of this chapter traces the escalation of the war – the multitude of events and players involved – as well as the long road to peace.

## Tracing war (1991–2002) and the long path to peace

Within weeks of the initial RUF invasion at Bomaru in 1991, the rebels successfully captured diamond fields in the eastern districts. Within a month, most of Kailahun was under RUF control. President Joseph Momoh responded by increasing his government troops to the encroached territories. However, for the SLA, troops were in short supply. At the time, a large contingent was deployed in Liberia under an ECOMOG intervention. As a result, reinforcements came from hastily recruited youth from the streets of Freetown, including 'hooligans, drug addicts and thieves' (Gberie 2005), and borrowed men from the United Liberation Movement of Liberia, a group countering Taylor's NPFL in Liberia (Richards 1996), as well as allied Guinean forces. Ultimately, the government and allied forces were able to temporarily halt the RUF, which retreated to the southern and eastern fringes of the country.

### *1992–1995: The NPRC and military rule*

While the rebel incursion threatened to bring down the APC government, in many ways the government in Sierra Leone under President Momoh was already collapsing. Momoh had stopped paying civil servants, teachers, soldiers and even paramount chiefs (Keen 2005). While the government had provisionally halted the rebels, the mission exposed the discontent of members of the SLA (Richards 1996). Months without pay crippled the morale of the frontline soldiers and led one hundred men to desert their posts (Gberie 2005). Their disenchantment with the government led to the first of three military coups during Sierra Leone's war. On 29 April 1992, under the command of Solomon Musa, a group of defected soldiers overtook the State House, driving President Momoh into exile to neighbouring Guinea. The military junta proclaimed itself the National Provisional Ruling Council (NPRC) to replace Momoh's APC regime and named Captain Valentine Strasser, who was only 26 at the time, its leader. The NPRC promised to end hostilities, renew legitimacy to government and end state corruption. For rural inhabitants and youth in particular, the change in government initially brought hope and anticipation for a better future.

The NPRC ultimately proved no better than its predecessor. In the months following the coup, it was largely preoccupied with establishing itself as the new sovereign authority and consolidating its power (Abraham 1997). In 1993, Strasser's government reportedly exported US$435 million in illicit diamonds to Sweden (Kpundeh 2004). Political representatives drove expensive automobiles and purchased European houses with public funds (Gberie 2005).

Meanwhile, the RUF intensified violence along the eastern border of the country in September 1992, and in the following months captured the central diamond district of Kono along with mines in Kailahun, Koidu and Pendembu (Abraham 2004; Richards 1996). The attacks forced mass migration from the instability of the countryside to the relative safety of towns and cities (Muana 1997). The NPRC responded to the attacks with Operation Genesis. In light of the need to increase the number of soldiers, new recruits, including significant numbers of children, came from the slums of Freetown.[8]

The NPRC mission lasted until the end of the following year, when the SLA recaptured lost territory, including the RUF's headquarters in Pendembu (Gberie 2005; Muana 1997). It appeared as if the RUF was

---

[8] It has been reported that most of the child recruitment into the SLA occurred during the NPRC reign (Coalition to Stop the Use of Child Soldiers 2008). McKay and Mazurana (2004) estimate that 3,500 children fought with the SLA over the course of the conflict.

in full retreat by the end of 1993 and many thought that the war was effectively over. In fact, from late 1993 and through all of 1994, Sankoh ceased his communication with the BBC. The perceived success of the mission led Strasser to declare a unilateral month-long ceasefire, ordering members of the RUF to surrender their weapons (Hirsch 2001). Ignoring the call, the rebels appeared to use the opportunity to regroup and devise a new strategy. By 1994, the RUF seemed suddenly invigorated, renewing attacks and ambushes on major highways linking the countryside to Freetown (Richards 1996). Violence once again gripped the country.

### 'Sobelization', the kamajors and private security firms

By the end of 1994, the RUF had established at least six permanent bush camps throughout the south and the east of the country from which it was able to carry out raids, and from December 1994 to January 1995, the RUF launched a new offensive. The rebels' apparent advance towards Freetown in early 1995 prompted aid agencies to evacuate their staff from the capital (Keen 2005, p. 40). The sudden renewed strength of the RUF was puzzling to many. Over time, reports of government soldiers leaving weapons behind for their RUF 'enemies' and RUF/SLA rotating control of the diamond mines for mutual profit confirmed the suspicion of an alliance (Abraham 2004; Keen 1997). In 1994, Strasser announced that at least 20 per cent of his forces were disloyal (Gberie 2005). The corruption of the SLA was coined 'sobelization' or 'sobels' – soldiers by day, rebels by night (Abraham 2004). Realizing that they could earn more through looting civilians and stealing national revenue through diamonds, young, ill-trained and poorly paid government soldiers attacked and pillaged innocent civilians for personal gain (Ukeje 2003). The RUF appeared to rely heavily, but not exclusively, upon arms and ammunition from disaffected government troops, which ultimately bolstered its strength and helped to explain its rather unexpected revitalization (Keen 2005).

To civilians, the RUF and the SLA became virtually indistinguishable. The distrust for government soldiers and fear of the RUF led to the emergence of the CDF – local men who sought to provide protection for innocent civilians and stage offensives against the rebels where the government had been unable or unwilling to do so. Among the Mende, these local men were known as the 'kamajors'. While 'kamajor' is a Mende word meaning 'hunter', the term eventually came to refer to anyone initiated into the militia, whether they had previously been a hunter or not (and most had not) and was used to describe more broadly based civil defence organizations (Ferme and Hoffman 2004, p. 76). Among the non-Mende, the CDF took more specific names (such as the Kapras and Gbetes among the Temne, the Donsos of Kono district and the Tamaboras of Koinadugu district). The kamajors, who had superior knowledge of the terrain near their home villages, were used as scouts during army patrols as early as 1991 and as the war progressed, a highly organized counter-insurgency movement formed. The kamajors were revered for their invincibility, mysticism and supernatural powers (Muana 1997). Through the use of native herbs, charms, sacred attire and prohibitions such as particular foods, having contact with a woman while in battle dress, looting villages and committing rape, the kamajors were said to be protected and impervious to bullets. As Ferme and Hoffman (2004) note:

The moral resonances of kamajor identity were made manifest in a series of taboos and restrictions imposed on individual combatants by their initiation into the militia. Every kamajor was required to pass through a series of instructions designed to instill the rules and behaviour expected of an initiate, and most importantly to provide them with the medicine that makes their bodies impervious to enemy fire. (Ferme and Hoffman 2004, p. 81)

Traditionally, kamajors had to be at least 30 years old, yet as the war progressed it recruited many children.[9] The kamajors were able to destroy major RUF training bases and capture rebel-occupied towns. Moreover, their perceived invincibility invoked fear in their opponents and many rebels refused to face the kamajor militia men, fearful of their supernatural powers (Muana 1997). While the taboos and prohibitions seen as guaranteeing immunity to bullets and death helped to limit abuses within the movement (Keen 2005), the kamajors were certainly not exempt from engaging in numerous human rights abuses during the war, including indiscriminate killings, torture and abduction (Human Rights Watch 2003c).

While the kamajors were critical to assisting the government, the loss of control over the diamond fields, the unreliability of the SLA and the continued brutality of the war and rising death toll led Strasser's NPRC

---

[9] McKay and Mazurana (2004) estimate that 17,216 child soldiers, who engaged in both supportive roles and active combat duties, were associated with the multiple civil defence groups during the war, 10 per cent of which they estimate were girls.

to enlist the help of private mercenary firms. In February 1995, a multi-million dollar deal was struck with the British-based Gurkha Security Guards (GSG) whereby in exchange for diamond concessions, the GSG trained the SLA in counter-insurgency operations and helped the government reduce rebel activities around key areas (Gberie 2005). The GSG contract was cut short when its leader, American Robert Mackenzie, was killed in an RUF ambush. Its rapid withdrawal forced Strasser to seek alternative reinforcement from a South African-based private mercenary outfit called Executive Outcomes (EO), which was led by retired white officers from the notorious apartheid-era 32nd battalion of the South African Special Forces (Keen 2005; Ukeje 2003). Employing Angolan and Namibian forces, EO was contracted to achieve four main objectives: 'to secure Freetown, retake the Sierra Rutile mines, destroy RUF headquarters, and clear remaining areas under RUF control' (Hirsch 2001, p. 39). Its monthly payment of US$1.5 million in diamond concessions, part of a complex deal with a diamond-mining company, depended on its ability to clear the mines from rebel control (Clapham 2003). By late 1995, with support from the kamajors, EO successfully reclaimed the eastern diamond fields within one month, and secured Freetown in less than a year (Clapham 2003). Suffering fewer than twenty casualties, including those from accidents and illness, the private firm succeeded in bringing temporary stability to the country (Singer 2003).

## 1996–2007: The Sierra Leone People's Party

With the success of the anti-RUF operations, attention turned to replacing the junta with a democratically elected government. Strasser's interest in the presidency sparked internal division within the NPRC, causing great upheaval. At only 30 years of age, he was constitutionally ineligible by 10 years to be leader of the country. Determined to run for office, Strasser threatened to fire anyone who failed to support his objective (Hirsch 2001). Before long, Strasser was removed from his position in a palace coup and was flown to Conakry. Brigadier Julius Maada Bio was installed as the new chairman of the NPRC in 1996.

### Elections, Kabbah and the Abidjan Agreement: 1996

News of the upcoming elections sparked renewed RUF hostilities across the countryside. The rebels called for the boycott of the poll and, as noted earlier in the chapter, the rebels symbolically amputated the hands of thousands of civilians: a clear message to prospective voters (Gberie 2005). Despite their tactics of terror, the elections went ahead as planned on 26 February 1996. After tallying the results of over 750,000 votes, Dr Ahmed Tejan Kabbah of the SLPP was declared the country's new president (Kandeh 2004). The next month, Maada Bio transferred power to Kabbah in one of the only instances of a peaceful transition from military to civilian rule in the country's history. With its platform slogan 'One country, one people', Kabbah's government declared its commitment to ending the war.

Peace talks with the rebels, initiated by Maada Bio, persisted over the next 8 months. The involvement of members of the RUF in the new government was seen as a possible way to end RUF insurgency and bring peace to the country. However, Kabbah initially deemed the inclusion of Sankoh and his top comrades in the new government as unconstitutional and unethical, and he refused to negotiate the issue (Hirsch 2001). Nonetheless, the Abidjan Agreement was signed by Foday Sankoh and President Kabbah on 30 November 1996, under the auspices of the UN, the Commonwealth, the Organization of African Unity (OAU) and the Côte d'Ivoire government (Hirsch 2001). Notable conditions of the agreement included the rapid withdrawal of EO forces, the initiation of demobilization and disarmament campaigns, the establishment of a Commission for the Consolidation for Peace to oversee the implementation of the agreement, and the transformation of the RUF into a legitimate political party (Clapham 2003). The agreement also required the government to take meaningful action to address the socio-economic dimensions of the conflict, specifically the marginalization of the rural population and its limited access to basic health and social services.

The peace agreement was never fully realized. It became clear that Sankoh and other RUF hardliners were reluctant to honour the agreement, perhaps because of the clear economic benefits of the war – particularly for the high-ranking RUF leadership. Moreover, key RUF commanders feared retaliation under conditions of peace (Keen 2005). Communication between the RUF and Kabbah ultimately broke down after radio interception revealed Sankoh's intention to sustain the war with the purchase of arms and ammunition (Hirsch 2001). In March 1997, Sankoh was apprehended at Mohammed Murtala Airport in Lagos, Nigeria, for the illegal smuggling of ammunition. At the request of President Kabbah, he was detained in Nigeria for nearly 18 months (Hirsch 2001). The absence of Sankoh ignited a power struggle within the RUF and several high-ranked commanders wanted him replaced, while Sam Bockarie (a former hairdresser and illicit diamond miner), his second-in-command and steadfastly loyal to Sankoh, refused and charged the men with treason (Hirsch 2001).

### The Armed Forces Revolutionary Council/RUF reign of terror: 1997

President Kabbah was wary of the sobelized army he had inherited from the NPRC. His appointment of former leader of the kamajors Chief Samuel Hinga Norman as deputy defence minister was done to enhance the role of kamajors, men he felt he could trust, in military operations against the RUF (Hirsch 2001). As a result, junior officers within the SLA lost considerable prestige. The favouritism of the kamajors, along-side rumours of downsizing and subsidy cuts to the army, sparked resentment of the Kabbah administration (Gberie 2005).

On 25 May 1997, a group of government soldiers broke through the gates of Pademba Road Prison in Freetown releasing about six hundred prisoners and arming many of them (Gberie 2005). Exploiting the rage of the prisoners at Pademba was a strategic move to unleash full-scale violence on Freetown. One of the released prisoners, who had been jailed since August 1996 for plotting a coup, was ex-army major Johnny Paul Koroma. Koroma was proclaimed chairman of the new junta government, which was named the Armed Forces Revolutionary Council (AFRC). Koroma announced that Sierra Leone's rebels and large parts of the country's military that had apparently been fighting each other for most of the previous 6 years had come together in a joint coup d'état. The prisoners and defected soldiers spilled into the city's main streets, raping, looting and murdering at random (Hirsch 2001). Over 250 police officers were killed, and within hours the State House had been taken over, driving Kabbah to Guinea (Gberie 2005; Kandeh 2004). It subsequently emerged that the coup was planned and executed by very low-ranking government soldiers, tapping into their collusion with the RUF.

As the leader of the AFRC, Koroma's first order of business was to announce the official inclusion of the RUF in the new government. Koroma called on Sierra Leoneans to rally behind his junta as he had brought peace by the 'only way possible: aligning with the enemy: the RUF' (Gberie 2005, p. 102). Acting as the RUF's interim leader in

Sankoh's absence, Bockarie accepted the invitation and began negotiations to install RUF commanders in cabinet positions. While still in detention in Nigeria, Sankoh was appointed vice-chairman of the AFRC and vice-president of Sierra Leone in absentia. The RUF power-sharing triggered an exodus of 400,000 Sierra Leoneans to neighbouring Guinea, Liberia and the Gambia in the 3 months following the coup (Gberie 2005).

### Enter ECOMOG: 1998

The AFRC/RUF junta was condemned outright by the international community, without a single organization or foreign government recognizing its legitimate right to rule (Hirsch 2001). The UN Security Council adopted a resolution that imposed oil and arms embargoes on the military government to force it to step down (United Nations 2005). Economic Community of West African States (ECOWAS) responded by deploying Nigerian led ECOWAS Monitoring Group (ECOMOG) troops to help restore Kabbah's government.

Within weeks, the ECOWAS Committee of Five (Nigeria, Côte d'Ivoire, Ghana, Guinea and Liberia) strongly encouraged members of the junta to sign a ceasefire agreement in Conakry, Guinea. The Conakry Peace Plan called for the disarmament and demobilization of the armed groups – and for the safe return of exiled President Kabbah to his position as head of state by April 1998 (Gberie 2005). The ceasefire officially began in January 1998 and was monitored by ECOMOG. In disregard of the agreement, the AFRC/RUF continued to smuggle arms and ammunition into the country from Liberia (Hirsch 2001). The junta's violations of the ceasefire were met with attacks from ECOMOG and kamajors with military reinforcement from a private security group, Sandline International, and financial backing from Canadian-based DiamondWorks (Gberie 2005). By mid-February, ECOMOG successfully drove the military government out of Freetown. On 10 March, President Kabbah was escorted back to the capital to resume his position. Shortly after Kabbah was reinstated, the government charged sixty people – members of the junta who were arrested, as well as junta collaborators – with treason. Among those accused for their role in the 1997 coup was Foday Sankoh, who was flown into Sierra Leone by the Nigerians to face the charges. Among dozens of others, Sankoh was ultimately convicted of treason and sentenced to death.

On 13 July 1998, the Security Council created the United Nations Observer Mission in Sierra Leone (UNOMSIL) and deployed seventy unarmed military observers who documented the human rights abuses over a 6-month period.[10]

### 'Operation No Living Thing' and the Lomé Peace Accord: 1999

Despite the success of ECOMOG, the rebels soon managed to capture the towns of Koidu and Makeni, killing hundreds of ECOMOG soldiers in the process. The apparent re-emergence of rebel activity once again caused much bewilderment. It was later revealed that the RUF had formed contracts, through Taylor, with British companies who supplied aircraft and mercenaries in exchange for diamonds, which helped explain their gain in momentum (Gberie 2005). The rebels eventually reached Freetown and once again broke through the gates of Pademba Road Prison, freeing RUF and ex-SLA prisoners awaiting appeal. The overriding motivation for the operation appeared to be Bockarie's determination to free Sankoh. Ultimately, however, Sankoh, who had been transferred from Pademba Road Prison just 2 weeks prior to the prison-break, was not among those freed, raising suspicions that the attacks had been anticipated by the government (Gberie 2005).

The RUF dubbed its reign of terror 'Operation No Living Thing'. Bockarie announced on the BBC newswire that it planned to kill everyone, '[down] to the last chicken' (Gberie 2005, p. 120). On 6 January 1999 the RUF and ex-SLA soldiers linked to the 1997 junta ravaged the capital city in what has been described as a 'regime of horror ... so intense and bizarre ... that it defies description' (Gberie 2005, p. 126). The rebels made little distinction between civilians and military targets, stating that they believed that civilians should be punished for what they perceived to be their support for the existing government. Resulting in weeks of arson, terror, rape, murder and dismemberment, innocent civilians and bystanders were attacked and killed, causing UNOMSIL personnel to be evacuated from the capital. By the time ECOMOG troops, aided by the kamajors, forced the rebels from Freetown, nearly 100,000 people had fled their homes, over 6,000 had been killed, thousands of children were reported missing and likely abducted by the rebels, and much of the city had been destroyed (Abdullah 2005).

---

[10] In October 1999, this observer mission was transformed into a peacekeeping one, known as the United Nations Mission in Sierra Leone (UNAMSIL).

President Kabbah was put under increasing pressure to bring peace to the country through negotiations. He was extremely reluctant to engage in peace talks with the RUF, but knew that peacekeepers would not be deployed without a signed peace agreement (Gberie 2005). The visit of the American Special Envoy for Africa, Reverend Jesse Jackson, led to the release of Sankoh from prison and to the commencement of negotiations in Lomé, Togo.

The Lomé Peace Accord was signed on 7 July 1999. The accord included a commitment to end all hostilities, the disarmament, demobilization and reintegration (DDR) of all combatants, the transformation of the RUF into a legitimate political party, the re-establishment of the Commission for the Consolidation of Peace and the creation of a Truth and Reconciliation Commission. The accord also stipulated a power-sharing arrangement, which granted RUF officials four cabinet posts and Foday Sankoh the chairmanship of the New Commission for the Management of Strategic Resources, National Reconstruction and Development and the vice-presidency (Abraham 2004). The most controversial part of the Lomé Accord was the blanket amnesty awarded to the rebels, which freed them of legal responsibility for the war between 1991 and the signing of the agreement, under the national penal code (Hirsch 2001). It was felt that without the amnesty, the RUF would not participate in the peace talks and the war would continue. Nonetheless, the UN refused to recognize the amnesty given that war crimes, crimes against humanity and other serious violations of humanitarian law were not subject to amnesty protection.

The accord, however, was unable to stop the war. Attempts to disarm and demobilize combatants took place as the RUF rearmed and resumed fighting. Attacks against Nigerian ECOMOG troops led to the total withdrawal of Nigeria's support for the ECOWAS mission in May 2000 (Gberie 2005). The RUF's abduction of 500 recently deployed Zambian peacekeepers of the United Nations Mission in Sierra Leone (UNAMSIL), which was launched in October 1999, sparked protests in the streets of Freetown on 8 May 2000 (Hirsch 2001). Nearly 30,000 people gathered around Sankoh's home demanding an end to the war and the release of the peacekeepers (Hirsch 2001). The peaceful demonstrations ended in bloodshed when Sankoh's bodyguards opened fire on the crowd, killing seventeen and wounding many more. Sankoh was put under house arrest, but managed to escape. Bizarrely, he returned to his house on 17 May to recover some items and was spotted by passers-by.

The government was alerted and attempted to arrest him, shooting him in the thigh. Civilians then beat Sankoh, stripped him naked and paraded him along the streets. Saving him from the violence of civilians, Sankoh was taken into custody by police and eventually transferred to Pademba Road Prison. The capture of Sankoh contributed to the eventual release of the UNAMSIL prisoners.

## The decline of the RUF and the brokering of peace

Gradually, towards the end of 2000, the strength of the RUF began to fade. Keen (2005) argues that six factors led to the 'softening' of the RUF, eventually paving the way to an accelerated peace process. First, was the combined assault of Guinean forces and the Civil Defence Forces. These forces dealt significant blows to the RUF who were increasingly trying to avoid confrontations. Second, was the international attention and pressure to crack down on 'conflict diamonds', which eventually had an impact on RUF activities and the capacity for smuggling. Third, were the sanctions that were being imposed on Taylor through the UN Security Council, which included a ban on Liberian diamond exports, the strengthening of the existing arms embargo and the grounding of Liberian aircraft. The diminished support from Liberia appears to have reduced rebel profits from the diamond trade. Fourth, was the strengthening of UNAMSIL. Having embarrassed the UN by capturing 500 peacekeepers, in May 2000, UNAMSIL was revamped with a more robust mandate, making it the world's largest peacekeeping mission with 17,455 peacekeepers by the end of March 2002. Fifth, was the intervention of the British and their attempt to retrain and reorganize the SLA. Finally, was the growing internal weariness within the ranks of the RUF. With Sankoh imprisoned, Issa Sesay emerged as the new leader. He appeared to be more motivated to crack down on human rights abuses, and to secure peace (Keen 2005). With all of these factors in place, the country was gradually pacified in 2001. In May 2001, representatives from both sides of the conflict met once again in Abuja to set the framework for another ceasefire which would ultimately bring an end to the war.

The war was officially declared over in January 2002. President Kabbah announced: 'Today we are happy that those flames of war have been extinguished' (BBC News 2002). The end of the 11-year war was marked by the symbolic ceremonial closure of the last disarmament centre in Kailahun district, where the war had begun in

March 1991, alongside a symbolic burning of arms in Makeni and Freetown. In May 2002, Kabbah won the presidential elections and the SLPP secured a majority in parliament.

Sierra Leone's Truth and Reconciliation Commission (TRC), conceived in July 1999 at the signing of the Lomé Accord, was established by an Act of Parliament in February 2000 to create an impartial historical record of violations and abuses of human rights and international humanitarian law related to the conflict. Having both fact-finding and therapeutic dimensions, the TRC intended to serve as the most legitimate forum for victims to 'reclaim their human worth and [as] a channel for the perpetrators of atrocities to expiate their guilt, and chasten their consciences. The process has been likened to a national catharsis, involving truth telling, respectful listening and above all compensation for victims in deserving cases' (Berewa, cited in Schabas 2004, p. 8). The TRC began its public hearings in April 2003 and held closed hearings at the district level for women and children. The TRC collected 8,000 statements and received an additional 1,500 statements from the Campaign for Good Governance. The TRC released it final report in 2004.

In August 2000, the UN Security Council created a 'Special Court' to try those persons who had borne 'greatest responsibility' for serious violations of international humanitarian law and the laws of Sierra Leone since 30 November 1996. The Special Court for Sierra Leone (SCSL) represents the first time an international war crimes tribunal has taken place inside the country where the conflict took place, making it easier for the population directly affected to follow its proceedings. There have been four trials at the SCSL, prosecuting key members of the RUF, AFRC and CDF, as well as former Liberian president Charles Taylor. In relation to the RUF, Foday Sankoh and four of his top commanders, Sam Bockarie, Issa Hassan Sesay, Morris Kallon, and Augustine Gbao, were indicted on multiple counts of crimes against humanity, violations of Article 3 common to the Geneva Conventions and of Additional Protocol II, commonly referred to as war crimes, and other serious violations of international humanitarian law. Ultimately, Sankoh died in custody on 29 July 2003 of natural causes. The chief prosecutor of the Special Court, David Crane, stated that Sankoh was granted 'a peaceful end that he denied to so many others' (BBC News 2003). Sam Bockarie also died in custody. The remaining three defendants were convicted of war crimes and crimes against humanity on 25 February 2009. These former rebel leaders became the first people in the world to be convicted for forced marriage and attacks on peacekeepers. They were also convicted of recruiting child soldiers. Issa Sesay was sentenced to 52 years imprisonment, Morris Kallon to 40 years and Augustine Gbao to 25 years.

Trials for Alex Tamba Brima, Brima Bazzy Kamara and Santigie Borbor Kanu of the AFRC concluded with the Appeal Judgment on 22 February 2008. The men were found guilty on multiple counts of crimes against humanity and war crimes. Brima and Kanu were sentenced to 50 years imprisonment and Kamara to 45 years.[11]

The trials for CDF commanders Chief Samuel Hinga Norman, Moinina Fofana and Allieu Kondewa concluded on 28 May 2008, and found Fofana and Kondewa guilty of war crimes and crimes against humanity. Fofana was sentenced to 15 years imprisonment and Kondewa to 20 years (Special Court for Sierra Leone 2008b). Hinga Norman, the former minister of interior and head of the CDF, died in Dakar prior to the announcement of a judgment.

Charles Taylor faces an eleven-count indictment for crimes against humanity, war crimes and other serious violations of international humanitarian law for his role in the war. On 25 March 2006, with the election of Liberian president Ellen Johnson-Sirleaf, Nigerian president Olusegun Obasanjo permitted transfer of Charles Taylor, who had been living in exile in the Nigerian coastal town of Calobar, to Sierra Leone for prosecution. Two days later, Taylor attempted to flee Nigeria, but he was apprehended by Nigerian authorities and transferred to Freetown under UN guard. The Special Court later announced that Charles Taylor would be tried at the International Criminal Court (ICC) in The Hague (Human Rights Watch 2006). This decision was made based on the perceived security threat to Freetown and the surrounding area if the trial proceeded locally.[12] If found guilty, Taylor is to be imprisoned at a detention facility in the United Kingdom, as per the conditional agreement forged between the ICC and the SCSL. At the time of writing, the trial of Charles Taylor continues in The Hague.

---

[11] The Court issued an indictment against a fourth AFRC defendant, former junta leader Johnny Paul Koroma, who is rumoured to have been killed, though his death remains unconfirmed.

[12] Taylor's transfer to The Hague has been criticized for making justice less accessible for those communities most affected by the war (Human Rights Watch 2006).

In March 2004, a proposal by the UN secretary-general was accepted by the UN Security Council that extended UNAMSIL's mandate to December 2005. This was made on the grounds that the country's progress to peace remained fragile and that the government was not in a position to assume full responsibility for security. In 2005, UNAMSIL withdrew all remaining peacekeepers and transferred non-peacekeeping responsibilities to a follow-on peacebuilding UN mission (UNIOSIL). In October 2008, UNIOSIL was replaced by the United Nations Integrated Peacebuilding Office in Sierra Leone (UNIPSIL). Authorized by the UN Security Council Resolution 1829, UNIPSIL is to ensure the continued support of the UN and the international community for the long-term peace, security and development of Sierra Leone.

Following elections in August 2007, the APC won a majority in parliament. While there were reports of voter coercion by party bosses and traditional leaders, observers characterized the elections as generally free and fair, adding that irregularities did not affect the final outcome (US Department of State 2008). On 17 September 2007, Ernest Bai Koroma was sworn into office as the elected president, replacing Kabbah.

In the aftermath of the war, the RUF became a political party. However, the party did not take part in the 2007 general presidential and parliamentary elections or in the local/municipal elections that followed.

Following years of strife, Sierra Leone has begun a long-term process of rebuilding. The war ultimately left the country with an economy in shambles, infrastructure destroyed, devastated educational and health systems, stockpiles of weapons, and generations of adults and children, both boys and girls, severely affected by the economic, political, social, psychological and physical health effects of the war.

When examining the war and the realities of young people in Sierra Leone (whether the early RUF sympathizers or the wartime child abductees who had little invested in the RUF 'cause'), it is clear that powerful structural considerations framed their individual decision-making and options. Profound economic marginalization, state corruption, structural violence, militarization, patrimonialism, social exclusion and historical and cultural realities shaped young people's opportunities and choices to take up arms. For those children forcibly abducted during the heat of war, the changing structural realities of the war inevitably framed their choices and prospects. It is the lives of this latter group of children that are the focus of upcoming chapters.

# 3 | Negotiating power: Research on and by child soldiers

C ONDUCTING research on former child soldiers raises a whole host of methodological and ethical dilemmas, particularly in relation to notions of power. In an attempt to mitigate the multiple research dilemmas, a participatory approach was employed that sought to engage a group of former child soldiers as researchers and collaborators. This chapter provides an overview of the study's methodology including information on the recruitment of participants, the research sample and how the data were collected and analysed. Before doing so, however, the chapter explores the notions of power and sensitive research and the ways in which they both shaped and embodied the research experience.

## On power, sensitive research and a participatory approach

I write and conduct research from a position of privilege and security as a white female academic living in Canada. I have not grown up within a context of war, nor have I been associated with a military or an armed group. The power and privilege of my social location sometimes brought automatic deference within the context of Sierra Leone, making me painfully aware of the ascribed power that I held within the context of this research. This, alongside the power differentials inherent to the research process, was a potentially lethal combination. It is within this context that some researchers have suggested that the possibility of exploitation is endemic to fieldwork (England 1994; Stacey 1991). In fact, research and fieldwork in and of themselves have sometimes been described as colonizing constructs, techniques of knowledge production that silences subjects, and crude exercises of power, with a legacy that Linda Tuhiwai Smith refers to as 'they came, they saw, they named, they claimed' (cited in Mutua and Blue Swadener 2004, p. 1). For the most part, researchers have suggested that the flow of power is unidirectional: the researcher and researched are often polarized into powerful/powerless categories whereby the researcher exerts power over the researched

(Thapar-Bjorkert and Henry 2004). Some have even suggested that it is impossible to conduct any research, particularly in the developing world, that is ethical and not exploitive (Wong 1998).

While such ethical issues are unquestionably present in research with both children and adults, issues of power in the researcher–participant relationship may present themselves more sharply when study participants are children (Mauthner 1997). Children and youth may find it more difficult to challenge adult authority and refuse to answer questions. They may also find it more difficult to act on their right to withdraw from a study. This may be the result of not knowing the practicalities of how to withdraw should they wish to, or of being concerned that they will suffer negative consequences if they withdraw (Mishna et al. 2004). Young participants may also communicate discomfort or desire to withdraw in indirect ways. Kay et al. (2002) suggest that interviewers need to be aware of more subtle signs that a child may no longer wish to discuss a particular issue in an interview, such as suddenly falling silent, and treat these as signals. As former child soldiers, many of the participants in this study went from a state of relative powerlessness prior to the war, to take up powerful positions within the armed group. During the conflict, some boys and girls became commanders of other child soldiers and held enormous power over civilians. In the aftermath of the conflict, however, these children frequently returned to a society where they found themselves rejected, marginalized and once again powerless. Power and status thus had important and complicated meanings for former child soldiers and given their militarized experiences of abduction, hierarchy and abuse by adult authority, many appear to have been distrustful and resentful of adults and highly suspicious of foreigners.

The notion of power was further intensified because of the sensitive nature of this research. Lee and Renzetti (1993) define a sensitive research topic as one that potentially poses a substantial threat for those involved in the research and which may have an impact on the collection, holding or dissemination of research data. Sensitive topics are ones that seek to explore deeply personal and valued experiences – experiences that those being studied do not wish to be misused. When conducting sensitive research, there may be psychological or social costs to those being researched, including guilt, shame or embarrassment. Importantly, the sensitive nature of the research can affect every stage of the research process, from formulation through design to implementation and dissemination (Sieber 1993). Throughout this project the research team was keenly aware of the wrenching nature of the stories sought, and the psychological risks that this might have entailed for the participants. While gaining an understanding of children's perspectives and experiences within the RUF's culture of violence is essential to challenging the narrow images and discourses of child soldiers, and to recognizing diverse realities of children caught up in the maelstrom of war, it can have serious implications. Participants were being asked to share potentially traumatic and painful circumstances of war and violence that could evoke varying levels of distress. Those who were still suffering from the trauma of war and its related effects could experience heightened anxiety by speaking about it in detail. Individuals who had begun to come to terms with their wartime experiences of physical, psychological or sexual violence and were beginning to move forward in their lives were being asked to reopen old wounds. Additional difficulties could potentially arise as a result of participants' discomfort and anxiety in openly discussing their experiences, or their fear of reprisal as a result of sharing their stories. Respondents could also worry of social stigmatization and judgment as a result of speaking about their direct involvement in violence.

These diverse issues undoubtedly represented a few of the 'ethical minefields' (Boyden 2004, p. 241) that required constant care, attention and mitigation. While it appears that the overwhelming number of children who participated in interviews and focus groups for this study found the experience to be something of a catharsis, a key facet of fieldwork was to pay scrupulous attention to the ethical dimensions of the research and to conduct follow-up visits and informal exchanges with all respondents to ensure that their safety and psychological well-being had not been jeopardized by their participation in the project.

Yet over the course of the project, gradual shifts in the negotiation of power affirmed the more complex and dialogical nature of the research relationship. Research participants gradually began to make demands on the research team, and, in a few cases, refused to answer questions. As Scheyvens and Leslie (2000) suggest:

[A] problem with the idea that research [on the] ... Third World ... is always exploitative is that this incorrectly assumes [that individuals from the] Third World have no power. The reality is that researchers rarely hold all of the power in the research process. Respondents can, for example, exercise control by withholding information from the researcher, failing to cooperate or refusing to answer questions. (Scheyvens and Leslie 2000, pp. 125–6)

Similarly, when conducting research with children, Barker and Smith (2001) maintain that the conceptualization of the research relationship as 'adult as all powerful' is overly simplistic. They argue that because children are the 'experts of the day-to-day spaces of childhood, adults' lack of experience of such places means that they are often the "novice" or incompetent adult' (Barker and Smith 2001, p. 146). In this sense, power in the research relationship, whether with child or adult participants, is never statically and evenly distributed. Instead, it can be characterized as fluid, negotiable and unpredictable and fluctuates depending on the different constellations of identity and power at play (Bhavnani 1993; Mutua and Blue Swadener 2004). As such, Thapar-Bjorkert and Henry (2004) encourage researchers to question the rigid demarcation between oppressor (researcher) and oppressed (participant) and to critically appropriate a framework that imagines power as shifting, multiple and intersecting (Foucault 1980). In this sense,

power is understood as not only top-down, but dispersed through both research relationships and the research process ... [T]his reconceptualization allows researchers to reimagine [their] participants as agents, thereby avoiding stereotypical constructions of the 'third world' as subordinate, the researched as powerless and the researcher as all powerful, while still acknowledging that there are differences and inequalities between researchers and research participants. (Thapar-Bjorkert and Henry 2004, p. 364)

Given the intricate and fluid realities of power, a methodological approach was needed that recognized children's inherent power and position as active participants in their own development and experts in their own lives. Alderson (2000) and Thomas and O'Kane (1998) have argued that reflexive, collaborative and participatory approaches to research, particularly when studying children, may not only work to neutralize power differentials and ethical concerns and engage children as active citizens, but may also increase reliability and validity. Similarly, Morrow and Richards (1996) articulate: 'Using methods which are non-invasive, non-confrontational and participatory ... might be one step forward in diminishing the ethical problems of imbalanced power relations between researcher and researched' (p. 100). Alderson (2000) notes that 'if children's social relations and culture are worthy of study in their own right, then who is better qualified to research some aspects of their lives than children themselves?' (p. 244). Alderson (2000) asserts that involving children more directly in research can 'rescue them from silence and exclusion and from being represented, by default, as passive objects' (p. 243). Moreover, she notes that doing research helps children, particularly disadvantaged ones, 'to gain more skills, confidence and perhaps determination to overcome their disadvantages than adult researchers working on their behalf could give them' (p. 253). It was in this spirit that this project drew upon a participatory research approach to studying the making and unmaking experiences of child soldiers in Sierra Leone.

Developmental and educational research, which historically has had an important influence on the nature of the research agenda concerning children, has tended to construct children as either passive objects of research, as problematic, or as vulnerable and incompetent (Munford and Sanders 2004). These powerful social discourses have meant that 'we do not have a culture of listening to children ... without the filters of adult perspectives and interests' (Munford and Sanders 2004, pp. 470, 472). In an attempt to challenge such discourses and to benefit from the unique knowledge and experience of former child soldiers in Sierra Leone, twelve adolescent researchers who had been associated with the RUF during the conflict were invited to participate in the project as collaborators and researchers. Besides the conviction that the adolescent researchers would enhance the richness of the project and therefore the quality of the data, the adult research team was keen to involve a group of young people in a purposeful activity that could prove to be educational and empowering. The adolescent researchers involved in the study were selected on the basis of their evident interest and enthusiasm for the project by research partners from Defence for Children International – Sierra Leone, and Forum of Conscience, who had ongoing contact with war-affected children through the course of their daily work.[1]

## Participant recruitment, data collection and analysis

The entire research team for the project was composed of a group of both Sierra Leonean and Canadian researchers. The Sierra Leonean researchers included eight adults (five male and three female) from

---

[1] The youth researchers were compensated for their work on the project in the form of educational scholarships or skills training to support their future endeavours.

two local NGOs in Sierra Leone: Defence for Children International – Sierra Leone (DCISL) and Forum of Conscience (FoC), as well as twelve youth researchers (six male and six female). The Canadian researchers included myself (the project's principal investigator) and Dr Richard Maclure of the University of Ottawa. Formal research training sessions and workshops were conducted with the adult and youth research team, which focused on the goals of the research, on interview techniques, conducting peer interviews, on the presentation of self during interviews and focus group discussions, on gender and culture in interviewing, on ethical issues including informed consent, confidentiality and anonymity, and on the potential challenges the researchers were likely to face in the field. As part of the training, researchers undertook mock interviewing and mock focus group discussions as a way to hone their new skills. While preparation and research training was extensive, in reality, the training was ongoing and the research team engaged in open dialogue and consultation throughout the project concerning the challenges brought forth by the research and fieldwork.

The selection of former child soldiers for participation in the study was facilitated by DCISL and FoC,[2] who had ongoing contact with war-affected children through the course of their daily work. Researchers from the two NGOs purposively selected a sample of seventy-six children (thirty-six boys and forty girls) with whom they were in regular contact in the eastern, southern and northern provinces and the western area of Sierra Leone.

To be included in the study, participants were required to have been associated with an armed group or armed force in Sierra Leone (whether by force or non-force) while under the age of 18. No stipulations were made regarding the length of time that children were attached to an armed group or armed force, or their assigned role within the group/force. At the commencement of the research fieldwork in 2003, all participants were between 14 and 21 years old and had been associated with the RUF.[3] The participants had all been recruited by the RUF when they were very young

---

[2] The researchers from DCISL were involved in all stages of the research process. Researchers from FoC were involved primarily in the recruitment of study participants in the northern and southern regions of the country, data collection in the north and south and the translation and transcription of these data.

[3] The purposive sampling method led to the eventual recruitment of eighty children – forty girls (all formerly associated with the RUF) and forty boys (thirty-six of whom had been associated with the RUF and four with the CDF). As a result

(ranging between 4 and 13 years of age), and most were not yet 18 years old at the end of the hostilities. All of the forty girls and thirty-six boys reported being abducted by the RUF and remained under their control for a period ranging from a few months to 8 years.

To supplement the data gathered from the child respondents, additional interviews and focus groups were conducted with seventy-two individuals. Forty interviews were conducted with institutional stakeholders (including representatives of the Sierra Leonean government, donor agencies, local community leaders and former adult ex-combatants), as well as focus groups with thirty-two parents/guardians of former child soldiers. These interviews and focus groups served to enhance and complement interviews with child respondents and enabled the research team to garner greater contextual information on the conflict, the role of children within the conflict, and broader community and family perspectives on the post-conflict psycho-social needs of former child soldiers.

The recruitment of participants for the study was, at times, challenging and several individuals politely declined the invitation to participate. In the post-conflict context there appeared to be a general wariness for individuals posing questions about wartime experiences. As Boyden and de Berry (2004) have noted, the realities of war often dismantle relationships within local communities and may lead to a profound loss of confidence in self and others. Profound ambivalence may be expressed about 'friends, neighbours, and kin, whether as betrayer or betrayed, victim or perpetrator, wrongdoer or wronged' (Boyden and de Berry 2004, p. 242) and this ambivalence may be even more profound in relation to strangers and foreigners. In addition, at the time when potential participants were being recruited for the project, Sierra Leone's TRC was travelling throughout the country gathering statements. Some potential respondents were initially reticent to participate in the project due to a fear that the researchers were affiliated with the TRC and the information shared during interviews could be divulged to either the TRC or to the SCSL. Among many potential child respondents, there was an immense fear of prosecution. This became

---

of the high numbers of former RUF child soldiers, it made sense to focus our attention on the experiences of those in the RUF. As such, data gathered from the four boys who were part of the CDF were used for general background information and were not included in the data analysis.

increasingly apparent when the country's erstwhile deputy defence minister and former kamajor leader, Samuel Hinga Norman, was arraigned before the SCSL. Potential participants expressed the belief that if such a powerful individual as Norman could be arraigned at the court, they could easily be in danger of prosecution. Moreover, as the majority of the potential participants appeared to make little distinction between the TRC and the SCSL at the time of the interviews, it became critically important not only to reiterate that all information gathered for the research would remain confidential and anonymous, and be used for research purposes only, but also to clarify that the team of researchers had no affiliation with the TRC or the SCSL.

Importantly, the youth researchers were involved in the identification and recruitment of study participants. Some children were initially reticent to participate in the study when first approached by adult members of the research team. However, when the youth researchers approached potential participants and disclosed that they themselves had been part of the RUF, explained the objectives of the project and laid out issues of informed consent, confidentiality and anonymity, children's fears were often greatly allayed and, after having been briefed by their peers, many agreed to participate.

What also appeared to be critical in the degree of receptiveness was the level of trust that a particular community shared with members of the research team. In cases where the research team was not well known in the communities where the research was being carried out, a trusted individual of the community often introduced the research team to the rest of the community members. The support of such people, including social workers, local authorities and ordinary people in the community, was invaluable to the recruitment of study participants and the ultimate successful completion of the fieldwork.

## Interviews and focus groups

A method of inquiry was needed that not only addressed the sensitive nature of the research, but also captured the diverse perspectives and meanings of children's experiences of armed conflict. Boyden and de Berry (2004) have argued that pre-coded research instruments such as questionnaires are extremely limited in their ability to capture the true nature of wartime experiences or the meanings for war-affected populations. Instead, they assert that greater attention needs to be paid to the shifting, ambiguous and elusive nature of the context and aftermath of war which, they assert, is best illuminated through qualitative approaches. In response, this project relied upon in-depth, open-ended interviews and focus groups as the main instruments of data collection. As garnering children's wartime and post-war stories and experiences was essential to the project, the intimacy of a one-to-one interview was particularly well suited to achieving this. The focus groups, where confidentiality and anonymity could not be assured, examined children's views on post-conflict policies and programmes for former child soldiers, a topic which boded well for a group discussion.

The design of research instruments involved the entire research team. In particular, the youth researchers were involved in the creation of interview guides, as well as questions to be posed during focus group discussions. Working in groups, the youth brainstormed on potential questions to pose to participants in light of the research objectives, and provided invaluable contributions to overall team discussions regarding inappropriate questions, as well as questions that they believed would be misunderstood or misinterpreted by participants.

Following the research training sessions and workshops, the entire research team embarked on fieldwork that lasted from May 2003 to February 2004. Travelling together, the adult and youth researchers conducted interviews and focus groups with the forty girls and thirty-six boys. One-to-one interviews conducted by the adult researchers usually preceded the focus group sessions led by the adolescent researchers.

The majority of child participants were interviewed twice, and, in some cases, three times. The adult Sierra Leonean research team conducted a first round of semi-structured interviews with the children in their native languages (Krio, Mende, Temne and Limba respectively). These interviews were audio-taped with permission and subsequently transcribed and translated into English. These first transcripts facilitated the study of the lives and family backgrounds of the children prior to the war, the circumstances of their recruitment into the RUF and their subsequent experiences with the rebels. Many months later, I conducted a second round of one-to-one interviews. These interviews, which served to probe topics covered in the first round of interviewing, as well as exploring other emerging themes, were likewise audio-taped, translated and transcribed. In 2008, several years after the initial field-work, I conducted a third interview with a handful of participants to follow up with them and to garner their longer-term experiences, and to explore changes in their perspectives over time.[4]

Focus group discussions, consisting of three to four children, were conducted in Krio by the youth researchers in 2003 and 2004 with the same seventy-six research participants who had participated in the interviews. The purpose of the focus groups was to explore the reintegration experiences and psycho-social needs of former child soldiers, to assess what they themselves deemed important for their well-being and healing, and how this could best be achieved. It has been suggested that focus groups are particularly useful when conducting research with children. As Mauthner (1997) argues: 'small group discussions allow children to set their own agendas and the research topic to be woven into children's talk about their daily lives and social worlds' (p. 26). By inviting adolescents to lead the focus groups with child participants, it was hoped that participants would feel more comfortable sharing their post-conflict experiences and needs in the presence of adolescents who had experienced similar events. While some focus group leaders requested that an adult, who remained silent during the focus group, be present during the discussion, the majority of focus groups were led entirely by the youth researchers. Focus groups were divided by gender whereby adolescent girls led discussions with a group of girls and adolescent boys led discussions with boys. As with the interviews, all focus groups were audio-taped with the permission of participants and later transcribed and translated into English. Once the focus groups were completed, the adult research team solicited feedback from the adolescent researchers on their experiences and perspectives of the focus group discussions.

### Questions of credibility

As with all self-report data, particularly in light of some of the violent events that these young people experienced and participated in, the interviews and focus groups with the children were invariably affected by their memory of events, as well as their willingness to divulge personal information. In post-conflict Sierra Leone the potential fear

---

[4] In most cases, it was not possible to find the respondents for a third interview, as they were no longer living in the communities where the first two interviews had been conducted. In addition, the research team sadly learned that three participants had died since our last interview.

of stigmatization, the aforementioned reality and concern surrounding Special Court indictments, and the ongoing anxiety concerning Truth Commission investigations may have prevented some young people from openly disclosing some of their experiences, particularly their active involvement in violence. Even when interviewed for a third time in 2008, well after the war had ended, a few participants continued to voice their fear of possible indictment by the Special Court. When questioned on the issue, participants reported being well aware that no children or former child soldiers had been prosecuted by the Special Court. Nonetheless, they continued to believe that they were not entirely 'safe' and thus chose to keep their former status as ex-combatants a secret.

It is possible that children altered or exaggerated aspects of their stories, particularly their status as victims. This is especially apparent in post-war contexts where individuals may be increasingly cognizant that emphasizing their helplessness, dependence and victim status, particularly to outsiders and humanitarian aid organizations, may be crucial to obtaining aid and assistance (Honwana 2006; Shepler 2005; Utas 2004). Given that the research team was composed of local NGO workers, as well as foreigners who were in close partnership with the NGOs, viewing the research team as potential donors proved problematic in the early stages of the research.

The unanimity in the ways in which children reported being recruited into the RUF (through coercion and abduction) inevitably raised concerns about the veracity of their accounts. Given the significance of embracing an identity as a 'victim', as well as the post-war context in which many children formerly associated with the RUF were fearful of recrimination, it was natural that some might be reticent to truthfully discuss how they came to participate in hostilities. Nevertheless, many respondents openly recounted acts of cruelty that they themselves had perpetrated during the war. In light of their openness in speaking of past experiences, including admissions among participants of violent acts that they had committed during the conflict, there was reason to assume that most, if not all, were honest in recounting how they were drawn into the RUF.

While the potential flaws of self-disclosure must be taken into account when considering the participants' narratives, a number of other factors minimized such tendencies and helped to ensure overall confidence in the authenticity of their personal accounts. During the course of the project, the research team developed a relationship of trust and friendship with respondents. This appeared to be facilitated by the NGOs' strong community relationships in some regions of the country, their reputation as defenders of children's rights in Sierra Leone in others, and by the researchers' own general knowledge of the background and context of these young people's disclosures. Over time, these relationships greatly facilitated in-depth discussions about the young people's experiences of conflict. Moreover, many of the youth respondents frequently visited and socialized at the local offices of the research team between interviews, and they continued to do so after the research fieldwork was completed. This gave the research team ample opportunities to not only informally probe their stories, and garner their trust, but also enabled the relationships to go beyond participants' initial interpretation of the research team as simply potential donors.

Other factors also helped to assure the authenticity of the accounts. An examination of participants' accounts over time, as well as opportunities to probe any discrepancies or contradictions in their narratives, was facilitated by ongoing informal visits with participants, as well as formal interviews several times during the course of the project. Where possible, the research team also sought the validation of respondents' accounts through community and family members and local authorities, which often provided vital corroboration of participants' narratives.

Nonetheless, Utas (2003) is critical of the use of formalized audiotaped interviews with populations of former combatants. He argues that in such contexts interviewees rarely display elements of agency and that based on his own experience using this approach 'every interviewee complied with ... preset frames of victimhood' (p. 81). It is without question that the young people in this study clearly articulated their experiences and status as wartime victims. Yet simultaneously, as the upcoming chapters will illustrate, most respondents were surprisingly forthcoming in also discussing aspects of their own accountability, their wartime commitment to and identification with the RUF, and sharing their active participation in brutal acts of RUF violence. Perhaps such disclosures can once again be linked to the longer-term nature of the research project and the young people's ongoing contact with the research team over time, potentially mitigating the limitations Utas sees in semi-structured interviewing. As Utas (2003) notes in relation to his own research sample of former combatants:

In order to more deeply understand individual motives and collective disposi-
tions underlying child and youth participation in civil wars, scholars need
longer-term personal contacts with their research subjects ... After some
months, when trust deepened between us, some of the youth ... recounted
stories closer to their own honest versions of their experiences. Time was the
most important ingredient in this arrangement. (Utas 2003, pp. 51, 80)

There are other limitations of the data that prevent the narratives from
being generalized to all child soldiers in Sierra Leone or all those formerly
associated with the RUF. The stories and experiences garnered through
interviews are only of those who survived the war and those who were
willing to discuss their experiences. Ultimately, it was apparent that participants took great risks to share their life stories and experiences. Several
participants reported that they had never before disclosed to anyone outside of their closest circle that they had been combatants in the conflict, or
that they had committed acts of severe violence. Many had told those close
to them that they had been victimized during the war, but that they had not
participated in violence. Some even reported hiding this information from
their closest friends, family members and girlfriends or boyfriends, largely
out of fear that they would be marginalized or rejected. Others, however,
chose to participate in the project because they felt that it would be
beneficial and cathartic. For example, one female participant expressed
the expectation during the interview that participating in the research
would help her emotionally and psychologically.

## Analysis and interpretation

Upon completion of the data collection, analysis of the interview and
focus group transcripts was essentially a phenomenological process that
involved careful reading and annotation of the collated information so as
to ascertain the meaning and significance that the boys and girls attrib-
uted to their experiences as child soldiers (Grbich 2007). With hundreds
of pages of interview and focus group transcripts at hand, an initial
inductive analysis of the data was conducted in Canada. Using an inductive approach was essential to ensuring that the voices and perspectives of
participants became the central component of the analysis and facilitated
an authentic presentation of children's experiences (Lyons 2004, p. 282;
Stasiulis 1993). Annotations of the transcripts consisted of themes that
were identified as recurring in the children's narratives. After the first
round of descriptive analysis, clusters of verbatim text were regrouped

according to thematic indices – a process that was facilitated by the use of a qualitative analysis software.

This initial thematic organization of the data, which was depicted in cognitive and visual maps (Miles and Huberman 1994), was then the subject of several days of in-depth discussions, dialogue and debate in Sierra Leone, where broad patterns of experiences and perspectives were recognized. The adolescent researchers provided their own critical reflections and interpretations of the data emerging from their role as researchers, as well as their own personal experiences as former child soldiers. Through this inductive analytical process, a common experiential process of the stages of children's immersion into the culture of violence and the world of armed conflict, as well as their eventual disengagement from the armed group, was identified. While the analysis showed that this process of gradual militarization and demilitarization was far from uniform, it nonetheless helped to illuminate the structural forces that facilitated children's socialization into armed groups, and the degree to which personal agency was a factor underlying their subsequent actions as child soldiers.

In the final phase of the project, acting as presenters and discussants, and performing theatre and music based on their experiences of conflict, the adolescent researchers, alongside a number of study respondents, participated in a community conference in Freetown to disseminate the research findings to the local community in Sierra Leone. In addition, following the conference, the adolescent researchers and many study respondents were actively involved in a seminar to begin to formulate policies and programmes based on the research findings. The final seminar provided a forum for reviewing and discussing the findings of the research, and proposing policy and programme recommendations to various representatives of civil society, government and the international donor community that attended.

## Assessing a participatory approach

As observed by others who have engaged children as participants in the research process (Alderson 2000), the involvement of the adolescent focus group leaders has been mutually rewarding. It greatly contributed to the depth of the oral narratives that were elicited during the fieldwork and to the insights that have helped to 'depathologize' children who were caught up in the fighting as victims, perpetrators and resisters of violence. Relying on sensitivity and intuition, focus group leaders reported being able to read the verbal and non-verbal cues of child participants. On several occasions, when respondents were evidently reticent to talk about their experiences at any length, the focus group leaders eased their anxieties through the use of humour, empathy and, above all, self-disclosure regarding their own past experiences during the war. Through their own candour and efforts to minimize the power imbalances inherent in the research relationship, they were able to foster group trust among the participants and a willingness to be open and candid about their wartime experiences. The following statement reflects to varying degrees what all focus group leaders reported experiencing:

One girl in my focus group was very shy ... she was so shy to talk. I tried to coax her to talk. I explained that I was a girl just like her. I told her what happened to me, that I became separated from my parents, that I was with the rebels, and that I was raped. Then she began to open up. (Female focus group leader)

In addition to their contribution to the research, the focus group leaders indicated in debriefing sessions, their involvement in the project appears to have strengthened their own sense of identity and purpose from participating in the study. All of them expressed an appreciation of the learning experience, both from the exchanges they had with peers in the focus groups and also with the research team as a whole. The experience likewise helped to reduce for at least a short period of time their sense of isolation and social exclusion. As they indicated, participation in the research provided an opportunity to develop friendships and to assume leadership roles. One focus group leader captured this common sentiment:

I enjoyed sharing ideas with other [girls] ... [T]hey would ask me what I thought about their situations and I gave them the best advice that I could. I think that I was a good leader. (Female focus group leader)

The evidence of self-esteem and burgeoning leadership skills exemplified by this statement has been among the most gratifying results of this project. Nevertheless, the research team remained cognizant of the limitations and risks of encouraging war-affected children to articulate their wartime experiences, particularly in group settings led by their peers. During the data collection phase, youth participation was limited to serving as focus group leaders. Moreover, although the enormous potential of engaging children as research partners is evident, the realities of distance (the author being permanently based in Canada), the stipulations of proposal submission (i.e., the need for a pre-determined research design in order to procure funding), and time frames (i.e., the contractual obligation to complete the project within a specific period) foreclosed any early 'ownership' of the project by the young subjects of research. For similar reasons, the preliminary analysis of the interview and focus group transcripts was conducted by the Canadian research team.[5] This was mitigated, however, by the community conference which provided a forum for reviewing and discussing the findings of the research, and proposing policy and programme recommendations to various representatives of civil society, government and the international donor community that attended. Throughout the project the research team was well aware of the potential social and psychological risks for the participants. The risk of emotional turmoil has become a feature of life in post-conflict Sierra Leone, and will likely underline all efforts to engage children as participants in research and in other forms of outside intervention. Yet by openly recognizing the risk, and by anticipating the necessary measures to minimize the effects of relived traumas, it would seem that in the long run the benefits of engaging children as partners far outweigh the potential limitations and drawbacks.

The following three chapters highlight the making and unmaking experiences of child soldiers and their pathways in and out of violence and armed conflict. The goal is to project the voices of the girls and boys in order to convey their experiences and perspectives. Nonetheless, capturing children's realities on paper may run the risk of trivializing their wartime and post-war lives, creating a situation of voyeurism, even disaster pornography. While I echo Lyons' (2004, p. 282) concerns about the inappropriateness of using marginalized children's voices to produce a western academic text, I am also cognizant of the openness advocated by Stasiulis' (1993) anti-essentialist position on 'authentic voice'. Moreover, as Honwana (2006) has articulated: 'the acknowledgement of the informants' agency in the process of telling their war stories is important. Even with the constraints inherent to their situation, they can choose which messages they wish to convey to the world and how they wish to communicate them' (p. 18). In light of these considerations, I have attempted to create a space where the voices of former child soldiers may be illuminated and communicated, while being mindful of both dignity and diversity.

---

[5] The raw transcript data were voluminous (hundreds of pages), and hence it is difficult to envision any other method of managing the data in a timely and efficient manner.

# 4 | 'Becoming RUF': The making of a child soldier

I am beginning with the young. We older ones are used up ... We are rotten to the marrow. We have no unrestrained instincts left ... But my magnificent youngsters! Are there finer ones anywhere in the world? ... Look at these young men and boys! What material! With them I can make a new world.

(Adolf Hitler, cited in Rempel 1989, p. 2)

The rebels attacked my village and I was separated from my parents ... [They] threatened to kill me if I made any attempt to run away. I didn't want to die so I joined them. I was afraid of being around these dangerous men with all kinds of weapons ... I had no mom, no dad, sister or brother ... I was alone for the first time in my life.

(Boy)

The making of an RUF child soldier is undoubtedly a complex and multi-faceted process that occurred gradually over an extended period of time. This chapter sheds light on the important context in which this process of RUF militarization began, and the means through which the transmogrification of disoriented youngsters into often obedient and militarized members of the RUF deepened. Drawing upon participants' narratives, the chapter explores boys' and girls' experiences with recruitment and the militarized training they received. It also examines the myriad devices and strategies used by the RUF to ensure children's compliance and strengthen their attachment to its formal and informal culture through the encouragement of solidarity and cohesion, role allocation and the use of rewards and promotion. Importantly, these devices and strategies, as well as the overall initiation process into the RUF's militarized world of violence and armed conflict, cannot be understood in isolation from the larger context. The final section of the chapter outlines the ways in which the RUF leadership drew upon broader structural and historical conditionalities and ultimately produced and reproduced a profound culture of violence. It is this culture of violence that is key to understanding children's progression towards 'becoming RUF'.

## Pathway into violence and armed conflict

With the gradual militarization of Sierra Leonean society, and the eventual war-torn situation and insecurity of people throughout the country, children inevitably reported experiencing forms of militarization and insecurity prior to their abduction by the rebels. However, it was clear that these experiences of insecurity and militarization were heightened – to the extreme – when they were coercively and violently separated from their families and communities and forced to join the RUF.

### *Abduction*

All of the participants interviewed reported that their pathway into violence and armed conflict began with an experience of abduction. As evidenced in the following narratives, there was little opportunity for children to opt out:

During one of their numerous attacks, the rebels succeeded in driving the pro-government forces from our community. We hid ourselves in our house. The firing was so intense. Most people were running helter-skelter. After the fighting and firing subsided, rebels entered our house and forcefully picked me among my brothers and sisters … Who would dare refuse? Not even if you were mad … So they took me away … I did not know what we were heading for and what they wanted to do with me. I was in total fear. (Girl)

The rebels entered our farm and captured my father and mother and killed them in front of me. After killing both of my parents I was commanded to carry looted items on my head and follow them. (Boy)

I was on my way to sell my [cakes]. You know our people took the whole business lightly at the time and said that the [rebels] would soon [retreat] after having collected a lot of food. So I went to sell cakes as usual. One of [the rebels] told me to go with them. I replied that I was on an errand for my mother. But they took my cakes and ate them and they took me away. (Girl)

I was attacked at school and forced to join the movement. I wanted to say no but they shot me in the leg and I had no options. The day I was abducted at school, it was as if death had come to collect me. (Boy)

The following participants described being injected with drugs immediately after their abduction:

I was captured by the RUF during an ambush. Everyone was kept in separate rooms and we were told we would be injected [with drugs]. The man who injected me told me that he was a doctor. He said that he was injecting me so that I would be given the mind to do what they needed me to do ... Afterwards, I felt very warm and my eyes became all red. The older men commented on our eyes and said that we had been over-drugged. They were afraid of us. (Boy)

I was captured in [region] and taken to a nearby village when I was 12 years old ... Immediately following my abduction, I was trained to use a gun and fire. After the training with the guns, they would bring [a civilian] for us to kill. Each one of us was forced to kill ... Soon after, I was injected with drugs ... I don't remember much after that, just going into action. (Girl)

For these young people, the abduction represented an abrupt and thoroughly traumatic turning point that fundamentally altered the course of their lives:

After my abduction I was in total fear and I thought I would die at any time. I wondered if I would ever see my parents again. The only thing I was thinking about was where my family was and how I could get to them. (Girl)

Following their abduction, a process of militarization into the dictates of the armed group began. Yet for the RUF leadership, significant challenges had to be overcome. Newly abducted children were clearly terrified, full of despair and profoundly disoriented. Moreover, they were highly uncommitted to the RUF as a whole. For the overall success of the 'movement', the RUF leaders needed to ensure that children gradually internalized and adopted the values, norms and practices of the militarized world that was forced upon them. In his important work on the making of torturers, Crelinsten (2003) argues that there is little difference between the training of soldiers in general, and the training of torturers in particular. According to Crelinsten (1995, 2003), much like the education and preparation of a soldier, preparation to become a torturer requires basic training, a hierarchical structure within which the torture unit operates and, importantly, a process of desensitization. Much in the way suggested by Crelinsten, to facilitate children's pathways into violence and armed conflict, the RUF leadership began children's initiation into the dictates of the RUF using physical, technical and ideological training.

## Physical, technical and ideological training

All of the respondents reported some form of physical and technical military training as part of their induction into the RUF. Yet the content and quality of training varied significantly. For some, training tended to be cursory when the RUF was engaged in protracted conflict and enemy attack was imminent:

I was given crash training in weaponry. It was at the time of the heart of the conflict, so the training was fast and intense. I learned to lay ambush and to crawl to avoid bullets. We were given crash training in pistol firing – they would place a target and if you missed hitting it on the third try, they would kill you. Two people were killed in front of my eyes because they missed the target. I hit the target on the first try so they gave me the name [nom de guerre] 'One Time Scratch'. (Boy)

I was trained to shoot a special gun that I used when we went to the war front. They taught us how to load our magazines, press the trigger, put it in rapid firing. We were also given physical training like jogging over long distances and training in ambush positions which included laying flat on the ground. (Girl)

Others, however, reported more lengthy technical and military training:

You were normally taught how to work the trigger and how to load the magazine ... We were also trained by jogging over long distances. We were taught to assemble, load and shoot guns, dodge enemy fire, how to disarm captured enemies and how to lay ambush ... The first weapon I touched was an AK-47 ... I was 9 years old ... I didn't know how to operate it so it fell and started firing by itself. After six months, I was given a G3 gun which I used from then on. (Boy)

I was given training on how to kill ... I learned to kill, to cut somebody's throat ... They trained us to use a gun. We were taken for training early in the morning to load the gun and fire ... and to dismantle a gun quickly ... Basically we were told to fire on people above the waist. This would ensure that they would die. If we just wanted to intimidate people and not kill them, we were trained to point the gun in the air. This was important because we were told not to waste any cartridges or ammunition. (Girl)

It is important to note that the transition and initiation into a world of technical training, weaponry and violence was not an easy one. Most participants were initially highly resistant to using weapons. As these girls indicated:

I wanted an education, not to know how to fire a gun. I didn't feel powerful, only bitter. It was not the place for a little girl to hold a gun. (Girl)

We were trained by a commander's wife – Mariatu. I felt very uncomfortable during the training. I was very nervous about it and I was trembling. But

Mariatu was encouraging us and each time we practiced firing the gun, she would tell us that we could do it. She said that she was a woman too, and that if she could do it, we could do it. (Girl)

Often, in situations where children were reticent to use small arms, girls and boys reported that to enable them to train and fight more effectively, they were given drugs and/or alcohol, which accords with other studies on child soldiers (Brett and Specht 2004; Honwana 2006; Wessells 2006). While information on the actual trafficking of illicit drugs by any of the parties to the Sierra Leonean conflict is scarce, there is evidence that the RUF strategically incorporated drug use into children's preparation for combat, particularly alcohol, the injection of cocaine and the ingestion of gun powder (see Clapham 2003). This 41-year-old former RUF commander interviewed for the research explained the rationale behind forced drug use among child combatants:

We were very much aware of the effects of drugs on children … Drugs and alcohol were prevalent and served as [a] prerequisite for combat activities. Fighting with a gun is not an easy task because it puts so much pressure on the mind. So we needed to free the mind by taking drugs, and it worked. (Former adult male RUF commander)

The apparent abundance of alcohol and hallucinatory drugs deliberately and unquestionably contributed to the creation of efficient and aggressive soldiers. Invariably, as discussed by other researchers exploring diverse contexts involving child soldiers (Honwana 2006; Stavrou 2004; Wessells 2006), the drugs were effective and engendered feelings of strength and a readiness to pick up their weapons and kill. As these children described:

[During training] when they saw how nervous and uncomfortable [the girls] were, they gave us drugs … Before the injection [in the arm], I was nervous, afraid and unsure of myself. Later, after the injection, I felt more confident. (Girl)

We were always drugged before fighting … The tablets were so powerful that you didn't feel anything after taking it … After [taking the drugs] the officer would slap your back two or three times and say 'good soldier'. (Boy)

Drugs were very common and prevalent … They were part of our rations when we were to go on the offensive. We did not normally go to fight without taking drugs or alcohol – marijuana, cocaine, and brown-brown [crack]. The effects of the drugs on some of the young people were really powerful and they could do anything when they were in that state. (Girl)

Importantly, as noted by Crelinsten (2003) and Kelman (1995), the training of an effective soldier may not only come from physical and technical training, but also from a strong belief and affiliation with the cause at hand. During interviews, children provided examples of the RUF's ideological teachings that reportedly made them more receptive to the cause of the rebels and thus more willing to fight. This was done both formally and informally. Formally, children reported being required to attend formal 'lectures' given by adult commanders that addressed the working 'philosophy' of the rebels and conveyed the urgent necessity to overthrow the corrupt and inefficient Sierra Leonean government:

When we were in northern jungle, they would gather us at what was referred to as the 'formation grounds' and they would address us. They used to call this our 'lecture'. They focused on the new recruits, as well as those who did not seem to be committed to the group. (Boy)

When we were recruited there was a meeting held with all the recruits. At the meeting they were preaching that those in power were not giving all people equal access to benefits and that [the rebels] needed to get control ... I was convinced by this meeting and it pushed me and motivated me to go to war. (Girl)

They told us that they were freedom fighters ... They called themselves the Black Guards of Sankoh. (Boy)

I did not willingly go and join them, but when I was abducted and my consciousness was raised about the movement, I became willing to fight. (Girl)

Children were also required to learn and repeat war songs that appear to have simultaneously inspired commitment and violence:

I enjoyed the [war] songs. They always inspired. It normally went like this: 'Commandos are brave, Commandos are intelligent, You don't fuck with us, Commandos hardly die.' (Boy)

Such convincing uses of lectures, propaganda, songs and ideological train-ing appears to have incited participants to see themselves as playing an important role in part of a noble effort, and to have encouraged them to ensure the ongoing security and integrity of the group (Kelman 1995).

More informally, training techniques were used to facilitate participants' use of violence. As an example, when committing violent acts, participants were forbidden to show any remorse, sadness or shame. Instead, they were encouraged and even coerced into participating in acts of celebration:

[Whenever we engaged in violence] you were not permitted to show [negative] emotions. Everyone always had to show happiness and laughter ... Sometimes we sang, shouted and danced for doing or seeing what we had done to people ... This was to train the children ... All of this mayhem and celebrating was part of the culture of the RUF. (Girl)

Some [fighters] even danced with the corpses of the enemy. (Boy)

Haritos-Fatouros (2003) notes that such 'mayhem' or 'madness' is a well-planned training method to minimize resistance by instilling compliance without question. Thus the children were 'carefully prepared to carry out orders to commit acts of cruelty and violence that had little or no personal meaning for them' (Haritos-Fatouros 2003, p. 46). Over extended periods of time, immersed in a social environment that rationalized violence, terror and cruelty, these came to be trivialized. As this boy commented:

Killing happened every day and we all became used to it ... It came to the point where you would come across a dead body near your door and you would just jump over it to get to your room. (Boy)

While diverse forms of training were inevitably a critical step in the militarization of the young, training alone, however, did not categorically tie children to the RUF and its 'cause'. Further along the continuum in the making of an RUF child soldier, children's civilian identities and self-concepts needed to be broken down and, on the path to 'becoming RUF', reality as children knew it needed to be reshaped. This reshaping of reality was accomplished through devices designed to enable children to carry out their roles effectively and in contexts of reduced strain.

## Reshaping reality and 'becoming RUF': Solidarity, role allocation and rewards

Crelinsten (2003) maintains that the system and routine of torture is most easily established within a closed (if not impermeable) world infused by a 'new' and alternative reality that is separated from that of conventional morality and is defined by the ideological dictates of the particular regime that holds power. Within this new reality, everything must be reshaped according to the new template: new language and vocabulary must be devised and social relations must be redefined.

Ultimately, through the creation of this new social order, there is a gradual movement from one world view to another – from a civic world based on principles of humanity, civic associations, empathy and caring, to a world of torture based on inhumanity, rigid hierarchies, detachment and cruelty.

Much in the way described by Crelinsten, the RUF leaders constructed a new (and closed) social reality that occurred in the self-contained setting of the Sierra Leonean bush (Richards 1996). The fact that children had been forcibly cut off from their former civilian lives and identities, as well as the influence of their families, friends and communities, inevitably facilitated the acculturation process into the RUF. Within the context of a closed RUF 'community', traditional family structures were replaced by militarized ones, rigid military hierarchies were imposed and new values of detachment, cruelty, terror, group solidarity and cohesion were propagated. Paul Richards' (2003) work, which has addressed the 'enclaved' nature of the RUF, offers helpful parallels. He writes: 'The RUF evolved ... from 1991 ... into a rather distinctive "enclaved" organization, with very few links to society outside the confines of its highly organized and strongly defended forest camps' (Richards 2003, p. 27).

As the upcoming section will highlight in greater depth, in order to maintain this closed reality, erode children's paralysing fears following their abduction and training, and enable them to engage in brutal forms of violence, specialized devices were employed by the RUF leadership to increase young people's compliance to the formal and informal culture of the RUF. Efforts to alter children's civilian identities and world views were accomplished by several means, including the encouragement of solidarity and cohesion, role allocation and through rewards and promotion, all of which are discussed below.

## Solidarity and cohesion

Membership of a group is usually of profound significance to human beings and provides a feeling of security, fills deep emotional needs and can often make situations easier to cope with (Haritos-Fatouros 2003). Creating a sense of belonging and camaraderie among the children proved to be an important means to ensure compliance, increase bonds among the rebels and demarcate clear boundaries between the 'in group' (members of the RUF) and the perceived 'enemy' (the government and its allies). The RUF invoked several techniques that aimed to incite cohesion and solidarity among the children, but particularly among the boys. This included severing children's family and community ties, encouraging peer mentoring, and tattooing.

### Severing family and community ties

Encouraging a family-like atmosphere among members of the RUF was important to assuring the overall solidarity of the group. The RUF appears to have been quite successful in instilling this sense of family-like cohesion. As this girl noted:

Once you were in RUF territory, your family was the RUF. (Girl)

An important means to achieve this strong sense of belonging was through the deliberate rupturing of family and community ties. For example, once abducted, children were encouraged to forget about their natal families:

The rebels tried to make me forget about my family. They told me my parents were dead and that the commander should be my new dad ... My commander took me wherever he went – this was to make me forget about my parents gradually. (Boy)

Another means to sever family ties was by forcing children to commit violence and atrocities against their own families and/or communities, a practice documented by researchers in other contexts, including Angola (Stavrou 2004), northern Uganda (McKay and Mazurana 2004) and Mozambique (Dodge and Raundalen 1991). As this participant explained:

They tried to spoil relationships among families ... that is why [the rebels] would assign you to attack your hometown – so that you would have difficulty returning. (Boy)

Given the potentially weak philosophical and political glue that bound young recruits to the cause of the RUF, extreme violence against one's family or community was highly effective in alienating children from their communities and, in the process, ensuring undivided allegiance to the RUF.

While adult commanders appear to have been strategic in their intentional severing of family and community relationships, they seem to have been equally strategic in their attempts to replace these severed bonds with relationships with members of the RUF, which was particularly apparent among the boys. The gradual development of relationships characterized by patronage and protection among boys and their male commanders is well illustrated by this boy who articulated the special and even nurturing relationship that he developed with his adult RUF commander:

I was a special boy in the bush. My commander loved me and I loved him. I would do anything for this commander because of my love for him ... I tried to impress him. My commander protected me and would often tell me to stay behind and not go to battle. It would have been much worse for me if I didn't have the protection of the commander. (Boy)

As addressed by William Murphy (2003) in his discussion of clientalism, patrimonialism and child soldiers in the contexts of Sierra Leone and Liberia, children became quickly dependent on armed commanders who offered a semblance of protection and opportunity in return for services of labour and combat. In such circumstances, children were easily inducted into the ideological dictates of militaristic violence that supplanted conventional and traditional norms (Murphy 2003).

### Peer mentoring

The use of peer mentoring was another effective way for the RUF to instil a sense of belonging within the armed group and socialize children into a new and highly militarized world. Throughout the conflict, the RUF encouraged children (mostly boys) to take on leadership positions with other children and, in particular, to act as role models and mentors, especially to new recruits. These 'mentors' were encouraged to actively recruit other children into the RUF during and following attacks on villages. As this boy indicated:

I recruited other children ... After we attacked a village, I would go into the houses and talk with the children. I would tell them that the RUF was great and I would tell them about the movement. I told them that they were in real danger if they didn't join ... I was very successful and I would come back with many children. (Boy)

Moreover, younger children appeared open and willing to be guided by older and more established recruits:

[When I was first abducted] I was very conscious that I had been separated from my father and mother and that was not easy for me. But I saw many other children of my age or just a little older carrying guns ... I was moved by meeting the other children ... I said to myself that if these children can survive ... why not me? We later became friends and they taught me how to operate an AK-47 ... They later found me a gun and I was under their Small Boys Unit. (Boy)

Importantly, Haritos-Fatouros (2003) notes that such techniques of social modelling may work to decrease the strain caused by committing acts that would otherwise be considered abhorrent.

### Tattooing

Yet another way of reinforcing group solidarity and ensuring attachment to the rebels was through tattooing, which was generally performed as a collective act, often after a successful battle when the mood was upbeat. In their discussion of gang membership, Decker and Van Winkle (1996) argue that the display of symbols among gang members, particularly tattoos, is a way of being acculturated into a group or 'learning' to be a gang member. They maintain that the display of tattoos is a way to

become encapsulated in the role of a gang member, especially through the perceptions of others, who, when they see the external symbols of member-ship, respond as if the person was a member. In a sense, exhibiting the external symbols of a gang is a way of 'trying out' a group identity. When that identity is confirmed by both gang and non-gang members in the community, the identity of an individual as a gang member is solidified. (Decker and Van Winkle 1996, p. 75)

Tattooing and other forms of scarification, which hold important cultural meanings in Sierra Leone (which will be addressed later on in the chapter), appear to have been a mechanism used by the RUF to promote group solidarity and cohesion, largely among the boys. While tattoos had the added benefit of demarcating and identifying RUF members and their battalions, male commanders appear to have used tattooing to enhance collective unity:

After a successful battle, the young people would get together to prepare food and cook. They would play very loud music and come together and rejoice. After, they would give each other tattoos. Sometimes they would name their group the Tiger group, the Lion Fighters or the Death Squad. [Did someone tell the young people to give themselves tattoos?] Yes, it came from the older commanders. (Boy)

I have two tattoos. One is a group identifier and the other indicates my post as a commander. (Boy)

Usually portraying words and images of brutality, tattoos reaffirmed the RUF's ferocity as a fighting force. The rituals of tattooing not only symbolized one's allegiance to the RUF, but also served as a form of social control, demarcating clear boundaries between the 'in group' (the RUF) to which they were bound, and the 'enemy' (the kamajors, ECOMOG and the SLA) who posed a threat to their existence. The symbolic power of tattoos was such that as one tattooed respondent remarked on meeting an ex-combatant long after the conflict had ended: 'When I saw his tattoo and he saw mine, we sat and talked together for a long time.'

In their discussion of the psychology and motivations of terrorists, Post et al. (2003, p. 176) emphasize the importance of group dynamics and group identity on the decision to commit terrorist acts. They suggest that as an individual succumbs to the larger organization, there is little or no room for individual ideas, individual identity and individual decision-making. As this occurs, individual measures of success become increasingly linked to the organization and stature and accomplishments within the organization. Individual self-worth becomes intimately tied to the 'value' or prominence of the group. As the individual and group fuse, the more personal the struggle becomes for group members. For individuals in such environments, they become unable to distinguish between personal goals and those of the organization (Post et al. 2003). Such observations are applicable to the RUF. As Richards (2003) has noted in relation to the RUF: 'As with many closed sects, the defection of one threatened the solidarity of all' (p. 28). Over time, the success or failure of the RUF group became intensely personal – if the group succeeded, then as an individual they succeeded; if the group failed, they failed. Pride and shame as expressed by the individual were reflections of group actions, not individual actions, feelings or experiences.

It is important to note that the encouragement of group solidarity by RUF leaders appears to have been directed specifically at males within the armed group. Whereas many boys discussed, often with great nostalgia, aspects of group solidarity and the development of a sense of group identity within RUF battalions and as RUF fighters, such discussions were notably absent among girls. Reflecting the patriarchal structures and interactions within the RUF, girls were relegated to a secondary status and there seems to have been little concern for the inclusion of girls within such militarized masculine structures of solidarity. Nonetheless, structures of solidarity among girls in the RUF did exist. However, it was not encouraged from the upper echelons of the RUF, but instead emerged informally and secretly by the girls themselves. These forms of solidarity were intrinsically linked to strategies of resistance against the RUF culture of violence. This will be discussed further in Chapter 5.

## Role allocation

Following their abduction and training, boys and girls were made to perform an array of tasks to support rebel activities. In most cases, children had *multiple* roles and were not assigned to any one task. The multiplicity of roles echoes the experiences of child soldiers in other contexts (Singer 2005b; Stavrou 2004; Wessells 2006). Children's duties often varied according to their age, physical strength and the circumstances of the armed group. However, roles tended to fall within the realms of domestic and supporting work, sexual violence and slavery, and combat activities. As has been noted by McKay (2005, 2006), regardless of their roles and duties, children's productive and girls' sexual labour was critical to the overall functioning of the armed group. Role allocation also worked to reaffirm the values, ideals and customs of the RUF.

### Domestic and supporting work

Boys and girls associated with the RUF were delegated to a wide variety of domestic and supporting activities that contributed to the daily operations of the armed group. Responsibilities included cooking, washing dishes, fetching water and firewood, laundering and taking care of younger children. Boys and girls also participated in pillaging villages for food and other goods. Most children were required to carry heavy loads of small arms, ammunition, food, young children and looted goods over extremely long distances. As this boy noted:

I did domestic work like washing, gathering firewood, fetching water, laundering ... I was given a weapon but I was unable to carry it because at that time I was only 7 years old. I had to drag it ... [We were] also used as carriers of their looted items ... At one time we went to fight in a nearby village and in the course of the battle my commander was shot. He was put in a hammock and we were told to carry him. (Boy)

For many children, the domestic work was difficult and strenuous:

We were ordered to beat the rice. We had to do it for hours and hours. My hands were bleeding and they would not let us stop. I was tired of the whole thing and in so much pain. (Girl)

Initially, [I] was cleaning rice with a pestle and mortar. Now it might look funny to me, but at that time, oh, I cleaned rice till my hands were blistered. The work we did for their women! (Girl)

Domestic work within the context of armed groups is often regarded as peripheral and insignificant (McKay and Mazurana 2004). It is increasingly being recognized, however, that armed groups cannot function without such labour (Stavrou 2004). Given an armed group's lack of resources, manpower, their need to keep moving and their often limited organizational structure, the domestic activities and loads carried by boys and girls are invaluable to the very survival and success of an armed group (Denov 2008). This was certainly the case with the RUF, as children's contributions were vital to the ongoing functioning and continued existence of the armed group. Importantly, while girls and the roles that they play are frequently deemed peripheral and insignificant by governments, national and international NGOs, policy-makers and programme developers, girls were *fundamental to the war machine* – their operational contributions were integral and critical to the overall functioning of the RUF. As this boy noted:

The girls were very important. They watched over the goods and did the cooking. The elders needed the girls and if any of the girls in our unit were harmed, one would be severely punished. In our unit, the girls had to be treated well, because if they weren't, they would try to escape and they needed them. (Boy)

### Sexual violence and slavery

For women and girls in the RUF, the provision of sexual services to the men and boys in the group was, perversely, included as part of their expected 'duties'. Indeed, all but two girls interviewed reported being subjected to repeated sexual violence, and gang and individual rape were common. The rampant nature of sexual violence accords with other research conducted on girl soldiers in Africa (see Coulter et al. 2008; McKay and Mazurana 2004; Schroven 2008; Stavrou 2004). As these girl participants remembered:

I had no relationships [during my time in the bush]. I was a mere sex machine. (Girl)

We were used as sex slaves. Whenever they wanted to have sexual intercourse with us, they took us away forcefully and brought us back when they finished with us. Sometimes, other officers took us up as soon as we were being finished with and subsequent ones were particularly painful ... I don't even know who might have been the father of my child. (Girl)

Alongside the widespread and repeated sexual violence, many girls were forced to 'marry' individual rebels. Euphemistically referred to as 'bush marriage' or 'AK-47 marriage', this was tantamount to sexual slavery whereby girls were deemed to be the (sexual) 'property' of specific RUF males. Moreover, numerous girls reported bearing children as a result of sexual violence.[1]

### Combat activities

Combat activities formed a critical part of many girls' and boys' involvement in the conflict. For the most part, children reported being involved in an array of activities, including frontline fighting, looting, burning villages, commanding other child soldiers, and the deliberate killing, maiming and torture of civilians:

I fought in battle so many times, it is uncountable ... Fighting in battle, carrying guns, and looting [civilian] properties were my jobs. In the bush I became a commander and I commanded a group ... of seven child soldiers. (Boy)

I was sent to the frontlines to fight, while the adults retreated back and remained at a checkpoint. This ensured that [the children] could never retreat back from the frontlines. It was very coercive and we were coerced into taking drugs. I became addicted to the drugs. (Boy)

Although girls tended to be relegated to activities that reflected traditional gender roles, including cooking, cleaning, looking after younger children and serving men, thus in many ways replicating the tasks that women and girls undertook in the broader society, as in the findings on girl soldiers by Keairns (2003), McKay and Mazurana (2004), Stavrou (2004) and Veale (2003), girls in this study also reported engaging in non-traditional roles such as active combatants. Most female participants reported that when first captured, they tended to carry out domestic roles. However, later on they became part of the fighting forces. Other girls reported being forced to participate in combat only in situations where there was a lack of military power on the side of the fighting forces. Yet, for many girls, combat

---

[1] The reality of sexual violence and its long-term impacts will be explored further in Chapters 5 and 6.

activities eventually formed the crux of their involvement in armed conflict. As these girls explained:

Our only motive to exist was killing. That is the only thing that we thought about ... I burned houses, captured people, I carried looted properties. I was responsible for tying people, and killing. I was not too good at shooting, but I was an expert in burning houses. This was less risky. We could just enter the house after the enemy had left the area and set it on fire with kerosene or petrol. (Girl)

On highways, we usually set ambushes especially when we needed food and other goods. We attacked convoys of vehicles including military trucks. We would lie flat on the ground in batches of ten or more depending on the type of ambush. The batches were stationed at different places along the same axis. When the enemy or trucks carrying goods entered into the ambush and got as far as midway, the commander would give the first shot and we would all follow until we got what we wanted. We always did it in areas where vehicles could not run at a high speed along hills, or on rugged parts of the road, or sometimes we even blocked the road with wood or old vehicles ... We killed people randomly when we overcame them. We took their goods and set fire to their vehicles. (Girl)

While domestic and supporting work, sexual violence and slavery, and combat activities were the foundations of the children's roles in the RUF, what was most apparent was the diversity and fluidity of roles that they undertook. The multiplicity of their roles is exemplified by these participants:

I did domestic duties for my boss' wife. I acted as watchman or bodyguard for my boss and his wives ... I also supervised the diamond mining to make sure that none of the miners stole any diamonds that were to go to the commanders ... I also went into battle. (Boy)

[The girls] were just mainly there to prepare the stolen food the [fighters] came with. We were cooks and they slept with us whenever they wanted ... But sometimes we would need all the manpower we had. The girls would then, under instruction and directions, engage in some fighting. (Girl)

I captured beautiful women for the commanders [to rape] ... I was also among those who would go and call civilians [hiding] in the bush and tell them that vehicles were ready to evacuate them. But of course they were being called to be killed or ... other violent acts like amputation. (Boy)

The roles allocated to children and the rigid hierarchies within which they were carried out were important as they appear to have deepened and solidified children's understanding of and compliance with the RUF's values, customs and institutional rules.

## Rewards and promotion

The RUF was indeed a 'total' militarized environment as its rules and structures disallowed alternative behaviours. However, unlike the inmates of most prisons or 'total institutions' as described by Goffman (1961), children in the RUF received (promises of) social and material rewards as positive reinforcement for actions that were deemed acceptable or encouraged within the group. For example, boys and girls in the RUF were promised significant financial benefits and social status in the aftermath of the conflict for their participation in the war. For children who had experienced profound marginalization and exclusion both prior to and during the war, enticements of social and economic rewards were highly alluring:

I was told ... that if the rebels succeeded, Foday Sankoh would compensate each and every one of us with money. I was happy about this. [It] gave me confidence and trust to fight with the rebels. (Boy)

They said they were fighting for freedom and justice ... They told us they were fighting to overthrow the government because their needs had been neglected for so long and there was so much corruption. They told us to be patient and loyal to them. They said we were all going to occupy very important positions in the government at the end of the war ... They said we would have opportunities to go overseas, and other grand things like that ... This gave us the motivation to fight. (Boy)

Moreover, the more aggressive and violent that boys and girls were seen to be towards the 'enemy' and the more destruction and looting they undertook, the more valued they were within the ranks of the RUF. As this girl noted:

I committed a lot of violence ... We were cherished by the senior officers for our wicked deeds. (Girl)

Engaging in extreme forms of violence during the conflict brought privileges such as better access to food and looted goods, and, in some cases, led to promotion within the ranks. Promotion to the rank of a 'commander' was deemed to be the peak of success within the RUF:

Very violent and obedient soldiers were given positions as commanders. You needed to show enthusiasm, be very active during combat and terrorize and abduct civilians ... I was very active in combat and also captured a lot of people, including children. This contributed to my elevation to the status of a commander. (Girl)

I was quickly given a lot of privileges. I even had my own vehicle. I was promoted to a captain's rank. I was among about twenty boys who were promoted ... If you were successful in your missions and you brought back lots of [looted goods], you were promoted. Also, we would normally fight alongside the elders and they would take notice of the ones that were very active and brave. (Boy)

Although a minority of respondents reported being promoted to a commander, those who did recalled this event with nostalgia and even pride. As these participants noted:

I became a boss among the children I captured ... I had my own group of children to organize and manage. I felt really proud to command the other kids. All of the kids admired me. (Boy)

I became a soldier and later a commander. My job was to mobilize soldiers and lead them to fight ... I was a commander not only for children but even for some older soldiers. (Girl)

The promotion enabled children to lead their own units of child combatants and contributed to their protection through their entourage of child bodyguards:

If you carried out amputations and were very brave in combat you were offered promotion ... I became a commander and I had fifty children to command. (Boy)

I was a commander not only for children but also for soldiers older than myself. Commanders were generally treated better regardless of their age or sex. I had six bodyguards ... They were very loyal and they did everything I ordered without questioning ... As commanders we needed bodyguards to boost our morale and to show other people our status. [This was important] because we didn't have badges, uniforms, or crowns to depict our status ... I was given a lot more status and protection as a commander. (Girl)

Promotions were highly significant in the lives of child soldiers. It often took them from dangerous tasks as combatants and allowed them to take on new roles away from the battlefield where they held safer, and more powerful and lucrative, positions. As this boy explained:

Before being promoted, I was given the dirty jobs, like carrying ammunition and fighting in combat. After I was promoted, I was allowed to man my own checkpoint. When people passed through this checkpoint, they had to produce a pass. Also, they had to give me money and food. The money was to give to my boss, but I would get some of it. I felt very powerful. By staying at this checkpoint, it also really reduced the risk. I no longer had to go to the frontlines to fight. (Boy)

Through violence, children accrued personal rewards and attained social prestige and power, all of which aimed to reinforce their bonds to the militarized world of the RUF.

## Understanding the RUF militarization process: Constructing a culture of violence

The RUF's militarization process, and the construction of a new social order and reality, although seemingly unique and distinct, was not created in a vacuum. Instead, the personal narratives of respondents not only capture their individual life experiences and their powerful initiation into a world of violence and armed conflict, but also mirror the traumatic events and contradictory forces that have been played out in Sierra Leone within the past several decades. As Abdullah and Rashid (2004) note: 'any research into the problem of juvenile combatants should start by looking at the partial disintegration of state and society in Sierra Leone in the 1980s and 1990s' (p. 240). In its militarization of the young, the RUF drew upon and ultimately reproduced existing Sierra Leonean militarized structures and systems. In this sense, although the RUF began as a force of opposition to socio-economic injustices perpetrated by the urban elite, the RUF was itself an offshoot of the violent and politically opportunistic structures that it opposed. As Kandeh (1999) notes: 'How political elites accumulated wealth and exercised power helped shape the dynamics of AFRC/RUF terror in Sierra Leone' (p. 364). As an example, the embroilment of the young in militarized politics was certainly not introduced by the RUF. Murphy (2003) suggests that prior to the war, Sierra Leone's governing elite recognized the importance of embroiling the young in their political operations for their own military and economic gain:

Politicians learn[ed] to exploit the main resources youths have to offer – physical strength, energy, and fearlessness – for their bodyguard services and the intimidation of rivals ... A new social system of violence produced a new youth stylistics which marked their dependence as much as their power. (Murphy 2003, pp. 69, 77)

Rosen (2005) notes that during the Stevens' era, members of the APC youth wing wearing red berets and red shirts bearing the logo of the rising sun became 'the political muscle whenever the APC wanted to display its power ... Youth set people on fire, burned down their houses, shot children, paraded citizens about naked and beat them, brought opponents before youth-run kangaroo courts, and hacked women and men to death with machetes' (p. 78). In turn, 'big men' offered young people forms of economic assistance and physical protection.

It would appear that the RUF drew upon and ultimately reproduced such structures of violence and patronage within their formal and informal culture, and, through their daily interactions, recreated relationships of patronage and deference between RUF adult commanders and their child soldiers. Children within the RUF gradually became clients to their military commanders, which provided them with 'coercive power and the economic spoils of war (or their promise) in exchange for military and economic services' (Murphy 2003, p. 77). As a patron, an RUF commander was responsible for his 'clients' and would also act as a resource for food, shelter, weapons and ammunition. Wholly dependent on their hostage-takers, children, particularly boys, developed bonds with individuals who actually were in positions to inflict severe distress on them with impunity, but could also provide them with relief and succour. In so doing, children became accustomed to complying with the orders and expectations of those who commanded them. The use of solidarity and cohesion, role allocation, and rewards and promotion further promoted and cemented the realities of patronage and deference.

As has been suggested by Richards (1996) and Ellis (2003), aspects of the RUF training and initiation can also be said to reflect culturally based structures and traditional initiation practices in Sierra Leone. For example, examining the traditional initiation process for Poro outlined below (Little 1965), one cannot help but make strong parallels with the RUF's process of initiation and acculturation. Particularly relevant to the Poro initiation process are the abduction from family, the deliberate use of fear, pain and deprivation, strict obedience to authority, the relative powerlessness of junior members and the segregation of initiates in special camps, all of which appeared within RUF practices:

The [Poro] procedure is partly ceremonial and symbolical and partly instructional, and it is designed, first and foremost, to turn the initiate into a good Poro man ... [T]he main function of initiation ... is to impress upon the new member the sacredness of his duty to Poro. This is done psychologically by *subjecting the youths to a number of terrifying experiences* ... [Initiates] also take part in a series of rituals involving the killing of fowl by brutal methods. The object is to demonstrate how the initiates, too, would be treated should they ever divulge any Poro secrets ... Boys ... undergo *common experiences of hardship and tests of endurance. Pain is inflicted deliberately upon them to instil habits of self-discipline and they are taught to obey the elders of the society without question.* This ritual takes place in the *special camp* in which the boys have been *segregated* ... Not only was [the Poro initiate] snatched, sometimes without warning, from the security of family and kinsfolk and exposed to terrifying experiences; but he was systematically deprived of sleep to make him still further open to suggestion. He was also subjected to a constant round of admonition, backed up by gruesome examples of the fate in store for him should he default ... *Junior Poro men had no rights within the society itself. They were completely without voice in its affairs although bound to carry out Poro commands.* (Little 1965, pp. 357, 358; emphasis added)

Other Poro practices of body marking and providing initiates with new names, and the overall goal of group solidarity, also appear to parallel RUF training and initiation whereby new RUF recruits were sometimes marked, branded or tattooed with an RUF insignia, and given a 'nom de guerre', all of which sought to encourage a sense of *esprit de corps*:

[T]he new [Poro] member takes his final vows of loyalty to the society in the presence of its spirits. As a sign of his incorporation, he carries out with him into the world, not only the *marks on his body* of the 'spirit's teeth', but *the new name* that Poro has bestowed upon him in the bush ... A good deal of the practical training, too, is calculated to produce among the initiates *a sense of esprit du corps and solidarity* as members sharing the same institution. (Little 1965, p. 357; emphasis added)

Ferme (2001) likewise notes in relation to initiation in Sierra Leone:

[F]or both men (who are scared and put through ordeals, as well as being scarified) and women (who undergo clitoridectomies), initiation is a violent, painful experience, one in which big women as much as big men wield the knife and in which the urgency of protecting secrets and bodily boundaries is inscribed in the initiate's flesh. (Ferme 2001, pp. 179–80)

Given the close linkages with traditional initiation practices, Richards (1996) argues that the young people themselves, as well as their families and communities, may have associated the RUF abduction with traditional initiation practices. He writes:

With initiation already deeply etched in the lives of many young people in the Upper Guinean forests, capture may serve to recapitulate aspects of the experience. Villagers apply an initiation 'model' to the disaster that has befallen them; they perceive that their children have been taken from them by force (as in initiation) and turned into alien creatures by the power of rebel magic. Offered rudimentary schooling in the bush and instruction to guerilla warfare, many captives quickly readjust to their lot. (Richards 1996, p. 30)

In a similar vein, Shepler (2004) suggests that armed groups in Sierra Leone, including the RUF, drew upon and reproduced several key cultural and historical practices in their recruitment and daily management of the young, particularly the practices of child labour, fosterage and education. Shepler notes that child labour, which practically defines childhood in Sierra Leone, was essential to the overall functioning of wartime fighting forces. For example, the RUF needed individuals to perform daily tasks, such as cooking, cleaning, fetching water and laundering within the armed group. These tasks are reflective of the overall daily tasks that are expected of children in Sierra Leone. Shepler argues that the recruitment of children for these tasks can be seen as being an extension of traditional cultural practices. The practice of fostering, where a child's primary caregiver is anyone other than the biological parents, is not only a form of exchange, but also an ongoing system extremely common to family structure in West Africa. Fostering is done to cement family bonds, create alliances and provide children with important social skills. Shepler suggests that the language of fostering was used in RUF abductions, with commanders 'asking' (albeit coercively) for children in ways that were reflective of cultural forms of fostering. Finally, Shepler maintains that the RUF drew upon pre-existing models of 'education', training and initiation in their practices. Ultimately, reflecting the significance of education, the armed group was sometimes constructed as a new form of schooling and apprenticeship. All of the aforementioned examples highlight the importance of historical and cultural conditionalities and structures on the eventual behaviours and realities that were the RUF.

The gendered oppression and gender-based violence that came to define the RUF was also a reflection of broader social structures and forces. Sierra Leonean societal arrangements have historically been shaped by patriarchal relations that have legitimized the economic, political and socio-cultural dominance of males over females. As Shaw (2002) aptly reveals, such arrangements date back as far as the slave trade whereby Sierra Leonean women were relegated to a life of agricultural labour, and domestic slavery as slave wives. When civic conflict expanded in Sierra Leone, the deep-seated gender differentiation that shaped the realities of women and girls became even more pronounced within the context of the 'militarized masculinity' (Enloe 2000) induced by the civil war. Importantly, the RUF drew upon and once again reproduced (to the extreme) the prevailing and often violent patterns of patriarchal hegemony. Girls in the RUF were forced to endure multiple and profound forms of gender-based violence and insecurity. Sexual violence was committed on a much larger scale than the highly visible amputations for which Sierra Leone became notorious. In contrast, boys were able to benefit from the RUF's rigid gender differentiation. For example, boys were more likely to garner status and power, gaining authority over younger boys, and, in some cases, rising to the ranks of a commander. For boys, to be a commander also meant having sexual licence over women and girls and abusing them with impunity. As these boys noted:

Once I became a commander, I could choose any girl that I wanted [as a wife] ... If they weren't willing to have sex with me ... I would force them ... I felt good. A woman is there to pleasure every man. (Boy)

As a commander, you got to choose the girl that you liked and wanted to be with. Girls were used as gifts. I had three wives. (Boy)

In contrast, although sometimes becoming combatants in their own right, girls rarely attained the same status as a male commander within the RUF fighting forces. Moreover, the systematic exclusion of girls from tattooing, peer mentoring and other efforts at creating solidarity among child soldiers is reflective of existing patriarchal structures that typically exclude women and girls and relegate them to a marginalized status. All of these powerful gendered forces and realities shaped girls' and boys' experiences and ultimately 'gendered' the militarization process.

These examples illustrate that the militarization process and the making of individual child soldiers cannot be considered in isolation or entirely divorced from the broader socio-historical context of Sierra Leone. Historical and structural features of Sierra Leonean society inevitably helped to shape and form the relations, actions and dynamics of RUF terror and the militarization process. The actions of individual actors also infused this process as they worked to produce and reproduce broader structures in their everyday activities.

However, it is important to recognize that while the culture of the RUF was reflective of existing structures in Sierra Leone, it was in no way an identical offshoot. In this sense, actors, in their ongoing actions and interactions, are able to contribute to and *alter* existing structures (Giddens 1977). While the RUF drew upon and reproduced many historical and structural realities of Sierra Leone's past, through ongoing actions and interaction of individual agents, the armed group also produced and constructed *new forms of violence and militarization* and created a closed world infused by a 'new' violent social order.

Within this new and closed world, extreme forms of violence, which far surpassed previous structures and interactions, pervaded both the formal and informal culture of the RUF (Abdullah 1998). I refer to this as the RUF 'culture of violence'. At the formal level, the command structures of the RUF, as well as the ways in which the RUF organized and carried out its missions, were forged and conducted within a framework of severe fear, brutality, detachment and inhumanity. At the informal level, the daily routines, informal values and interactions within the armed groups, which were steeped in rigid hierarchical and patriarchal power relations and threats, were similarly propagated and sustained through extraordinary violence and cruelty. Interviewees spoke of those with power, almost always male, exercising their authority by shouting commands and threatening children with death if they did not comply. Failing to perform one's duties in a timely or efficient manner often led to harsh punishment, and even death. At the outset they were treated harshly as outsiders, essentially as prisoners of war who had to be forced into docility. Once children were absorbed into the ranks of the RUF, often after the trauma of witnessing unspeakably brutal acts and the shattering of their natural centres of social support, sheer survival necessitated adhering to the dictates of the rebel community into which they had been drawn:

If you refused or failed to do what you were told, they would put you in a cell or tie you up. In some cases, one of [the commanders] might pass a command saying 'Kill that person for not taking orders.' (Girl)

The RUF was a strict group. They punished anyone who disobeyed orders. The common punishments for children were beatings, detention, disarmament, and starvation. (Boy)

An aura of terror, repeatedly articulated, was a key factor in ensuring cohesion and obedience within the group. Such terror is said to reduce initiative and resistance and increases the feeling of dependency on superiors (Haritos-Fatouros 2003). Moreover, terror and irrational punishment from which there is no escape is known to produce learned helplessness[2] whereby an individual fails to take steps to avoid punishment as they believe that their efforts will have no effect (Hiroto and Seligman 1975).

Within the RUF, violence and the threat of violence appears to have permeated every aspect of children's daily lives. As this girl noted:

There wasn't a single day in RUF territory that was trouble and violence free. People were always maltreated and any wicked act you can think of in this world was perpetrated by the rebels. (Girl)

It was within the context of this profound culture of violence that the reconfiguration and 'making' of children's militarized identities deepened and solidified. The process of acculturation into the RUF was a gradual yet calculated one. While the new social reality created by the RUF drew upon historical and cultural practices, it simultaneously rejected traditional values and cultural and community norms, such as respect for the authority of traditional elders and senior members of the community and cultural respect for women. Consequently, the traditional gerontocratic ties were materially reversed (Murphy 2003). Moreover, by engaging children in physical, technical and ideological training, as well as encouraging solidarity and cohesion and offering symbolic and significant rewards and promotion for violence, the RUF leadership aimed to increase young people's compliance to the RUF. In this sense, these devices, alongside the culture of violence, together played a powerful and essential role in breaking down children's civilian identities, introducing them to a 'new' social order and further entrenching the process of militarization and the progression towards 'becoming RUF'.

Inevitably, the violent structural realities of the war framed and shaped children's choices and prospects. It is important to recognize, however, that children were not simply passive recipients of the RUF culture. Children's experiences of 'being RUF' and the diverse ways in which children responded to the culture of violence will be explored in the next chapter.

---

[2] Learned helplessness thus refers to a situation in which an organism, after experiencing a series of inescapable aversive situations, ceases to try to escape further negative consequences (Hiroto and Seligman 1975).

# 5 | 'Being RUF': Victimization, participation and resistance

War is a total social phenomenon; violence is personal, transformative, and identity making for all involved, victims and perpetrators.

(Shepler 2003, p. 61)

As time went on and the killing happened every day, we all became used to it. After some time, the violence became part of me.

(Boy)

Once abducted into the RUF and the process of militarization had begun to take its course through the devices highlighted in Chapter 4, boys and girls became embroiled in a profound culture of violence. Yet how did children respond to the culture of violence that surrounded them? What did it mean to 'be RUF' once the process of militarization was well under way? This chapter traces children's daily lives and experiences during the heart of their time as child soldiers. It highlights the multi-faceted world that girls and boys contended with – one in which the realities of victimization, participation and resistance were experienced and carried out by children in a shifting and dialectical fashion. The chapter also explores the extent to which children took on an RUF persona, as well as responded to the RUF's culture of violence. Although caught in structures of profound violence largely beyond their control, children were not merely passive recipients to such structures but were actively implicated in, contributed to, reproduced and, ultimately, transformed the RUF.

## Experiences of violence and armed conflict

While all participants were exposed to very similar circumstances and realities, children's experiences as soldiers and their reactions and responses to those experiences were neither straightforward nor uniform. Instead, experiences turned around the shifting realities of victimization, participation and resistance.

## Victimization and insecurity

Within the RUF culture of violence, all the study respondents reported suffering devastating forms of abuse from those who commanded them and in many ways echo the brutal victimization experiences of child soldiers found in other contexts (Betancourt 2008; Boothby 2006; Honwana 2006; McKay 2004; Stavrou 2004; Wessells 2006). The violence and victimization experienced by participants ranged along a continuum from verbal abuse to outrageous acts of cruelty. As these boys remembered:

The senior commander was horrible. He used to beat us with an iron cane. I was feeling so afraid ... I thought I was in the circle of death at any moment. (Boy)

All those that showed signs of fear were initially beaten mercilessly. They wounded some with their knives and tied others down and starved them for days. (Boy)

The victimization permeated all RUF ranks and ages and became a regular currency even among the very young:

There was a very young commander who was directly above me. He was only 12 years old. I was 14 at the time and it was unusual that they would give a command post to someone who was younger than one of the members of the group. I think that it was because he must have been related to one of the older commanders. Anyway, this young 12-year-old commander was very horrible to us. He would wake us up in the morning and shout at us and yell obscenities about our mothers. He would yell at us to get up immediately to find food. But there was no food to find and he knew it. He would even fire at us with his gun to run faster. (Boy)

During their time with the RUF, children were also witnesses to brutal forms of violence against men, women and other children, both combatants and civilians, which were clearly intended as public displays of horror. As these participants described:

My commander captured a girl with her [baby] sister and her mother. He shot the mother and the little baby dead. He left the adolescent girl alive but told her to remove her dress and he raped her ... He told us to form a circle around him and we all had to watch. (Boy)

The worst day for me was the day they captured my mother and me. They cut her throat right in front of me. (Girl)

Most days were awful because the rebels almost always did wicked things to people. The beating of people, they tied some, the starvation, the systematic raping of young girls against their will ... I never thought I would survive their physical torture. (Boy)

They split open the stomachs of pregnant women and removed the foetuses. These foetuses, as well as their mothers died shortly after ... Other people were also amputated ... It was so horrible. I nearly fainted during these times. (Girl)

While many contemplated attempting an escape, the culture of violence and terror that surrounded them prevented them from doing so:

I thought of trying to escape by just leaving with my gun, but I decided against it ... I didn't want to get captured into another group. I thought that in the end, it was safer to stay with my group than be captured by another, where I could be worse off. (Boy)

In some ways, the RUF was indiscriminate in its brutality. This is important to note, as the victimization experiences of men and boys, whether physical, psychological or sexual, are often minimized or dis-regarded. In others ways, however, the violence had significant gen-dered dimensions, rendering the experiences of girls unique to them. The reality of repeated sexual violence was the embodiment of the RUF's patriarchal power relations. As has been found in other studies of girl soldiers (Coulter, Persson and Utas 2008; McKay and Mazurana 2004; Stavrou 2004), sexual violence, whether gang rape, individual rape or rape with objects, was a daily occurrence for most girls in this study, not only wreaking physical, emotional and spiritual havoc, but also putting them at high risk of increased exposure to HIV/AIDS. These narratives reveal the profound brutality of these acts:

One afternoon, two rebels raped me. It was very painful. I cried right through the act. But even when I cried for mercy, they wouldn't listen to me. They tied my hands ... After the first man raped me I was helpless. By the time the second guy was on top of me, I didn't even know what was happening. When they had finished, I had blood between my legs and I couldn't walk because of the pain ... I felt very awful. I was ashamed of sitting among other people. I really felt like just dying. (Girl)

Girls were dying of rape all around me. Every young girl was terrified of rape. The first time I was raped was by the commander who abducted me ... He left me bleeding. I was so afraid and I thought I was going to die like the other rape victims … This commander continued having sex with me against my will. Other officers also came around and had sex with me. Even the young boys were attempting it. (Girl)

Rape was just normal with the group … When I was newly captured, I was raped … I was too small to be raped … I cried and pleaded with the man to let go of me. He didn't. He went right on and did exactly as he wanted … That night I cried and cried … For a whole week I sat and grieved. (Girl)

Girls sometimes became pregnant as a result of rape, although many of the babies died soon after birth due to malnutrition, lack of health care and disease and, in some cases, abuse. As these girls explained:

I became pregnant twice [from begin raped]. But both died soon after and during combat. Other girls were experiencing the same thing, although some had live births while others experienced stillbirths. (Girl)

The child [I gave birth to in the bush] survived only three days. It died on the third day. I was glad. There was no food. I didn't want the baby and I didn't want that man's baby. I was glad that it died. (Girl)

The girl and I slept in the same room and in the middle of the night I would hear her shouting and crying and saying to the man: 'leave my pants', 'don't touch me'. The man said that he needed a baby now and that he wanted a woman to give him a baby. His wife wasn't getting pregnant. When the baby finally came, the woman took the baby from the girl and was maltreating it. She wouldn't care for it and was abusing it. It eventually died. (Girl)

Although most of the worst excesses of violence on girls and women appear to have been perpetrated by boys and young men, particularly the recurrence of sexual assaults, physical and sexual violence seem to have been a currency of interaction and authority among females as well:

[One] woman found out that a girl was impregnated by [the woman's] husband and she told [the girl] to come to see her. The girl went to see her and the woman tried to strangle and kill her. Later on in her pregnancy, the woman would try to punch the girl in the abdomen and was trying to kill the baby. (Girl)

Female officers treated us like slaves. The females were even more wicked to us than the men … I was raped by a male officer [and he was] interested in having further relations with me, but my female commander stopped him. Little did I know that she was also after something. She was a lesbian and each time we went very close to the men, she would punish us. We were four in her group and she slept with all of us. At night, she told us to 'play love' with her. (Girl)

Incidentally, none of the boys interviewed for the study reported being a victim of sexual violence. However, given the reality that boys may be highly reticent to reveal their experiences of sexual victimization due to stigma or shame (Mendel 1995), study participants, both male and female, were asked if they had ever witnessed a male being a victim of sexual violence. None of the participants, boys or girls, reported witnessing such an act.

It is without question that girls' and boys' experiences within the RUF brought forth a profound sense of *insecurity*. As has been demonstrated in recent academic and policy literature on security studies, the concept of 'security' no longer refers solely to the security of territory or of states. Instead, with the increasing recognition of 'human security', individuals and communities are seen as the key point of reference and it is argued that security policies must be more highly integrated with strategies for promoting human rights, democracy and development (Weissberg 2003). The UN defines human security in the following terms:

Human security means ... protecting people from critical (severe) and pervasive (widespread) threats and situations ... [I]t means creating political, social, environmental, economic, military and cultural systems that together give people the building blocks of survival, livelihood and dignity. (United Nations Commission on Human Security 2003)

The security of the young participants was thus constantly at risk within a multitude of domains. Girls and boys lacked access to adequate nutrition and health care, and lived in contexts of dire poverty. Forcibly separated from their families and communities, the security and survival of traditional communities, cultures and values were severely jeopardized:

There was never enough to eat ... [W]e had no medicines to take care of our wounds ... I constantly missed my family and longed to be with them and to live the way we used to. (Girl)

Moreover, as demonstrated above, children's personal and physical security was constantly in peril through acts of torture, rape and abuse. With no serious possibility of escape from the authority of RUF leadership, the children faced the untenable choice of either conforming to the forces of violence that had overwhelmed them or suffering harsh consequences for refusing or failing to conform.


## Participation

Children's experiences as victims of violence are highly disturbing and reveal the constraints and authority structures that ensured their subservience. Yet focusing solely on situations of victimization obscures the layers of complexity that surrounded children's experiences in the RUF. It is equally important to trace the ways in which children became engaged as active participants and combatants.

As time wore on, girls and boys who were victimized by their commanders eventually became their unwitting soldiers and allies. The 'enemy' was thus transformed from the individuals who captured and coerced them, into those who fought against these same individuals. However, the transition from 'victim' to 'perpetrator' was a *gradual* process. As these respondents noted:

When they captured me and took me to Kono, I was afraid of the different types of guns because I knew they were meant to kill ... They started eroding the fears from me gradually. (Boy)

I didn't have the mind to kill someone initially ... but later on I enjoyed the wicked acts. (Girl)

What appears to have facilitated the transition between victimization and perpetration was the RUF's strategic efforts at *desensitization to violence*. Kelman (1995) has observed that when individuals perpetrate acts of violence and torture, over time and with gradual exposure, they tend to see themselves as performing a routine, even a professional job. This sense of the routinization of violence was expressed by a number of respondents, many of whom came to view participation in killing as simply a normative act, whose senselessness they had learned not to question:

Killing was just part of the normal activities of the RUF ... Overcoming the enemy was part of our job ... Once you were part of the fighting force, you should be seen killing someone even without a reason. This shows that you were committed and ready to work with them. (Girl)

[Killing] was an acceptable thing to do ... we just considered it normal. (Boy)

Desensitization to violence can come in a variety of forms, and can include the use of language. Research in a multitude of disciplines has shown that language plays an important role in how we think, feel and behave (Haritos-Fatouros 2003). It can also be used as a disengaging mechanism to reduce strain, and as a way to increase bonding among group members (Cohen 2001; Sykes and Matza 1957). Crelinsten (1995) maintains that within contexts of organized torture, new language and vocabulary are frequently devised to coincide with the creation of the new reality. He notes that the language of torture is a language of euphemisms, black humour, sick jokes, obscenities of the worst kind and cruel ironies. As examples, torturers use euphemisms such as 'tea parties' or 'tea party with toast' to connote applications of torture techniques. Such euphemisms serve as a disengaging mechanism which makes the reprehensible acceptable, turns atrocities into a game or a respectable act and, ultimately, reduces anxiety on the part of the torturer (Haritos-Fatouros 2003).

Euphemistic language used as a form of desensitization was apparent within the informal RUF culture. One girl participant noted the use of the term 'washing' to connote killing among the rebels:

[Before they branded me] I didn't cry openly, but I cried in my heart. If you cried openly they would ask you: 'Do you want us to *wash you* or to *brand you*?' 'Washing' us meant killing. (Girl)

Other euphemisms came within the context of organized amputations of civilians. The sheer brutality of amputations was cloaked in the euphemistic phrases of 'long-sleeves' (an amputation done at the wrist) and 'short-sleeves' (an amputation done at the elbow). As this boy explained, this language became part of the wartime vernacular:

On one of our amputation days, I was given a lot of people to do the amputation operation on … We normally asked [victims] whether they wanted long or short sleeves. (Boy)

A final example of the RUF's use of euphemistic language, black humour and sick jokes came from this participant who described the reaction of RUF adult commanders to the sight of dead bodies. He noted:

The fighters … joked about killing and dying. When we were captured … we saw a lot of corpses. Some of the corpses were the rebels' friends. The corpses were swollen and almost rotting. When they saw a fellow they knew they said: 'John has had too much food, man. Look how bloated his stomach is! He has never been better fed in his life!' They treated it quite lightly. But the rest of us were very upset by the very sight of corpses or of people being tortured. (Boy)

In describing the process of violent desensitization, Bandura (1999) argues that individuals may not initially recognize the changes they are undergoing. At first, they perform milder aggressive acts that they can tolerate with some discomfort. After their self-reproof has been diminished through repeated enactments, the level of ruthlessness increases, until eventually acts originally regarded as abhorrent can be performed with little personal anguish. In this vein, both boys and girls in this study revealed that they slowly began to perpetuate the very culture of violence that had been initially terrifying to them:

[Among the RUF] our only motive to exist was killing. That is the only thing that we thought about ... I burnt houses, captured people, I carried looted properties. I was responsible for tying people and killing. (Girl)

I was given a lot of people to do the amputation operation on. We had very crude machetes ... [W]e refrained from using sharp ones because we believed that more pain would be inflicted if we used dull ones. (Boy)

Emulating the violence and the gender-based oppression of his adult male commander, this boy disclosed his perpetration of sexual violence:

I used to peep in while my boss was having his way with other women. I got one of the boys in my unit to come with me while I selected the woman I wanted [to rape]. I told the boy to bring the woman to me, just as my commander had asked of me. She was an older woman. I didn't select her because she was beautiful but because she was newly captured ... [Why was it important that she be newly captured?] Because I knew that she was afraid and that she would obey me. I felt more powerful because she was afraid. [So what happened?] I got the woman to do exactly what I saw the commander do with his woman ... Sometimes I would choose beautiful women ... If they weren't willing I would force them. [How did you feel about this?] I felt good. A woman is there to pleasure every man. (Boy)

Similarly, this boy described how he drew upon and imitated the deference, patronage and brutality of his own adult commander:

In the bush I became commander and I commanded a group that was called the 'petty group' because all the soldiers were very small boys. There were seven of them. I was appointed as the commander of this group by my own commander and I felt very proud of that ... My group ... loved me. I protected them and gave them things that they didn't have in action, like extra bullets ...

I wasn't very good at [using weapons]. They took us to a base to learn how to use the weapons. I didn't learn very well. At one point my gun misfired and I was nearly killed ... I really had fear in my heart. (Girl)

However, as the conflict dragged on, and through ongoing observations and relations with their commanders and other child soldiers, the participants became increasingly aware that carrying a gun often increased their power within the ranks of the RUF and, in some cases, decreased their chances of victimization. As these participants described:

The gun made everyone powerful. As long as you were armed even the older commanders were more careful in their treatment of you ... You were recognized as somebody if you were carrying a gun. When you had a gun, you felt that you were strong. (Boy)

I felt powerful when I had a gun. As long as you are holding a gun, you have power over those who don't. It gave me more status and power. (Girl)

I always felt powerful with my gun ... when you have a gun, you can force anyone to do anything for you. You can even capture five big men if you have a gun. Otherwise who was going to listen to me as a small boy? (Boy)

The gendered dimensions of the conflict once again became apparent within the context of small arms use. Although girls reported that their status as combatants tended to be low in relation to that of most boys, girls revealed that carrying and using arms nonetheless gave them a sense of power and control that they otherwise lacked in the norms of gendered inequity within the RUF:

I was not very powerful in my own group, but I had a lot of power over civilians. The commander would give us each a civilian – he would say, 'this one is yours, this one is yours,' and you would kill the one that was given to you. At that time, I was quite enthusiastic about it – I was proud and confident. I felt good ... That was one way of building confidence in me that I am just like them. (Girl)

Moreover, for many girls the gun offered important protection from abuse and exploitation from those *within* the RUF. In light of this, girl participants came to see small arms as a way to increase their safety and security and, reflecting both their agency and resourcefulness, over time became eager to possess their own weapon. As these girls commented:

I was eager to become a soldier and have my own gun so that I would be able to resist threats and harassment from other [RUF] soldiers. (Girl)

The gun became my bodyguard and protector. The gun was power and that's why I was anxious to have one. (Girl)

The young people's feelings of power and confidence in relation to handling weaponry must be seen, however, within the context of (gender) dependency and subservience. Through the use of small arms, the participants appear to have experienced a sense of release from previous relations of victimization and submission. More specifically, some youth participants were able to reframe and transform their original fear of small arms into instances of power that afforded them, *albeit minimally*, a greater sense of security.

### Negotiating (in)security: Girls and 'marriage' to a powerful commander

Marriage and sexual relations are often referred to as necessary exchanges for the survival and protection of girls associated with fighting forces (Dinan 2002). In what have been called 'sex for soap' exchanges, some females may try to negotiate their hygiene and food securities 'by using their positions as women (being [sexually] available to men)' (Lyons 2004, pp. 191, 271). Others may seek protection from physical and sexual abuse through sex or marriage (Ibañez 2001). Depending on the severity of the power dynamics, marriage and sexual relations may be perceived as either active or passive on the part of girls.

As noted earlier, the reality of sexual violence was a devastating feature of everyday life for girls in this study. Amid a powerful patriarchal structure, girls became mere 'property' of males, with their bodies being used as resources to be exploited, and even as gifts and rewards. Through sexual violence, girls' bodies became both literal and figurative sites of combat. Yet while girls in this study were constantly aware of the potential threat and danger of sexual violence by their adult commanders, as well as other males within the armed group, they were not entirely passive. Within a context of constant insecurity, girls realized the importance of actively aligning themselves with a high-ranking male, who could, in some cases, provide a degree of protection:

It was more advisable to have a husband than to be single. Women and girls were seeking [the attention of] men – especially strong ones for protection from sexual harassment. (Girl)

Although these 'marriages' to individual male commanders were often highly repressive, violent and abusive, they were seen by girls as preferable to the alternative of being ongoing victims of gang and individual rape by countless members of the fighting forces. As this girl explained:

When one of the commanders proposed love to you, sometimes you had to accept even if you really were not willing to co-operate. This was preferable to being gang-raped. (Girl)

'Marriage' to a powerful commander not only protected girls from daily sexual violence and physical abuse by other males in their group, but also tended to elevate their overall status within the armed group. Once 'married' to a male commander who held a senior rank, girls could actually benefit by gaining access to more food and a higher social status within the group:

Girls who were wives of senior officers were treated according to the status of their husbands, so it was good for any girl to have a senior officer as a lover. They had more power and status. (Girl)

The girls who were serving as wives were treated better, and according to the rank and status of their husbands ... At the beginning, I was raped daily. At least one person would come to me for sex ... I was every man's wife. But later, one of them, an officer, had a special interest in me. He then protected me against others and never allowed others to use me. He continued to [rape me] alone and less frequently. (Girl)

However, girls' relative security under such repressive circumstances must be acknowledged. While 'marriage' may have rendered a girl more secure, the context in which she benefited from a certain level of protection was still very insecure. Nonetheless, 'marriage' to a powerful male in the fighting force can be seen as a clever strategy to actively seek out protection, power, status and survival. This reality has also been discussed by Utas (2005b) in the context of Liberia, where he highlights one young woman's shrewd social navigation tactics, including aligning herself to a powerful male commander to assure her own security, power and overall well-being. For the girl participants in this study, although bush marriages may be perceived as a form of sexual slavery, they also appear to have served as a way for the girls to attempt to reframe their victimization and, however minimally, transform it into a slightly more secure space.

### Modes of resistance: Subverting RUF authority
For boys and girls living among the RUF, where obedience to authority and conformity to the values of the armed group were imperative to

their very survival, there was little room for defiance or opposition. Nonetheless, while interviews uncovered experiences of victimization and participation in violence, they also highlighted the unique, and often subversive, ways that children resisted these same forms of victimization and participation. Four forms of resistance will be discussed, namely girls' resistance to sexual violence, the establishment of close and sometimes secret friendships with other girls and women, refusal to comply with RUF orders, and methods of escape.

Girl participants' abhorrence and disgust with ongoing sexual violence was clear:

I felt so depressed about the rape incident and since that day I hated the man and I still hate him. He was so dirty with a very awful odour which suffocated me and made me vomit. (Girl)

In response, girls were found to engage in forms of resistance that were intended to protect them from sexual violence. For example, one girl would pretend that she was menstruating which thwarted any potential sexual victimization:

[To avoid being raped] I would fix a pad as if I was observing menstruation. (Girl)

Other girls reported using violent forms of resistance to retaliate against male perpetrators of sexual assault:

I stabbed one guy to death – he was always harassing me for sex. On that day he wanted to rape me and I told him that if he tried, I would stab him. He underestimated me and he never knew I had a dagger. He met me alone in the bush on my way to town after using the bush toilet. I knew that he and others were observing my movements ... and I took the dagger along [to protect me from] rapists. As he attempted to rape me, I stabbed him twice ... I was tired of the sexual harassment. He later died [from the stabbing]. (Girl)

I always wanted to take revenge against men [because they raped us]. This is why I was so wicked and aggressive to men during the conflict. Men are heartless and some of us [girls] were killing them for their wicked acts. (Girl)

Girls also resisted the culture of violence through the establishment of close friendships and sometimes secret solidarity among other girls and women. Although some would argue that the creation of strong female relationships can be considered a common survival strategy used by war-affected females historically, one must consider the unique context in which the girls were living. Within the context of the RUF any form of socializing or sharing of their current thoughts, feelings or information about their former civilian lives was strictly forbidden and highly punishable, even by death. As this girl explained:

If we came from the same place and we knew each other, we would share a few jokes or sit together and share thoughts and memories of home. This would go on until perhaps one of the commanders came and said, 'What are you sitting here for? What are you doing?' We would then pretend we were doing something else so that they would not learn of what we were actually engaged in. Because at those times, if you were caught in acts like that, you [could be killed]. (Girl)

Under these circumstances, girls took considerable risks in fostering supportive female relationships and defied the rules of the armed group. These relationships not only brought a degree of solace, comfort and solidarity, but also created a unique physical and emotional space for compassion, from which males were inherently excluded. This girl's comments underscore the importance of sharing her experiences with other girls:

One day a girl was brutally raped and she bled so badly she died ... I had heard about it and was so affected by it, but I was afraid to discuss it ... Two girls began discussing it and I overheard them. We all sat down and started sharing our stories [of rape] ... I felt much better after this because I thought that I was the only one to have this happen to. (Girl)

Another girl, who became pregnant as a result of rape at the age of 12, illustrated the reliance of the younger and inexperienced girls on the older women for knowledge and mentorship, as well as the unique sense of community among girls and women:

I heard from the older women in the bush that if you didn't menstruate for two months, you were pregnant. I didn't menstruate for more than two months, so I went to an older woman and told her. She told me that I was pregnant ... I really didn't believe it and I began to cry. So after the woman told me that I was pregnant, I continued to go to other women in the group and tell them the same thing. I kept hoping that they would tell me something different. They all said the same thing and I was devastated. (Girl)

While pregnant, this participant reported enduring ongoing verbal abuse by the boy soldiers. When this occurred, however, the older women offered her protection and validation:

[The boys] would come around and taunt me and say 'Out of all the girls here, only *you* are pregnant.' They made fun of me and kept repeating and pointing at me: 'Pregnant woman! Pregnant woman!' I was so humiliated. [But] when the boys did this I would swear at them and all the women in the group would also come around and swear at them and abuse them back. (Girl)

This sense of female solidarity in a male-dominated environment was further revealed by this same girl in her description of the eventual delivery of her child:

The delivery happened in the bush ... The men stayed away ... The older women helped me. They knew what to do. (Girl)

Given the dangerous and volatile context and the repercussions of being discovered for socializing, engaging in personal discussions and building a sense of solidarity can be considered more passive forms of resistance. Such communicative structures among girls, whether formal or informal, open or secret, were instrumental to their psychological and emotional well-being during armed conflict.

Alongside resistance to sexual violence and developing forms of solidarity, it became apparent that, at times, boys and girls also resisted RUF authority, command structure and participation in violence. For example, participants reported risking their well-being and their lives to protect civilians from the violence of the RUF. As this boy explained:

One day, another boy and I were asked to attack a woman, but [instead of attacking her] I helped the woman escape. My friend reported me and I was severely punished. I was tied and beaten mercilessly by every officer who came around ... Three times daily – morning, afternoon and evening. They often used electric cables and sometimes military belts. (Boy)

Resistance also manifested in refusing to ingest the drugs that were mandatory in preparation for combat. Participants found ways to avoid drug use:

[In preparation for combat] we were given cassava with gun powder underneath it to eat. I managed to get rid of the gunpowder without anyone noticing ... I would also hide during the time that the commanders began distributing the drugs. (Boy)

Resistance among both girls and boys also came in the form of mobilizing themselves to plan an escape. Some girls and boys fled from their captors, fully aware of the consequences of violence or death if they were discovered:

I was about 10 years old at the time ... Several of us small children sat together and planned our escape ... We decided that when and if we are attacked by the CDF, we will not go with the rebel group, but we will go with the CDF. Everyone knew about the plan so when the CDF did attack, we ran away. (Girl)

My first attempt was when I had no gun. I was just carrying loads. We met heavy attack from the CDF forces. We scattered and there was a group of us who were trying to find our way to Freetown. But we were caught. They executed three of them right away. The other three of us were put in cells and were not fed. They told us that they would have killed us but that the only thing that saved us was that they needed the manpower. After this the RUF began to brand people to prevent such escapes. If people did manage to escape it would be revealed that they had been with the RUF and would probably be killed by the enemy. (Boy)

Another girl explained the circumstances surrounding her attempted escape:

I became very tired of always carrying the loads. Myself and a group of about five others decided that we would attempt an escape. We decided to use the opportunity of fetching water to do this. But one girl was not involved in the plan and she overheard us talking about it. She informed the commander about our plan ... [W]e were [punished] and confined to a small space and starved for several days. (Girl)

In the above case, when the respondent was asked why she thought that her colleague had revealed the group's plan of escape to the commander, she replied:

I think that [the girl who revealed our plan to the commander] had a vested interest in having us all stay with her. If we escaped, she would have no friends or companions and she would be left to do all the chores and work by herself. (Girl)

By deceiving her fellow captives by reporting the plan of escape to the commander, the girl in question is herself actively using a survival strategy and a form of resistance. This demonstrates that while children acted in solidarity in some moments, in others they were in conflict and competition in their strategies of survival and resistance. Although a few were able to escape, many more respondents were unsuccessful in their attempts. Nonetheless, it was clear that they demonstrated a capacity to organize and to act both individually and collectively with extraordinary courage.

While there were differences in children's responses to the culture of violence, what the boys and girls all had in common was that following their coercive introduction to the war system, they eventually began to understand the intricacies and internal workings of the system and subsequently created different ways to master it. This was invariably shaped by the unique individual (psychological, personality, maturity, physical and mental strength, health) and contextual (structural, spatial, relational, geographic) opportunities and circumstances of each child. Several factors appear to have been salient to modes of resistance, including age and length of time with the rebels. Boys and girls who had more life experience and maturity appear to have been able to evaluate, appraise, calculate and, ultimately, negotiate their situations with seemingly greater ease and confidence. There were, however, clear exceptions, as the study revealed several instances of very young children – as young as age 10 – who actively planned and executed a successful escape from the RUF. On the whole, it would appear that younger children who had less life experience and a limited understanding of the war dynamics, and who were suddenly catapulted from the safety of their families and communities, relied more heavily upon modes of calculated acquiescence than bold resistance. It would also appear that girls and boys who lived among the RUF for longer periods of time, and had time to observe, learn and understand the system, were more skilled at creating effective means of ensuring their security. For example, it took time and experience to discover that carrying arms, which was initially experienced as frightening and embittering, could actually be protective. A final factor that appears to have propelled girls and boys to develop strategies of resistance was the continued and unrelenting victimization. Girls, in particular, who lived among the rebels for long periods of time and grew tired and weary from massive sexual, physical and psychological insecurity developed bold strategies of resistance for their very survival. For example, the young woman who reported killing the man who attempted to rape her explained that she had grown 'tired of the sexual harassment'.

It is important to recognize, however, that children's abilities to resist during armed conflict cannot be constituted as full emancipation. Invariably, the broader social, economic and political forces in Sierra Leone, both prior to and during the war, the violent forces of the RUF, as well as the pre-existing inferior social status, particularly of women and girls, shaped and organized the social actions of child soldiers and the degree of agency and resistance that the children exhibited.

These broader social and historical conditions are, of course, also highly relevant to understanding participants' wartime victimization and participation experiences. Through children's narratives, we can observe the bounds within which the RUF commanders appear to have operated during the height of the conflict and how this affected the children themselves. Particularly noteworthy are the ways in which the RUF leadership drew upon and reproduced powerful historical realities and practices of patronage, exploitation, enslavement and extreme violence within their ongoing relationships. The victimization experiences of girls are a case in point. Shaw (2002) regards the capture, brutality and enslavement of Sierra Leonean girls and women during the war as comparable to the realities of women during Sierra Leone's slave trade. As with women during the slave trade and nineteenth-century colonialism, girls and women in the RUF were relegated to a life of agricultural labour and domestic slavery and were viewed as commodities. That a young RUF soldier could treat his 'wife' in a similar fashion to a nineteenth-century slave suggests that the exploitation, abduction and murder that underlay the slave trade in fact became inscribed into the cultural patterns and practices of life in Sierra Leone, and ultimately shaped RUF practices (Shaw 2002). Moreover, as addressed in Chapters 2 and 4, the connected realities of violence, protection and patronage feature prominently in Sierra Leone's history (Kandeh 1999; Murphy 2003; Reno 1995; Richards 1996). The patronage networks between RUF leaders and their child (mainly boy) soldiers, and the ways in which the young people themselves appear to have emulated such relationships with their peers and subordinates, can arguably be linked to these historical realities. Ultimately, the children's narratives of victimization and participation provide insight into the social context of RUF practices and the ways in which the RUF leadership appears to have drawn upon and propagated deeply rooted social and gendered practices and expectations within their own relationships.

## 'Being RUF': Identity construction in the culture of violence

Given the process of 'making' outlined in Chapter 4, alongside children's experiences of victimization, participation and resistance highlighted above, it is critical to consider how such realities and experiences affected children's sense of self-concept and identity. What did it mean to 'be' RUF? Was this an identity that children genuinely embraced?

According to Erikson (1963), it is during adolescence that people first confront the problem of identity and begin to explore the ideological and occupational options and social roles available in society, with the aim of eventually consolidating their beliefs and values into a personal ideology. Similarly, McAdams (2001) suggests that adolescence is an essential period when young people are first confronting their identity issues and actively formulating integrative life stories and narratives to address the many psycho-social challenges they face. Consequently, young people 'may be more likely to encode personal events occurring during these years as relevant to their psychosocial goal of formulating an identity' (McAdams 2001, p. 110). If, as Erikson and McAdams suggest, the developmental process that accompanies adolescence is a crucial life-course moment, then the significance of being abducted, brutalized and militarized, all in a relatively short period of time, can be viewed as both momentous and life-changing. Moreover, if, as McAdams argues, young adolescence is the period whereby life stories, and thus identities, are being formulated and encoded, then indeed the experience of child soldiery can also be seen to 'disrupt' conventional narrative and developmental processes as a result of indoctrination into a world of violence and terror.

The degree to which children reported taking on an 'RUF identity' – that is, a genuine belief in and commitment to the RUF 'cause' and its objectives and goals – varied significantly. Moreover, as the following section will highlight, given the ever-changing circumstances of their wartime lives, children's sense of identity was not stagnant or fixed, but altered throughout their time with the rebels. In this sense, children did not always remain within a single identity construction, but frequently drifted between personas and identities at different stages of the conflict.

## Acquiescence and suspended identities

As with entry into a 'total institution' (such as a prison or an asylum), which deliberately strips the identity and previous sense of self from individuals who enter it, abduction and indoctrination into the world of the RUF represented a 'massive assault' on the identities of those held captive (Schmid and Jones 1991, p. 415). Developing a survival strategy, some children reported publicly acquiescing to the RUF culture of violence and attempted to give their commanders and colleagues the impression that they fully identified with the cause of the RUF. This girl explained her resourceful tactic to both show her 'dedication' to the RUF and simultaneously avoid warfare:

I had to show that I was committed to working with them ... I was responsible for cooking and I always did it well because I did not want to leave the [domestic duties] for jobs like combat that were more deadly. (Girl)

Demonstrating a (false) degree of commitment to the group to ensure their long-term survival is reflective of Schmid and Jones' (1991) notion of a 'suspended identity'. This concept relates specifically to individuals who find themselves in circumstances where it is necessary to accommodate a sudden but encompassing shift in social situations. These circumstances can range from meteoric fame to confinement in total institutions, which place new identity demands on individuals while seriously challenging their prior identity bases. According to Schmid and Jones (1991), after coming to believe that they cannot be 'themselves' in these new social situations because they would be too vulnerable, individuals decide to 'suspend' their previous identity and take on a 'false' identity for the duration of their time within the social situation, which emanates directly from feelings of vulnerability, discontinuity and differentiation from others (p. 419). Importantly, as Schmid and Jones note, this bifurcation of self is not a conscious decision made at a single point in time, but represents conscious and interdependent identity preservation tactics, formulated through ongoing self-dialogue and tentative interaction with others.

Applying Schmid and Jones' framework to the sample of child soldiers in the RUF, some children appeared to draw a distinction between their 'true' identity (their pre-soldier identity, which remained a subjective or personal identity) and a 'false' RUF identity created for the world of armed conflict, which served as an objective or social basis for interaction. In this sense, during the heart of their time with the RUF, some children saw themselves as playing a 'part'. Acting in accordance with RUF expectations and behaviour, children covertly preserved a sense of compassion associated with their pre-war identity. As an example, several girls reported secretly refusing to kill during battle. These children often shot their weapons in such a way that human targets were able to escape without being hurt:

While on patrol if we came across [unknown] people they would order us to kill them. But I was not really interested in killing people ... [I] would normally fire, intentionally not aiming well. [I] would then report that the mission was completed without really killing the people. (Girl)

[I]n combat I was just firing sporadically. I was not really aiming at anything at all. I wasn't interested in harming anyone. (Girl)

This boy remembered the specific event that made him realize that he could no longer be 'himself' within the RUF. He recounted:

A man was severely beaten and amputated because he tried to prevent [the RUF] from taking his goat away. One arm was amputated to scare him but he still persisted until the other was cut off too ... I felt so bad and that was the time I really became frightened. I couldn't eat for that day and even got fever in the evening. The barbaric and terrifying behaviour of the other soldiers made me very sad and scared. My mind kept telling me that anything could happen to me from that moment on. (Boy)

He later noted:

I knew that I had found myself in a difficult situation so I just had to bear it ... I just kept quiet and stayed cool to myself ... I was always pretending. (Boy)

For these children, this was not a form of identity transformation but was rather a form of identity construction. This 'false identity' was essentially created for survival in an abhorrent world.

## Identifying with the RUF

Some children, mostly boys, reported an attachment, commitment and dedication to the RUF and its values, goals and beliefs. These boys reported that during the height of the conflict they came to recognize themselves as RUF fighters, warriors and commanders:

I was a warrior because I was a commander with my own bodyguards. I gained this position because I was brave and obedient ... I was appointed as the commander of a group [of small boys] [and] I felt very proud of that. (Boy)

Another boy expressed his strong dedication and affiliation to the RUF when he reported his fervent sentiments concerning the CDF, ECOMOG and other allied government forces:

I hated them. I *truly* hated them. They were the enemy. (Boy)

In recounting their lives in the RUF, several boys indicated the pride in the status that they had achieved, as well as an accompanying sense of nostalgia. As they became inured to the violence that surrounded them, these children became effective soldiers who not only embraced the values of the RUF, but who also appear to have had little compunction over the suffering that they inflicted on others. As this boy explained:

On one of our amputation days, I was given a lot of people to do the amputation operation on … [One man] pleaded that I kill him. But I considered killing not to have a very big effect because once the person died, everything was finished. I had to give him short sleeves on both hands. He jumped after me, wailing. I felt so good at that time because I was superior. (Boy)

It is nonetheless important to keep in mind the context in which these children were living. The moral compass that children may have had at other moments in their lives appears to have been lost in a context of extreme violence, drug use, perverse authority structures and mentorship. As this boy explained:

You couldn't tell if it was good or bad while you were with your group of commanders. (Boy)

Moreover, previous studies of coercive persuasion and the so-called Stockholm syndrome, in which terror-prone victims develop emotional fealty to their tormentors as a form of survival conditioning,[3] reinforce interpretations of the unwitting desensitization of child soldiers and their subsequent participation in atrocities.

The differences in identity construction attest to the fact that children's responses to abduction and coercion by the RUF, and the degree to which they embraced the militarized values and personas, were wide ranging. Some children were highly obedient and publicly acquiesced to RUF commands for their own survival and safety, yet privately rejected or resisted the culture of violence. Others became highly integrated with the values and culture of the RUF and actively engaged and participated in brutal and excessive forms of violence. Importantly, given the changing context of their wartime lives and circumstances, children often moved within and between the above-mentioned identity constructs and were not relegated to a single and solitary form during their time with the rebels.

Gender appears to have been a salient factor in identity construction within the RUF. Overwhelmed by patriarchal, militarized structures of

---

[3] See Pavlos (1982) and Galanter (1989).

violence on all sides, girls, like their male counterparts, were easily socialized into the norms and behaviours that once again helped to reinforce these structures. At the same time, however, it is evident that many girls did not entirely succumb to the RUF's totalitarian system of militarized masculinity. Some resisted, on occasion at grave risk to their safety, while, as noted earlier, others sought a 'feminist' space with other girls and women that provided a modicum of temporary solace. Importantly however, it would appear that perhaps due to the realities of ongoing sexual victimization, girls' secondary status and social exclusion from the patriarchal RUF structures of power and privilege, and the lack of corresponding mentorship that was offered to the boys, relatively few girls reported a strong identification with the RUF or actively embraced such a persona during the conflict, although a minority of girls did report this.

In stark contrast to the formulaic and unidimensional imagery of child soldiers that are commonly depicted in the media and in popular discourse, child soldiers existed in a hazy realm where they suffered horrible abuses, were engaged in brutal acts of violence and, nonetheless, heroically resisted the violence that surrounded them. To be a child soldier in the RUF meant that the realities of victimization, participation and resistance were experienced in an irregular, changing and dialogical fashion. Bringing forward these complex sets of realities forces a more intricate picture of these children, who sometimes actively sought power, resisted authority, planned and mobilized for escape, experienced profound violence, perpetrated severe violence, and whose resilience and ingenuity become clearly apparent.

The wartime experiences of these young people were, without question, life changing. Nonetheless, the extent of the many changes that occurred was, in some ways, more clearly revealed in the conflict's aftermath. It was in this post-conflict period that children were faced with another powerful shift in their circumstances.

# 6 | 'Put dey gon don': The unmaking of a child soldier

You were only recognized as somebody if you were carrying a gun.
You felt like you belonged.
You felt powerful and protected ...
Without your gun you were shit.

(Boy)

At the conflict's end, with the disbandment of the RUF imminent and with the guns gradually falling silent, returning to a civilian existence became an ever-increasing reality for the child soldiers in this study. However, given the profound meaning that holding a gun roused, disarmament and returning from the bush was an invariably complex and sometimes conflicting experience. As indicated by the participant in the above quotation, for some children, putting down the gun often meant relinquishing power and protection, renouncing a part of their identity and losing a sense of belonging. For others, it meant a newly found freedom and relief from a militarized world that they had longed to escape. For most children, it meant each of these realities (and others) simultaneously. As discussed in the book's introduction, there has been a tendency to assume that in the post-conflict period, former child soldiers are destined to a life of pathology, disorder and deviance. Although the process of disarmament, demobilization and reintegration may be highly challenging, for both the child soldiers themselves and the communities that are expected to reabsorb them, such assumptions are overstated and premature. In fact, the 'unmaking' of child soldiers – the ways in which these young people leave the world of violence and their struggles to redefine themselves following demobilization – remains poorly understood. This chapter traces the initial phases of this process of 'unmaking' and, in particular, examines the individual and structural factors that influenced children's demilitarization experiences immediately following the war. Such individual and structural factors include individual identity construction, as well as formal disarmament, demobilization and reintegration programming, family and community acceptance, access to education and employment, and issues related to gender-based violence and health.

## Pathways out of violence and armed conflict

For participants in this study, the pathway out of violence and armed conflict was often as sudden, unexpected and disorienting as their pathways into armed conflict through abduction. Participants left the world of the RUF through a variety of means, including rapid escapes, unanticipated liberations or through spontaneous reintegration.[1] These pathways out of violence were often fraught with fear and uncertainty, and the first phase of a long and arduous journey back to a civilian existence.

### Escape

A minority of children escaped from RUF captivity and attempted to make their way back from the bush on foot. Such physically and psychologically laborious passages normally entailed crossing enemy checkpoints, days without food or water and the constant fear of being discovered as former RUF combatants and subsequently being killed. This boy explained the myriad hardships associated with an escape and the ongoing stress and emotional strain that accompanied it. His narrative also illustrates the profound loss of significant friendships that are invariably tied to demobilization and escape:

[My friend Mohamed] had been shot in the eye ... His eye was badly damaged and he was suffering a lot. I kept telling him 'let's go, let's escape'. Finally, one night he was in so much pain that he decided to try ... We were asked to go and find food. There were some ducks around and we were running after them, trying to catch them. At that point, Mohamed said, 'let's escape'. And we did. We walked in the bush for two days until we came to Grafton ... There was a checkpoint that was being manned by the CDF and they interrogated us. We told them that we were victims, running from danger. They were suspicious of Mohamed because of his eye ... I gave my shirt to Mohamed to put over his own so that the RUF branding on his chest was hidden ... Eventually they let us go ... We reached a final checkpoint and once again

---

[1] This term will be explained below.

we were interrogated by ECOMOG. I advocated on behalf of Mohamed and told them that he had been shot by the RUF. The men took pity on Mohamed and gave him a handkerchief to cover his eye. I was so scared because I was sure that they would be able to find us out – they were so powerful ... Mohamed could not see out of his eye and it was very smelly, so once we passed the checkpoints, we were trying to find a hospital. But when we got [to a hospital], it was completely empty. So from there we went to a pharmacy – but again no one was there. There was a woman who lived upstairs and she took pity on us and gave Mohamed a new cloth for his eye. He then decided that he would go to find his family as they lived in the area. So we parted ways ... We embraced. We were both crying. We shook hands and cried again and then parted ways. As I was walking away I kept turning back to see him and he was doing the same. We kept looking back and waving ... I never saw him again [long silence]. (Boy)

While these children had freed themselves from the RUF, in doing so, they had also made themselves 'enemies' who were vulnerable not only to the RUF, but also to CDF and ECOMOG forces. As such, to ensure their very protection and survival, escapees needed to continue to rely upon the many militarized skills that they had learned and developed over the course of their captivity. In this sense, while they were on their way 'back' to civilian life, they remained highly militarized.

## Liberation and release

For other children, the pathway out of violence and armed conflict occurred rapidly and often without warning. Some children reported being discovered by UN troops following an ambush or were serendipitously found while in the bush. Once discovered, the UN troops assembled the children and, in most cases, brought them to reception centres for formal demobilization or to their natal communities. As this girl noted:

Following an ambush, UNAMSIL collected all the child soldiers ... from our rebel held area. They took us to a displaced camp and we were temporarily kept by [a child protection agency]. We were later taken to a DDR camp and sent to train in vocations of our choice. (Girl)

## Spontaneous reintegration

Others experienced 'spontaneous reintegration' or self-demobilization, whereby children exited the RUF under an array of circumstances and made their way directly to their communities, returned to new communities or drifted to camps for the internally displaced in search of alternative forms of support. Spontaneous reintegration essentially refers to situations where children did not undergo any formal demobilization process.[2] As this boy explained:

After an attack, I managed to survive and I was not captured by the enemy. I got rid of my rocket launcher and just kept my gun. I was alone and so it would have been hard to identify me as a soldier. I was so small too – no one would have guessed I had been a soldier. One driver came by and picked me up. I never told him that I was part of the RUF – I just said that the rebels had attacked the village I was in. The man dropped me off in Freetown – and I had no idea where I was … [i]t was 400 km from where I had been with the rebels. Another man picked me up and again I said that I was a lost child. I stayed with the man for one month. Unexpectedly, I ran into an old friend who also had been with the rebels. He was shocked to see me – he thought I was dead. He introduced me to his family, who said that they knew my family. They told the man I was staying with, that they knew my family and that they would take me to them … I was not [formally] demobilized – I thought that [demobilization programmes were] the government's way of gathering soldiers to prosecute them. (Boy)

Spontaneous reintegration was preferred by many children, as the anonymity provided them with a degree of protection from potential post-conflict discrimination and ostracism. Nonetheless, without formal mechanisms of assistance, this pathway out of violence left most participants to fend for themselves (and their children born within the RUF) under extremely challenging circumstances, and as McKay (2004) has noted in relation to the self-demobilization of child soldiers, it also concealed their need for physical or psycho-social support.

Regardless of the means through which children exited the armed group, the sudden separation from the RUF was another major turning point. Much in the way that they were initially abducted, children were catapulted from a life that they had been a part of for significant periods of time, and, in some cases, from a life that they had grown partially accustomed to. Within a period of weeks or even days, participants were abruptly disconnected from their militarized lives and were

---

[2] It is possible that some children who escaped or were liberated by UN troops also chose not to participate in DDR and thus experienced spontaneous reintegration.

propelled into a new existence with a unique set of civilian norms, values, expectations and actors.

## Reshaping reality and 'becoming a civilian': Demilitarization and the process of unmaking

The pathway out of violence signalled the unmaking of their militarized lives as child soldiers. Whether entering a DDR camp, an internally displaced camp or reintegrating directly into a community, participants were compelled to begin an unsettling process of transition and adaptation to a completely different social context. Suddenly, the RUF networks and relationships they had developed, alongside the militarized skills that had helped them to survive the war, were no longer of benefit to them. Moreover, the formal and informal RUF values of detachment, cruelty, terror, violence, group solidarity and cohesion were, in the post-conflict context, no longer propagated or encouraged. Similarly, rigid military hierarchies ceased to be imposed upon them and there were no commanders shouting orders and demanding compliance. Instead, in the post-conflict world outside the RUF, there existed an array of possible options, and the necessity for independence of thought and action. In essence, there lay a new 'civilian' reality ahead of these young people – one that, for some, had become a vague and distant memory of the past. Ultimately, for the second time in their lives, there was a necessity (and often a profound desire) to move from one world view to another – from a world of inhumanity, rigid hierarchies, detachment and cruelty to one based on principles of humanity, civic associations, empathy and caring. In contrast to young people's initiation into the RUF, which had been carefully contrived to facilitate and ensure their adaptation and compliance to the militarized system, in the aftermath of the conflict, children were left to build and reshape their identities and their place within a new civilian reality largely in isolation.

Several individual and structural factors were highly significant to and profoundly influenced this process of unmaking. At the level of the individual, participants were left to reconstruct 'civilian' identities, within a context of torn allegiances in the war's aftermath. At the structural level, formal disarmament, demobilization and reintegration programming, family and community acceptance, access to education and employment, and the reality of gender-based violence and health significantly shaped the process and experience of demilitarization. Each of these factors will be discussed.

## Individual identity construction: Torn allegiances and duelling identities

In the post-war period, participants were not able to simply return to their communities and live their lives as if their RUF captivity had never occurred. As has been reported in studies of child soldiers in other contexts (Betancourt et al. 2008; Betancourt and Tanveer Khan 2008; Chrobok and Akutu 2008; McKay 2004; Stavrou 2004), participants reported experiencing ongoing psycho-social after-effects of the war, such as disturbing memories of violence and abuse, nightmares, anxiety, anger, fear and depression, which reportedly pervaded their daily lives. Furthermore, the struggle to disengage from RUF values and culture was not always obvious or straightforward. In theory, the term 'demobilization' connotes the formal disbandment of armed groups, and demobilization efforts typically attempt to quash formal and informal command structures. In reality, however, relationships, informal systems of support and mentorship often continued among former RUF members several years after the end of the conflict. As this girl noted:

For a few years after the conflict ended, I was still living with the people who first captured me. The commander got a house for us to live in. The commander was living there with his three wives and the radio-man [communications person] from the bush. (Girl)

This boy continued to see one of his former RUF commanders, who still provided him with money and mentorship:

I still see one of my [former] commanders and he gives me money and clothes to wear. I recently went back to see him but his wife said that he had gone traveling. (Boy)

In many ways, some children had not completely detached from the RUF, either psychologically or socially. For example, although evidently focused on his present circumstances and the need to plan for his future in post-war Sierra Leone, the following boy longed to see his former RUF commander and the boys who were under his command during the war:

Now that the war is over ... I have to make new friends and adapt to new ways ... but I would like to see the boys who were under my command, just to know if they are okay. [And] I would really like to see my former commander. (Boy)

Undeniably, the formal demise of the RUF brought children critical relief from wartime violence, terror and abuse, whether as victims, aggressors or resisters. Yet simultaneously, for a number of participants, it also meant separation from significant relationships. According to this participant, a special post-conflict bond appeared to exist, largely among male members of the RUF:

We still like to see each other and we always meet with great joy. I would really like to see the commander who recruited me ... I don't know where he is ... I think he might provide me with assistance now. I also see another commander sometimes. He gives me advice – he's like a mentor. He tells me that he can't protect me now – now I have to protect myself. When I see these people, we share experiences together that I can't share with other people. (Boy)

For some participants, the RUF was often the only 'family' they had ever known. When this 'family' was disbanded at the end of the war, this sometimes led to a sense of loneliness and isolation. For example, one girl participant, who had been abducted by the RUF at approximately age 4,[3] explained that the values, norms and culture of the RUF were not something that she temporarily accepted in order to survive the war, or that they represented a 'false' or suspended identity. Instead, the culture of violence and the RUF had been the only way of life that she had ever known. She explained:

I grew up with the RUF. All I knew was the behaviour of the RUF. I did not join them from the outside but *grew up* with them. My only family and friends were members of the RUF. The only parents I know are the Major and his wife [who abducted me] ... but they don't even know where I am now. (Girl)

The significance of RUF relationships, and their subsequent demise, often led to torn allegiances and a deeply personal struggle – that is, being conflicted between their 'RUF' sense of self and their post-conflict 'civilian' identity. As this respondent explained:

Even when the war was over, I still saw myself as a soldier ... I certainly did not consider myself a civilian. (Boy)

This participant articulated that even after he had successfully escaped from the RUF and was reunited with family members, he continued to identify with the RUF:

---

[3] As this participant was a very young child when she was abducted, she was unsure of her precise age at abduction.

When I managed to reunite with my family, the war was not yet over. We were in an area where ECOMOG was patrolling. Knowing that the RUF was close by I began to laugh and say 'ECOMOG are such fools, don't they know that our people [the RUF] are all around? They will all be killed!' After I said that the girl [I was with] looked at me and said 'don't you see what you are saying? *You are still with them* [the RUF]' ... From that moment I realized that I really needed to change my thinking. But the girl wasn't convinced and she went to my uncle to tell him that I was still willing to fight with the RUF. My uncle called a family meeting and told me that I should be thinking about my future and going to school. I told him that I didn't need school – the RUF will be giving me money when I leave here. (Boy)

For some children, shedding their militarized sense of self was filled with uncertainty and hesitation. For one girl, her reticence to cast off her military identity and her acquired sense of power was evident in her actions in a 'disarmament, demobilization and reintegration' (DDR) camp. Maintaining her persona as a leader of child soldiers in the camp, this participant was elected 'head girl', a position of coordination and responsibility that enabled her to exercise control over other girls:

I was elected as 'head girl' [in the DDR camp]. I felt very good about this ... I would delegate who would do what chore and they had to listen to me ... If they disobeyed me I would punish them ... I would starve them for a day ... I liked it ... I had more power in the camp than I had in the bush. (Girl)

The struggle to disengage from her former RUF lifestyle, identity and sense of power was also evidenced in her other activities in the DDR camp. When she and several other former combatants did not receive their financial benefits on time, they organized a violent attack against the DDR programmers. Significantly, to prepare for the attack and to build courage and strength, the group of children organized themselves to purchase and take drugs – the same technique that they were taught as RUF fighters:

We were very angry about not getting our money ... [To build up courage] we took drugs and went as a group to physically attack the DDR programmers for not giving us our money. (Girl)

Feelings of severe guilt and shame, previously noted by Boothby et al. (2006) and Betancourt and Khan (2008), also contributed to the challenge of post-conflict identity construction, particularly in light of having committed wartime violence and abuse. Participants were plagued by persistent feelings of guilt:

Since I've come back ... I often think about those wicked acts I did and they make me feel horrible. I wish I hadn't done them. I feel the guilt. (Boy)

While trying to leave Bo ... I saw my best friend running away from the heavy gunfire. I called to her ... 'Please come!' ... Our commander gave me a gun and told me to fire at her. I refused at first, but he threatened to kill me ... I ask myself again and again the same question – why didn't you disobey the command? (Girl)

At the same time, some participants reported engaging in acts of reconciliation as part of their post-conflict identity construction. As this participant explained:

During the war, the rebels killed my father right in front of me. He was killed by a young child soldier. At that time, I couldn't cry, because they told me that if I cried, they would kill me. But I cried in my heart ... [After the war] I was lucky enough to go to school through the help of an NGO. At school, in my class, I saw the very boy who killed my father. Every time I would look at him, he would bow his head down and he wouldn't look at me. Finally after some weeks, I went up to him and he was very scared. I said to him: 'The war is over. We are all brothers now.' (Boy)

Participants found themselves torn between a powerful militaristic identity that they had assumed at a time when violent conflict pervaded some of their most formative years and an abruptly new context of societal demilitarization that they knew required them to remake their own character and assume a new set of values and relationships. It was a major turning point that required a profound personal struggle. However, unlike the establishment of his or her persona as a child soldier – a role that was largely learned under profound coercion and from other soldiers – a participant's struggle with questions of identity in the post-conflict context was a largely solitary activity and participants responded to the struggle in individualized ways.

While individual identity construction (and its associated realities of uncertainty, hesitation and guilt) was a critical element in becoming a civilian, this occurred alongside powerful structural factors that also shaped participants' post-war experiences. These structural factors are addressed next.

## Disarmament, demobilization and reintegration programming

The difficult and complex transition from a militarized life in an armed group to a civilian life has been well documented, and over the past several decades has garnered much attention by scholars, psychologists, militaries, policy-makers and governments alike (Helmus et al. 2004; Marlowe 2001; Solomon 1993; Staub 1989). To ease the transition, national and international efforts have sought to conceptualize and implement post-war development assistance projects and programmes. What is known as 'disarmament, demobilization and reintegration' (DDR) programming is increasingly being utilized as a technical solution to militarization and as a means out of organized violence. DDR efforts have been supported by the World Bank and UN agencies such as the United Nations Development Programme (UNDP), UNICEF, United Nations Development Fund for Women (UNIFEM), International Organization for Migration (IOM), International Labour Organization (ILO) and other NGOs. According to the Integrated DDR Standards (IDDRS) initiated by the UN in 2006, 'disarmament' is defined as:

the collection, control and disposal of small arms, ammunition, explosives and light and heavy weapons of combatants and often also of the civilian population. Disarmament also includes the development of responsible arms management programs. (United Nations 2006, p. 6)

Formal disarmament processes usually occur following formal peace accords and involve the surrender, registration and destruction of weapons and ammunition. Combatants are normally gathered in pre-determined assembly areas and, in some cases, material goods or cash payments are provided as an incentive for handing in of weapons. Importantly, however, achieving 'peace' is not simply about disarming militarized populations, but it is also about breaking down the command and control structures operating over militaries, thus making it more difficult for them to return to organized rebellion (Spear 2002, p. 141). 'Demobilization', therefore, is the complex process by which armed forces and/or armed groups either downsize or completely disband, as part of a broader transformation from war to peace. The IDDRS defines demobilization as follows:

Demobilization is the formal and controlled discharge of active combatants from armed forces or other armed groups. The first stage of demobilization may extend from the processing of individual combatants in individual centres to the massing of troops in camps designated for this purpose (cantonment sites, encampments, assembly areas, or barracks). The second stage of demobilization encompasses the support package provided to the demobilized, which is called reinsertion. (United Nations 2006, p. 6)

Perhaps the most important and long-term stage of DDR is 'reintegration'. Reintegration aims to assist ex-combatants and the community in the difficult transition to civilian life, facilitates and supports combatants to be productive members of society by providing alternative employment support options, and seeks to promote broader social acceptance and reconciliation. The IDDRS defines reintegration as follows:

the process by which ex-combatants acquire civilian status and gain sustainable employment and income. Reintegration is essentially a social and economic process with an open timeframe, primarily taking place in communities at the local level. It is part of the general development of a country and a national responsibility, and often necessitates long-term external assistance. (United Nations 2006, p. 19)

DDR programmes have been continually regarded as crucial to increasing security, public safety and protection in the aftermath of conflict, as well as promoting peace, and have figured prominently as part of UN operations in Angola, Burundi, Cambodia, El Salvador, Guatemala, Liberia, Mozambique, northern Uganda, Sierra Leone, Sudan and Tajikistan, to name a few. Given their unique political and socio-economic contexts, DDR programmes in each of the above-noted countries have been unique, but nonetheless hold similar overarching goals and objectives.

DDR programmes have provided mixed and, to a great extent, untested results (Muggah 2006), yet have been met with considerable criticism. For example, research has indicated that there is a serious lack of long-term strategic planning when it comes to DDR and issues tend to be dealt with on an ad hoc basis (Specker 2008). Some have asserted that reintegration programmes have suffered from chronic underfunding and it has been argued that resources are often used for the disarmament and demobilization phases, leaving limited resources for the reintegration phase of the process (Specker 2008). Other critiques have centred around the exclusionary practices of many DDR programmes, particularly the neglect or systematic exclusion of women and girls (Farr 2002; McKay and Mazurana 2004; Stavrou 2004). Others still have observed that DDR programming is often 'quick and dirty', as noted by Ismail (2002) in relation to Liberia: 'identification, registration and interviews took place inside one hour and counseling took another two. This lost sight of the psychological and social needs of the child and of the communities that were expected to re-absorb them' (p. 127). Another concern has been highlighted regarding recipients of DDR programming. It has been suggested that humanitarian agencies often consult with local people of power and influence in their programming and rely upon them to identify programme beneficiaries. As a result, DDR 'benefits' may go to those who are connected to local power networks and remarginalize those who lack social resources (Shepler 2004). The reality of community resentment of DDR processes has also been raised whereby programming is often perceived by the wider community as rewarding perpetrators of wartime atrocities and neglecting broader populations of war-affected youth and adults (Chrobok and Akutu 2008). Some have also underscored that programmes often overlook local and traditional customs in their design and implementation (Specker 2008). Despite such criticisms, DDR programming continues to be a central component in post-war reconstruction efforts.

### DDR in Sierra Leone

Although former UN Secretary-General Boutros Boutros-Ghali called for a demobilization and reintegration effort in Sierra Leone as early as 1995 (Agence France-Presse 1995), plans for DDR in Sierra Leone were not made explicit until the following year within the terms of the 1996 peace agreement. Sierra Leone's National Committee for Disarmament, Demobilization and Reintegration (NCDDR) was formed in July 1998 in the aftermath of the junta period in anticipation of a negotiated peace settlement. The Sierra Leonean government and international partners, including ECOMOG and UNAMSIL, conducted a formal DDR programme in three phases between 1998 and 2003.[4] Phase I began in 1998 and was led by Kabbah's government after it was returned to power. However, the process was largely unsuccessful as only 3,183 ex-combatants registered for disarmament and demobilization (Molloy 2004; UNICEF 2005). Phase II began in 1999 following the signing of the Lomé Peace Accord and continued until 2000 when the war broke out anew. During this period, which included an interim phase from May 2000 to May 2001, 21,526 combatants were demobilized (UNICEF 2005). The bulk of demobilization occurred when UNAMSIL was strengthened and reinforced following the British intervention in 2001 and 2002. During Phase III, 47,781 combatants were demobilized, bringing the total to 72,490 (Miller et al. 2006).

---

[4] Programmes of reintegration continued after 2003.

The DDR process in Sierra Leone was conducted at reception centres placed around the country and involved the assembly of combatants, the collection of personal information, the verification and collection of weapons, the certification of eligibility for benefits and transportation to a demobilization centre. In the initial phases of DDR, to qualify for entry to the programme each combatant was required to present a weapon at any of the official reception centres. As a prerequisite for participation in the programme, every candidate was required to respond to questions and to disassemble and reassemble a gun, normally an AK-47. This 'one-person, one-weapon' approach was later changed and group disarmament was instituted where groups would disarm together and weapons would be handed in jointly.[5] At the reception centres, ex-combatants normally received basic necessities, reinsertion allowances, counselling and transportation to a local community where they elected to live permanently. Once in the community, many ex-combatants were involved in training programmes designed to ease their re-entry into the local economy.

Sierra Leone's DDR programming has been regarded as highly successful in increasing the country's security and viewed as a model on which other DDR processes could be based (Women's Commission for Refugee Women and Children 2002). However, the process was far from perfect. Malan et al. (2003) note that in 2001 there were delays in demobilization at certain cantonment sites and some combatants refused to leave camps because of the slow release of entitlements. Moreover, during July and August 2001 there were riots, demonstrations and beatings of NCDDR staff in the demobilization camps in Lunsar and Port Loko (Malan et al. 2003). Recent research by Peters (2007a) has thrown into question the long-term success and overall effectiveness of the DDR process. He notes that most ex-combatants have not been able to achieve sustainable livelihoods due to failures in DDR programming. Similarly, Humphreys and Weinstein (2007) found little evidence in support of claims that DDR effectively broke down factional structures and facilitated reintegration in Sierra Leone. In fact, their data suggest that combatants not exposed to DDR programming appeared to reintegrate just as successfully as those who participated in the programme.

---

[5] Weapons were collected, tagged, disabled and transported to storage centres. Later on, the weaponry was destroyed under the supervision of military observers and recycled into productive tools (Miller et al. 2006).

**Children's experiences of DDR**

Within the Lomé Peace Accord, explicit provisions were made to ensure the inclusion of child soldiers within the DDR process. The eligibility criteria for proving child combatant status required that children were between the ages of 7 and 18, had learned to cock and load a weapon, had been trained in an armed group and had spent 6 months or more in an armed group (UNICEF 2004, p. 2). According to UNICEF (2005) and the Monitoring and Evaluation Unit of NCDDR, 189 children were disarmed in Phase I of the DDR programme, 2,384 children in Phase II (including the interim phase from May 2000 to May 2001) and 4,272 children in Phase III, bringing the total number of children to 6,845. According to the final report of the TRC (Sierra Leone Truth and Reconciliation Commission 2004, p. 324), of the total number of children demobilized, 3,710 had been with the RUF, 2,026 with the CDF, 471 with the SLA and 427 with the AFRC; and 144 were with other factions or were non-affiliated.[6]

Children registered with Sierra Leone's DDR could choose from several programmatic options (Peters 2007a). In the first option, a former child soldier could re-enlist in the new Sierra Leonean Army and become a soldier. According to NCDDR (2004), only a few thousand ex-combatants chose this option. A second option was to return to school to continue their education, for which educational support was provided for a pre-determined period of time. According to NCDDR, this option was chosen by 20% of ex-combatants (NCDDR 2004). A third option was to engage in skills training, such as carpentry, masonry, hairdressing, tailoring or soap-making, and a monthly allowance of approximately 60,000 leones (approximately US$15) was attached to this package, alongside a basic toolkit that was received upon graduation from the programme. The majority of ex-combatants (51%) chose this package (NCDDR 2004). A fourth option was an agricultural package which was normally a training programme with a

---

[6] There are statistical inconsistencies in the TRC report which affect the numbers cited here. In Vol. 3B, ch. 4, p. 324, the TRC maintains that 6,774 children went through DDR and references the National Committee for Disarmament, Demobilization and Reintegration's (NCDDR) submission of 4 August 2003. However, this submission of 4 August 2003 in fact does not provide statistics. Instead, the NCDDR's submission for 3 March 2003 indicates that 6,845 children went through DDR – a figure that is frequently cited by other authors, organizations and UN documents (Miller et al. 2006; UNICEF 2005).

monthly allowance and toolkit. This sometimes took the form of a one-off package of farming tools, rice and seeds. An estimated 15% of ex-combatants chose this package (NCDDR 2004). A final option was to enlist in public works employment opportunities (such as road construction projects) in which ex-combatants received 'food for work' and, in some cases, a small allowance (Peters 2007a).

Despite the programmes offered, most boys and girls in this study's sample *intentionally* and systematically avoided the entire DDR process, which has been reported in other research and reports on child soldiers in Sierra Leone (Mazurana and Carlson 2004; McKay and Mazurana 2004). Among the interviewees, fear of stigmatization and criminal prosecution in the aftermath of the conflict were participants' main reasons for avoidance. As these participants noted:

No, I didn't go through DDR. I was too afraid. I was afraid that people would be able to identify me and single me out as one of the bad people of the war. I didn't want anyone to learn that I was in the bush. I didn't want my name advertised – I'm ashamed of that and very afraid. (Girl)

[My uncle and I] went to the displaced camp in Freetown. My uncle was concerned about the drugs and the trauma I went through. He suggested that I go through DDR but I refused. I was afraid of the DDR. I thought that it was a ploy by the government to take revenge on the ex-combatants ... I don't regret not going through DDR. I still think that it will be used to identify me and I will be exposed for my participation in the conflict. I sometimes see former RUF colleagues in the street and I don't trust the ones who went through DDR. I just nod hello, but I don't talk to them. (Boy)

I didn't go through DDR. My aunt who found me after I came out of the bush told me that if I went, my name would go on a computer and they would use it later to prosecute me. If I went through DDR they would know that I was a combatant and I don't want anyone to know. (Girl)

Other children reported that they wanted to participate in DDR; however, there was no programme available in their area. This girl explained:

No, I didn't go through DDR. I dropped my gun a few months after the ceasefire actually gained ground, and by then so many new faces were coming into [town]. So I disguised myself within the new faces. Later on we were told that the UN was coming to register [ex-combatants] for DDR and that we would be given money, but we never saw this happen. They only concentrated on big towns and some of us could not go to the big towns because we didn't have relations to stay with. (Girl)

For those few children who went through a DDR programme, their recollection of the process closely resembled the procedures noted above. As this boy explained:

At the demobilization camp they wanted to make sure that you were really a soldier. So they asked you to dismantle a gun, put it back together and then to fire, although there were no bullets. You then filled out a form, giving your name, former commander, training base, and you were given a card and basic needs. We had to live in the DDR camp for two weeks. Then they let you choose whether you wanted to go to school or whether you wanted to learn a trade. If you wanted to go to school they would arrange it for you. If you wanted to learn a trade they would give you about 360,000 leones (approximately US$93) to help you set up. They would also give you an allowance of 60,000 leones (approximately US$15). I decided that I wanted to go back to school to Makeni. (Boy)

Some children reportedly enjoyed and benefited from the DDR programme:

In the [DDR] camp, I really liked it. We had recreational activities – we went to concerts and did interesting things. (Girl)

Yet many of those who went through the programme expressed their disillusionment with a process they felt did not meet their needs and was undermined by corruption, mismanagement and false promises. This led many to drift away from the programme without acquiring the proposed skills or financial benefits:

I liked the idea of learning, but there were constant delays in the process – and the [managers of the programme] were very crooked ... They were not teaching us well and we were not paid on time or we were not given our allowances at all. As a result, we had no materials to use to continue with the program – there were no sewing materials. So I drifted from the program. (Girl)

Oh the false promises! ... We expected so much because the [skills training] program started very nicely, but later, we were not given what we were promised, they were not paying allowances on time and there were a lot of strains in receiving what was due to us. They were not even listening to small boys like us. They ate a greater part of our money. (Boy)

The short-term nature of the programme and its lack of sustainability were perceived as particularly problematic. In many cases young people were unable to make effective use of their training because of the weakness of the economy. Moreover, as has been noted by Hanlon (2005), the length of time in training was viewed as insufficient to provide the skills necessary for an individual to launch a small, sustainable business. Furthermore, once the programme ended, normally after a few months, participants who had no support systems or families were often left to fend for themselves and their children. While both sexes were inevitably affected by such realities, post-conflict vulnerability appears to have been more acutely felt by girls due to their peripheral social status as females and the continuing risk of sexual assault (Denov 2006). The ongoing predicament of girls in post-conflict Sierra Leone is reflected in this brief story recounted by a girl participant. Soon after the end of the conflict, with no place to live and no money, she accepted an invitation to live with an NGO worker who ended up sexually abusing her and abandoning her once she became pregnant with his child:

At the beginning, the DDR program provided me with a place to stay. Then suddenly they told me that the program was ending and I had to find a new place to live. I had nowhere to go! There was this man – an NGO worker at the DDR camp. He was always kind to me and I felt that he was trying to court me even though he had a wife at home. He invited me to come live at his house. I didn't want to go to live with him. I didn't fully trust him, but I had no alternative. After a while he began to make [sexual] advances on me ... I became pregnant. When I found out I was pregnant, I thought that he would assist me in getting an abortion, because he wouldn't want his wife to find out. He didn't ... [H]e told me to leave the house. He will not support this new baby ... I have no place to go and I now have two babies to take care of. (Girl)

Left to care for her two children, both less than 3 years old at the time of the interview, this girl was selling chewing gum and relying on handouts from strangers to support herself and her children. These gendered realities highlight the need to further explore the unique experiences of girls in DDR programming.

### Gender and DDR
An examination of DDR programmes in a variety of contexts, including Angola, Mozambique, Liberia and Sudan, has uncovered important examples of the systematic exclusion of women and girls (McKay and

Mazurana 2004; Stavrou 2004). Such exclusionary practices were also apparent in Sierra Leone, as the number of female combatants was grossly underestimated by those responsible for planning and conducting the DDR programme. Informed by conventional views of gender roles, which tend to regard armed conflict as a phenomenon occurring between males, in the early phases of the programme girls were consequently considered to be ineligible by programme planners, who were largely male. Mazurana and Carlson (2004) argue that women's lack of representation and exclusion at the decision-making and planning levels of DDR created a bias in the programme design and implementation that contributed to females' marginalization during the process. The Coalition to Stop the Use of Child Soldiers (2004) indicates that of the 6,845 children formally demobilized, a mere 529 were girls.[7]

The very small proportion of demobilized girls stems in part from their inability to benefit from the initial 'cash for weapons' approach to DDR, which was highly exclusionary. In Phases I and II of the programme, the 'wives' of male combatants, as well as their dependents, were not eligible for entry. Many girls reported being ordered to hand in their weapons prior to demobilization, and were left behind as their male colleagues were transported to assembly centres. Other girls indicated that their guns were taken away by their commanders and were given to male fighters, or, in some cases, sold to civilians who then reaped the financial benefits of the DDR programme. On other occasions, girls used small arms that were provided communally and thus did not possess their 'own' weapons and were simply not deemed to be primary fighters. Following complaints by male ex-combatants about the inadequacy of DDR assistance to support their families, wives were able to apply for micro-credit at the end of Phase III; however, they had to be identified by their husbands. This therefore excluded abducted wives who had escaped and also forced others to remain in such unions (Mazurana and Carlson 2004).

Alongside exclusion, fear of stigmatization and a lack of information (or the spread of misinformation) combined to ensure that relatively few girls and women were formally demobilized. Among the girls who were

---

[7] There are inconsistencies in the number of girls formally demobilized. Mazurana and Carlson (2004) draw upon World Bank figures and note that 506 girls went through DDR. In the TRC report, figures of 513 are cited for the number of girls formally demobilized.

interviewed for this study, many were convinced that participating in DDR programming would have hindered their chances of reintegration into their communities. Girls feared that public acknowledgement of their role as 'fighters' via the DDR, a role which counters accepted traditional norms for females, would increase the likelihood of being cast out of their families, stripped of their social standing and losing their potential marriageability. For many girls, the risks of participating in DDR, and exposing their former roles as fighters, far outweighed the potential benefits.

While most girls experienced systematic exclusion from DDR in Sierra Leone, some who registered for DDR later chose to leave the programme for reasons of security. More specifically, the ongoing threats of sexual violence that continued in the demobilization camps impelled this girl to leave the programme, even if the alternative meant living on the streets of Freetown:

The [demobilization] centre became chaotic and disorganized ... [T]here was no order ... The officers [at the camp] who were on night duty were not able to control the boys [former combatants], so the boys were coming over to [the girls] and harassing us for sex. I didn't feel safe and my friend and I decided to leave and go to Freetown because of that. Since we came to Freetown I have been living in the street. (Girl)

Ultimately, by downplaying the integral roles of female combatants, the DDR programme had the effect of extending gender-based insecurity and power differentiation into the post-conflict era and left most girls to fend for themselves and their children under extremely challenging circumstances. In spite of the critical roles girls played during the conflict period, they were rendered invisible in the post-conflict context. It should be noted, however, that in response to the absence of girls in DDR, UNICEF created the Girls Left Behind Project at the end of Phase III of DDR. In the Kono, Bombali and Port Loko districts where the project was in operation, over 1,000 girls had been identified who had not gone through the DDR process, and 714 girls were provided with services by the time the project ended in February 2005 (Coalition to Stop the Use of Child Soldiers 2008).

## Family and community acceptance

Family and/or community support is undeniably critical to war-affected children's long-term well-being and overall successful reintegration

(Betancourt and Khan 2008; Betancourt et al. 2008; Kostelny 2006). It has been suggested that a trusting relationship with a caring adult, as well as living with parents, may be a critical factor in children's recovery from the scourge of war (McKay and Mazurana 2004). As a result, those children who have family and community support are likely to fare much better than those children who experience post-conflict rejection and social exclusion. Importantly, upon return to their communities, children in this study were overcome by fear – this time, of condemnation by those who might learn of their past affiliation with the RUF, which was widely reviled in the post-war period. Children's fears were well founded, as they reported experiencing profound forms of rejection as a result of their status as former RUF soldiers. As these participants explained:

Since I came back, I have not been one year with my people, but there have just been problems, problems, problems ... You know, they don't love me any-more ... They despise me now ... I want them to accept me, to forgive me and allow me to be part of the community. (Girl)

[My community] refers to me as part of the 'evil ones'. (Girl)

When I arrived, my mom was overjoyed to see me. She cried and cried. She thought that I was dead. When I told my family what happened to me, and that I had been with the rebels, they told me to leave ... After a while, friends and family intervened and convinced my family to take me back. But the neighbours told their children not to talk to me – they found out that I had been with the rebels, because I was friends with one boy who was known to be a rebel. The community reaction tormented me. I found that my friend was much more helpful and supportive to me than my own family. They refused to talk to me and refused to include me in anything. My mom was particularly bad about this. Finally, my friend told his father about my mother's reaction. His father knew my father and told him. My father, who was living away from my mother, came to her to try to convince her to treat me better. My mom couldn't be convinced. She left the house and it was only because the elders went to talk to her that she finally came around. I really felt at that time that this woman was not my real mother. I felt that a true mother would not treat her son like that. (Boy)

Given the profound psycho-social impact of family and community rejection, participants made concerted efforts to conceal their former status as RUF combatants as much as possible.[8] Many had hidden their

---

[8] It should be noted that the experience of 'unmaking', particularly as it relates to community acceptance, appears to be significantly different for those children who

wartime experiences from close family and friends and vowed never to reveal their RUF status in the future. As this boy explained:

I won't tell anyone that I was a combatant … I will never even tell my future wife or even my children that I carried a gun and fought with the RUF. (Boy)

For fear of stigmatization and retaliation, children also altered their behaviour, avoided travelling to certain areas of the country, were highly cautious in cultivating new relationships and, in some cases, withdrew from social situations altogether:

When I'm walking outside, I'm always afraid that I'll see someone that I hurt during the war. I avoid going out as a result. (Girl)

I used to move around with friends and go out a lot. I don't like to hang around people much anymore because I'm afraid that if I am hanging around someone for too long, eventually I may reveal my past inadvertently. I don't want anyone to know that I was an RUF combatant. (Boy)

Sometimes to gain acceptance I tell people that I fought with the CDF. (Boy)

While children reported hiding their former RUF status quite effectively, others were not able to conceal their RUF affiliation as a result of brandings. In the aftermath of conflict, branded children reported feeling deep shame, and experiencing stigma and rejection by community members. This girl explained the powerful impact that her brandings had on her post-conflict life and on her (in)ability to put her RUF affiliation behind her:

[The RUF] left a farewell 'gift', an everlasting farewell gift with me … I am carrying on my breast right now. They wrote 'RUF' on me and they wrote 'AFRC' on me … What they did to me was calculated on their part. They knew that once they put this brand on me, if I went off to some other place, the people on the opposing side would kill me. That is why they put this on me. They wanted me to always be with them. They wanted to make me incapable

---

fought with the CDF. Anecdotal interviews conducted with former CDF child soldiers, as well as the perceptions of RUF study participants, revealed that many former CDF fighters were and continue to be unafraid to reveal their wartime affiliation. In fact, former kamajors interviewed for this study reported openly disclosing their former status to others with confidence and pride. In some areas of the country, particularly in the south and east, CDF fighters are often regarded as heroes who protected the country from the violence of the rebels, thereby in some cases facilitating their community acceptance and long-term reintegration.

of leaving them. That is why they did this to me … It is the most painful part of life right now. (Girl)

Children's experiences of post-war stigmatization and social exclusion were not only psychologically and emotionally detrimental, but they also may have an important impact on long-term socio-economic well-being in Sierra Leone (Betancourt et al. 2008). The World Bank (2007a, p. 10) has noted that lack of family connections is a major source of vulnerability and poverty, especially in rural Sierra Leone. Indeed children were well aware of the long-term socio-economic impact of such exclusion:

Now that the war is over, I'm afraid that I won't get the jobs that I want and people will point fingers at me … I'm not convinced that I will be what I want to be. (Boy)

Following their return from the bush many children had been unable to reunite with family members, or their families had been killed during the war. These children reported a severe sense of isolation and some were in fostering situations where they felt unwanted and abused:

In the household where I am living there is a certain lady who treats me badly. During a quarrel, she called me a 'rebel' and said that she shouldn't be wasting her time talking to an illiterate rebel girl like me. (Girl)

Well, take the household that I am living in now, for instance. There is a certain relative of mine there who attributes every little fault of mine to what she calls my 'rebel disposition and habits'. Any small disagreement or misunderstanding that we have she will yell at me and say, 'Your rebel games don't try them with me, you hear that? Don't try them with me. It is the same rebel actions that you are still up to.' … It hurts. I sit and cry. (Girl)

Girls appear to have experienced unique forms of rejection and stigma. For example, significant reintegrative challenges were experienced among girls who chose to remain with their RUF 'husbands'. This girl explained:

My father refused to accept me because of the background of my boyfriend. He doesn't trust me anymore and he just thinks I am still RUF because I still maintain an RUF relationship. But this is the only man I trust now and my father cannot get me another love. My entire family is angry with me and they have put a condition that if I don't forget about my boyfriend, they won't accept me. I am not going to become educated as I had aspired, I may never be accepted by my family because I can't afford to lose my source of comfort [boyfriend] just to please my family ... My concern is for my children, for having a rebel father, I don't think they will wholeheartedly be accepted in our home. Some people may discriminate against them in future or it may work against them if they are competing for something with other people that have a decent background. This worry is often expressed by my mother in the absence of my boyfriend. (Girl)

Importantly, girls appear to have suffered rejection not only as a result of their former affiliation with the rebels, but also because they had been victims of sexual violence. As has been noted in other research on wartime sexual violence (Fox 2004; Human Rights Watch 2003b; McKay and Mazurana 2004; Twagiramariya and Turshen 1998), given the importance placed upon virginity at marriage, girls were often deemed 'unmarriageable' following disclosures of rape. This girl explained the implications of being raped:

I am from a Muslim family and we believe that a girl should marry as a virgin, so depriving me of the honour and respect I would have enjoyed from my husband always troubles me, especially when I think of the way it happened. I regret not leaving [my village] when I had the chance before it was taken over by the RUF. (Girl)

Moreover, in a society where girls are valued primarily for their future roles as wives and mothers, and where marriage is often the best option for obtaining economic security and protection, being 'unmarriageable' often left girls feeling profoundly at risk. As this girl expressed:

I'm afraid I won't get a husband to marry me because of my past with the rebels ... My aunt told me that no man will marry me now [that I am no longer a virgin]. I feel a sense of despair. What will happen to me? How will I manage? (Girl)

For all of the post-conflict issues raised thus far, it is critical to note that the challenges may be even more pronounced for girl mothers, who return to communities with children who were conceived through sexual violence. As noted by McKay and Mazurana (2004), these children are evidence of violated community norms, including the importance of maintaining virginity until marriage, knowing a child's paternity and community-sanctioned notions of marriage. Moreover, in a patrilineal society, access to land, which often depends on the father, is impossible for these children, thus making their futures potentially bleak. These girls and their children often faced profound community rejection and insecurity:

When I came back to my people I used to feel really bad about it all ... I used to say to myself, 'These people are going make a mockery of me ... and my condition [pregnancy].' These thoughts tormented me. So I used to lie face down on a pillow and tie my stomach very tight with a piece of cloth. I had heard stories that it would induce abortion. It was only when my pregnancy grew mature that I gave up. (Girl)

The child now lives with my aunt. We don't have any relationship. I know that he is badly treated and gets no support. They call him 'rebel child'. (Girl)

Although participants, both male and female, and their children appeared to face diverse forms of social exclusion in the aftermath of conflict, purification ceremonies and rituals reportedly facilitated the process of demilitarization and community reintegration. While the process varies in different communities, rituals may combine prayer, song and dance and may be conducted by religious or traditional leaders and healers. Alongside welcoming the child back to the community, rituals seek to drive out dead spirits, provide a symbolic break from the past, call upon the protection and assistance of ancestors and protect the community from evil influences. One Sierra Leonean traditional leader interviewed by Stark (2006) described the cleansing process of a group of war-affected girls in the following manner:

The way I saw the girls, I knew I should cleanse them before their minds were set. I went to the ancestors and asked them how to help the girls. The ancestors instructed me in how to cleanse them. I went to the bush to fetch the herbs for the cleansing. I knew which herbs to pick because the ancestors told me. I put the herbs in the pot and boiled them. I poured a libation on the ground and also drank some of it. After boiling the herbs, I steamed the girls under blankets and over the boiling pot for their bodies to become clean and their minds to become steady. After the steaming, we all slept in the same house. The next morning we all went to the bush. In the bush, I gave them some herbs to drink. We spent the day cooking, singing and eating, and telling stories. On the third day I brought the girls to the riverside. I washed the girls one by one with black soap and herbs. After the washing, they put on new clothing and we all came to town dancing and singing. (Stark 2006, p. 207)

Given that communities and families in traditional societies may experience shame because they failed to protect their children during the war, spiritual and religious rituals may be important for the community as well as for the children themselves (Betancourt 2008; McKay and Mazurana 2004, p. 50). Incorporating both social and political elements,

Honwana (1998) notes that traditional African treatment necessarily transcends the individual to involve the collective body and a largely holistic approach. Rituals can thus facilitate the process of healing, reconnect the child to the community and facilitate social reintegration, spiritual transformation and positive psycho-social effects.[9]

The respondents in this study noted that community-cleansing rituals helped them to successfully reintegrate into their communities. Traditional rituals and ceremonies were said to provide the children with a feeling of acceptance and importance, and an opportunity to begin afresh following the scourge of war:

I used to have frequent bad dreams and it became a concern to my parents, so my father took me to an imam who prayed for me and gave me some treated water in a bottle for drinking. I was also to rub the water on my body before bed every night. This has helped me so much and it has even brought me closer to God. (Girl)

Because I refused to go to DDR, my uncle decided to use native herbs to help me. He got the herbs from the bush and my grandmother boiled them. I drank some of the mixture, rubbed it on my joints, and then they put a blanket over me and I inhaled the steam from the mixture. During my sleep my grand-mother performed a ceremony. She passed a mixture over my body and placed it around my heart. The ceremony was performed just once ... I felt different after the herbs. (Boy)

Importantly, where family or community support structures did not exist, participants actively formed and created their own support structures and informal peer-support networks. The practical support and kindness offered by friends was deemed as crucial to their healing and problem solving:

[When I am feeling sad] I come to the workshop. You see [my boss] does not give me much pay but he understands the way I feel most of the time. That is why even though the others have left, I am going to stay. When I am with him I don't have time to worry too much. Once you are fixing those carburettors, you have to concentrate so much that you forget your worries ... And he speaks to me as if I were his own son. That is why I have been on that work training all this time. (Boy)

---

[9] As noted by Williamson (2006), some traditional practices are harmful. As a result, it is 'necessary ... to determine what a practice involves before encouraging or supporting its use' (p. 197).

Moreover, respondents had often formed critical bonds with other former child soldiers during the conflict and often lived with them following their release from the armed group. These networks reportedly provided participants with mutual social, economic and emotional support and acceptance:

I am living with my best friend [from the RUF] and her mother. This is her home and she is generous to me. She also understands me. (Girl)

Community and family acceptance appeared critical to participants' view of their reintegration experience. The greater the perceived support from family and community members, the more likely it was that respondents viewed their reintegration experience in a positive light.

## Economic marginalization: Education and employment opportunities

The depressed economy of Sierra Leone has remained a major source of concern in relation to post-conflict reintegration (Hanlon 2005; Silberfein 2004). Loans and grants were designated for rebuilding Sierra Leone and some debt forgiveness was announced. However, not enough funds were being made available to resuscitate the economy. Silberfein (2004) notes that 'Sierra Leone has evolved into an AID-dependent state that has not been able to wean itself off foreign assistance. The economy grew about ten per cent from May 2001 to April 2002 and prices fell as well, but much of this phenomenon was the result of an unsustainable level of aid money' (p. 231). It has also been argued that international financial institutions, including the International Monetary Fund (IMF), have also been active in reconstruction and yet have also compounded the economic challenges. In particular, the IMF's insistence on privatization of public enterprises has made rebuilding the country's infrastructure a challenging task for a government whose budget comprises 65 per cent foreign aid (Freeman 2008). Moreover, international insistence on removing trade barriers has meant that cheap Asian rice has flooded the local market and small farmers are unable to compete (Hanlon 2005). A report assessing Sierra Leone's National Recovery Strategy highlighted the poor economy, inequality and corruption and its impact on marginalized groups in Sierra Leone, including former child soldiers:

There are more jobless youths, women and men roaming the streets of major towns and in the countryside today than before the war ... Economic inequities continue to exist. The national economy cannot engage ex-combatants who have been demobilized and other jobless citizens. Economic disparities and inequalities, fuelled by blatant corruption and decisionmakers that seem trapped in crisis management mode, continue to characterize social dynamics in the country. (Moore et al. 2003, pp. iv, vi)

Ginifer (2003) came to comparable conclusions: 'Economic stagnation and a lack of infrastructure creation also seem to be factors hurting both Sierra Leone and the reintegration process ... In an unstable Sierra Leone these could be worrying factors for peace in the country' (p. 51). These realities underscore the economic situation into which youth are supposed to be 'reintegrating'. Education and employment, key issues for post-conflict reintegration, are integral to this context (Betancourt et al. 2008; Boothby, Crawford and Halperin in 2006). Rapid educational reconstruction in the wake of severe and prolonged civil strife is widely considered essential for cultivating societal reconciliation, peaceful civic relationships and the reinvigoration of war-torn economies (Kagawa 2005). Besides inculcating knowledge and skills essential for employment and economic growth, education is seen as an indispensable basis for diminishing the corrosive divisions of the past (Tidwell 2004). Education is also regarded as essential for instilling stability and normalcy in the lives of children who have experienced the turbulence and trauma of civil war (Kuterovac-Jagodic and Kontac 2002). In place of violence, fear and uncertainty, the re-establishment of schools and other forms of education can be a significant 'life-affirming activity' that restores hope and purpose for war-affected children (Machel 1996, p. 92). Through the development of curricula that are sensitive to children's wartime experiences and the application of pedagogical practices that help to strengthen children's confidence and self-esteem, post-war schooling may offer possibilities for learning and play in safe and structured environments that enhance the psycho-social welfare of war-affected children. In a statement to the UN Special Session on Children in 2002, the director of Forum for African Women Educationalists (FAWE) in Sierra Leone stated that peace is a phenomenon that needs to be taught and learned: 'Sustainable peace must be built on a bedrock of quality basic education for all children' (Thorpe 2002, p. 3).

The government of Sierra Leone has made significant efforts to improve access to education in the post-conflict context, with particular attention to girls and those in the northern and eastern provinces

(Ministry of Education, Science and Technology 2007). The Ministry of Education undertook several measures to increase primary school enrolments and retention rates: a reduction in the duration of regular primary schooling from the pre-war 7-year span to 6 years; the free provision of core textbooks and learning materials for all pupils; a universal school feeding programme; and the abolition of primary school enrolment fees and payments to sit for the national primary school leaving examination (Ministry of Education, Science and Technology 2003). For older children who were forced out of school because of the war, or who were prevented from attending school at all, the government established the Complementary Rapid Education for Primary Schools, a programme enabling young people to complete primary school equivalency within a 3-year period. By 2004, an estimated 25 per cent of Sierra Leone's national budget was earmarked for school reconstruction and renewal.

International aid agencies also rallied to directly assist in rebuilding the country's shattered school system and in extending education to as many children as possible throughout the country. The Sababu Project, a World Bank initiative, focused on rehabilitating 600 primary and junior secondary schools within a 5-year period, and the UNICEF-sponsored Community Movement for Education facilitated the construction of more than 1,000 low-cost school structures that provided space for 375,000 children within a span of 3 years (UNICEF Sierra Leone 2005). Alongside multilateral and bilateral assistance, numerous faith-based organizations, and international and national NGOs such as Plan International, World Vision and FAWE, have likewise been actively involved in establishing community schools, hiring teachers and providing teaching and learning materials (Maclure and Denov 2009).

Such initiatives have had a significant impact, and estimates indicate that enrolments have tripled since the late 1990s, although the government currently faces a bottleneck for secondary school entry due to the increased graduation from the primary levels. The current rate of expansion will likely ensure the feasibility of attaining the Millennium Development Goal of universal primary schooling by 2015 (Bennell et al. 2004).

Despite such successes, important limitations remain. In comparison to other developing countries, Sierra Leone's educational opportunities continue to lag behind. According to the World Bank (2006), in Sierra Leone, at the age of 12 only 68% of children are in school compared to more than 85% of all children in developing countries. The World Bank (2007b) also notes that 25–30% of primary-school-aged children (more than 240,000) are currently out of school and girls, children living in rural areas, children living in the poorest households and those from the northern region continue to be particularly disadvantaged. Moreover, while the Education Act stipulates the right to free basic education for all, public schools are reportedly continuing to charge extra fees unchecked (Kemokai 2007). Hanlon (2005) notes that an estimated 375,000 children could not attend school in 2005. A recent UN report notes that just half of Sierra Leone's primary schools are functioning, many of them in inadequate conditions, and secondary school attendance is only at 44% (IRIN 2008a). Furthermore, an assessment of the country's National Recovery Strategy found that 'currently the numbers of primary school teachers nationwide remained insufficient. An additional 8,000 teachers were required in 2003, but with the Ministry of Finance's ceiling of 25,000 teachers (already reached) only 3,000 were approved to be hired effective 2004' (Moore et al. 2003, pp. 43–4). Pupil to teacher ratios have reached 118:1 in some parts of the country (Hanlon 2005).

While participants in this study cited educational opportunities as their top post-conflict priority, the vast majority were not in school at the time of the interviews in 2004:

This war has made progress impossible for me. I want to go to school. So I am appealing to the government to support me, and children like me, to return to school. That is what I really want for myself. We are ready to learn. (Girl)

It is the educational opportunities that I want ... You see, having lost both parents in the war, an education would serve as my mother and my father. (Girl)

I really want to go to school so that I'll become prestigious [sic] like the schoolgirls I see in uniform everyday. I admire them so much. (Girl)

A minority of participants were able to attend school, mostly through the support of relatives. In some cases, the participants helped to pay their fees by selling in the marketplace or carrying loads following their school shift. However, even for those in school, they emphasized that their access to education was highly precarious – the person who was providing them with support to pay their fees, books and uniform could easily, and at a moment's notice, halt their support, forcing them to leave school.

Although children in this study expressed their faith in education as a panacea for their future prospects, in reality education may actually have little impact on their ability to attain future employment. As Farrell (1999) has argued, 'In very poor societies [where] almost everyone is engaged in subsistence survival ... education can have very little effect on occupational mobility because there are very few occupational destinations into which one can be mobile' (p. 168). As an example, the Youth Reintegration Training and Education for Peace programme provided 55,000 youths with counselling, life skills and agricultural skills development. However, a follow-up survey found disappointing results in job placement and creation of productive activities. Moreover, the skills acquired reportedly faded rapidly in the absence of financial support to entrepreneurship initiatives (Hansen et al. 2002).

Sierra Leone's Poverty Reduction Strategy Paper (Government of Sierra Leone 2005) cites the importance of youth employment in maintaining peace, yet it continues to be a significant post-conflict challenge. Hanlon (2005) notes that 'there is a total lack of job opportunities' (p. 466). In Sierra Leone, an estimated 70 per cent of youth are unemployed or underemployed (United Nations Development Programme 2008b). Male idleness (defined as not in school or working) begins at a very young age. By ages 9–14, one in every ten young males is inactive, rising to three in ten by ages 20–24 (World Bank 2007b). Importantly, a quarter of these 20–24-year-old men say that there are no jobs available, so it is not even worth looking for work. Women and girls' no-school and no-work status increases rapidly: by ages 15–19, two in every ten females are not working or in school. Their greater inactivity is partly, but not fully, due to motherhood, as by the age of 20 most inactive young women cite labour market reasons as the main reason that they are not working or looking for work (World Bank 2007b, p. 23).

Furthermore, according to the World Bank (2007b) Sierra Leonean youth[10] assert that jobs are awarded through connections, rather than skill, and this is borne out by evidence that demonstrates that adults have higher employment levels even if they have the same level of education as youth. Indeed, the World Bank (2007b) notes that less than half of young workers receive payment for their labour, compared to two-thirds of adults, even though youth might be more educated than

---

[10] Here, reflecting Sierra Leone's national definition of 'youth', youth is defined by the World Bank (2007b) as anyone between the ages of 15 and 35.

adults; formal employment opportunities are significantly lower for youth regardless of their higher employment levels; and public sector employment opportunities are mainly for adults older than 35 years.

Peters (2007a) has argued that politics and corruption continue to play a role in the economic marginalization of youth. He suggests that urban-based elites, including politicians, have a vested interest in maintaining an abundant flow of young Sierra Leoneans who are willing to sell their labour for low wages. Should youth be engaged in gainful employment, particularly in the realm of agriculture which provides three-quarters of the jobs in Sierra Leone (Freeman 2008), they would become unavailable to work as cheap labour in alluvial diamond pits from which elites in Sierra Leone derive their wealth: 'a free and successful peasantry would undoubtedly reduce the supply of cheap labour and start to demand political recognition. For the elites, it is better to keep the countryside poor and needy' (Peters 2007a, p. 49).

The structural realities of a poor economy, lack of infrastructure, embedded corruption and inequality create a context whereby young women and men who are unable to progress via education or employment find themselves increasingly exploited, and have few routes of escape. This has meant that for their livelihoods, most respondents in this study were engaged in petty trading, agricultural labour, mining and odd jobs at very low pay or they were relying on the support of others who were engaged in such work:

I do mining and the person that we mine for provides us with food as payment ... I transport gravel and I grind the materials with rocks, stones and irons. There is not enough food at home. (Boy)

I sell cigarettes in the backyard of the house where I am staying. (Girl)

I sell chewing gum on the streets to support me and my two children. Normally, I eat once a day. But there are some days when I go without eating. (Girl)

I carry loads for people in the marketplace to earn money. I earn about 2,000–3,000 leones [less than US$1] each day. (Boy)

Right now ... we face difficulty with getting food and some of us want to go to school but there is no way. Then there are some of our sisters who have given birth to children with the soldiers. They do not even have places to be right now. So we are asking the government to make all efforts to provide for our ... education and our feeding. (Girl)

In response to continued social and economic marginalization, some girl participants had turned to prostitution in order to cope and survive in the post-war period:

I now live on prostitution ... I live in the street exposed to all kinds of danger. I am tired of living in the street. (Girl)

The poor economy and lack of education and employment opportunities for these young people inevitably set the stage for a highly marginal post-conflict existence, as well as a sense of frustration and disappointment at the chronic lack of prospects to assist and facilitate the long-term reintegration process.

## Gender-based violence and health

Just as gender was critical to understanding the lived realities of children during the conflict, it was equally significant in the post-conflict period. Aside from the aforementioned structural and individual predicaments, girls faced unique challenges that had a profound impact on their daily post-conflict lives and the process of unmaking. In particular, girls were left with the physical and emotional scars of the gender-based violence they suffered during the conflict. As a result of sexual violence, girls reported suffering genital injury, infections, vesicovaginal fistula and complications from self-induced or clandestine abortions, all of which brought both physical pain and psychological anxiety. As these girls noted:

Ever since I was raped, I get horrible stomach-aches. The pain comes and goes but it remains one of my biggest problems now ... I have gone to the hospital. The doctor told me that this pain is a result of the rapes. (Girl)

This is my worry ... I don't get pregnant and I think something might have happened to my womb during the time I was raped. (Girl)

Girls also reported being frightened of having contracted HIV/AIDS as a result of being raped. However, at the time of the interviews none of the participants (boys or girls) had been tested for the virus and thus their HIV/AIDS status remained unknown.

Alongside physical pain, sexual violence left devastating psychological after-effects, as has been reported by female survivors of wartime sexual violence in a myriad of contexts (Fox 2004; Physicians for Human Rights 2002; Sideris 2002; Twagiramariya and Turshen

1998). These included persistent anguish, flashbacks, shame, fear of sexual victimization, difficulty re-establishing intimate relationships and a distrust of men. Depression and poor self-esteem were common:

I feel depressed most of the time. I sometimes feel there is no hope for me … I just think of ending my life. (Girl)

Despite ongoing war-related reproductive health problems, services have seldom been available to girls for a variety of reasons. Sierra Leone's health care system, which had virtually collapsed during the war, continues to be severely constrained in the post-conflict period and with only US$34 spent per person per year, the system's recovery is highly problematic (Médecins Sans Frontières 2006). As a report by Médecins Sans Frontières (2006) indicates: 'Sierra Leone's health conditions are still at disaster levels. The slaughter once delivered by machetes and automatic weapons is now more stealthy and routine' (p. 3). According to the World Bank (2003), 70% of health facilities were not functioning at the end of 2001. In 2002, health expenditure made up only 1.7% of Sierra Leone's GDP, compared with 2.5% in other sub-Saharan African countries (World Bank 2007a, pp. 31–2). Salaries of health care workers average only US$48 per month (Hanlon 2005, p. 464) and most tend to be de facto volunteers (Van Gurp 2009). As health care workers pay for their medications up front, sub-standard doses of often inadequate drugs may be prescribed which negatively affects clinical outcomes, as well as contributes to the emergence of resistance (Van Gurp 2009). Overall, faced with the shortfall of subsidies from government and international sources, most public health structures apply a system of cost recovery, requiring patients to pay for most services (Médecins Sans Frontières 2006).[11] As an example, a cesarean section costs the patient 100,000–200,000 leones (approximately US$25–50), supposedly to cover the cost of intravenous drips and medications. A vaginal delivery also incurs costs, thus creating important disincentives to seek formal medical assistance and making hospitals places of last resort for patients (Van Gurp 2009). Moreover, the Ministry of Health tariff of charges is often added to by health

---

[11] Government policy on user fees does grant exemptions where sick people are unable to pay. However, Médecins Sans Frontières (2006) has noted that of the exempt categories (children under 5, breastfeeding mothers and elderly people) only 3.5% of patients actually received an exemption.

workers, and the official 'list prices' are highly negotiable and vary greatly across the country (Médecins Sans Frontières 2006). Perhaps not surprisingly, it is estimated that 80 per cent of women give birth at home without ever consulting a medical official or midwife and are instead supervised by an untrained 'traditional birthing attendant' (IRIN 2008b). Médecins Sans Frontières (2006) indicates that one in six women will die from having babies during their lifetime and one in six babies will die at birth. These are just a few examples of how particularly vulnerable groups, such as women, children and victims of sexual violence who may need ongoing healthcare, face dire realities in the post-conflict period.

Given the profound state of poverty in which the vast majority of the girl participants continued to live, and despite ongoing reproductive health issues, most were unable to access appropriate health care. This, alongside the lack of accessible health facilities and lack of money for transport and medication, has meant that not only has the health status of girls been poor, but also that most have had to suffer in silence, which inevitably affected their reintegration experiences.

On 29 February 2008 the Sierra Leonean government launched a maternal mortality strategic plan (backed largely by the UK Department for International Development), which focused on eradicating redundancies from the various government agencies involved in reproductive and child health, while promoting preventive activities like immunization and women's rights generally (IRIN 2008a). With one of the highest maternal mortality rates in the world, and only six obstetricians for the entire country, the Chief of Obstetrics at the Princess Christian Maternal Health Hospital in Freetown shared his scepticism of the government's response: 'We need a new health system not a new strategy. Only education combined with a health system that actually provides results can change things' (IRIN 2008b).

When exploring the post-conflict realities of the girls, what once again stands out is that in spite of the critical roles they played during the conflict period, girls were largely invisible in the post-conflict context. Excluded from DDR, left to contend with the severe and lingering after-effects of sexual violence, rape-induced pregnancies, profound social exclusion as a result of being victims of sexual violence, and little opportunity for education and/or employment, girls were often left destitute and dependent, an embodiment of the stark gender divide and its consequences of female vulnerability in Sierra Leone. While demobilization ostensibly signalled an end to violent conflict it did little to reduce gender disparities.

Following the end of their captivity, having been associated with the group that 'lost' the war, children were once again catapulted into social isolation and uncertainty, only this time into a post-war context of espoused national disarmament and demilitarization. Liberation from an oppressive environment which had victimized them, but which paradoxically they had come to reinforce through their own violent actions, generated feelings of loneliness, resentment and abandonment – very similar to how they had felt after being abducted by the RUF away from their natal communities. The energies that they had channelled outwards towards crushing an enemy, obtaining material gain and asserting power over others were abruptly redirected towards reflection and doubt, and the need to reconstruct new personal identities that depended not on skills of military prowess and courage under fire, but on extraneous factors such as access to education, remunerative work, health care, and family and/or community support – factors that were sorely lacking for many former child soldiers when the war was ended. A return to a post-conflict situation meant an abrupt end to their structured world and their identities within that world. In its place came a new reality characterized by diffuse values and expectations, the diffusion of authority and the exercise of individual autonomy. This new demilitarized environment, so different from the violent totalitarianism of the RUF, created profound uncertainties for the participants and caused them periods of anguish; it also generated feelings of regret at having wasted a substantial portion of their formative lives. Moreover, this new environment, plagued by structural inequalities, community rejection, lack of educational and employment opportunities, and economic and gendered exclusion and exploitation, provided a highly uncertain and dubious backdrop for post-conflict reintegration.

# 7 | *New battlefields*

Sometimes I think that I am a good person.
But then how can I say that I'm a good person after all
the horrible things that I've done?

(Boy)

Helping children recover from ... their [wartime] experiences
and ensuring their long term reintegration into their communities
remains a considerable challenge.

(United Nations 2007)

While Sierra Leone is slowly recovering from the brutal civil war, remnants of the violence remain apparent throughout the country; the sight of amputees and crushing poverty are only a few of the daily reminders of the brutal violence of the past. In addition, less visible markers of violence inevitably pervade the hearts and minds of all those who lived through the war. For the participants in this study, the remnants of violence are powerful and ever-present, although often concealed and spoken of only in highly selective contexts. As this final chapter will illuminate, the narratives gathered from the young people reveal some of the post-war opportunities and challenges for former child soldiers. The chapter addresses some of the new and figurative battlefields that exist at the war's end – for both the child soldiers in this study, as well as the many institutions working on their behalf. The chapter begins by summarizing the link between structure and agency in the process of making and unmaking, underscoring the utility of Giddens' concepts in enabling a greater understanding of the wartime and post-war lives of child soldiers. It then explores the continued process of unmaking in post-conflict Sierra Leone. The chapter concludes by drawing attention to the lessons that can be heeded in utilizing the framework of structure and agency within the long-term context of reintegration.

## Structure and agency in the making and unmaking of child soldiers

The making and unmaking of the seventy-six child soldiers in Sierra Leone who took part in the research embodied powerful passages and poignant journeys in and out of the world of violence and armed conflict. Importantly, however, as the data have revealed, navigating and traversing such passages was blurred, convoluted and filled with contradictions. Giddens' interconnected concepts of 'structure', 'agency' and, in particular, 'the duality of structure' provide a useful lens and framework from which to gain a deeper understanding of the complex lives of this cohort of former child soldiers in Sierra Leone. Through the application of these concepts, it is possible to observe the full force of children's ability to contribute to their social world, through both action and inaction, while recognizing the limitations imposed by structure and social context.

Indeed, structural considerations were critical to understanding children's wartime and post-war realities. Impoverished and wholly dependent on established adult authority structures, children in Sierra Leone were clearly overwhelmed by tragic socio-economic forces both during and following the conflict. During the conflict, with no institutional and family buffers to withstand a social movement that defined itself by acts of violence and terror, sheer survival compelled children to become the agents of practices that reinforced and reproduced the system into which they had been co-opted. Caught up by structures of predatory commerce, militarized violence, patronage, gendered oppression and state failure, children were easily socialized into the norms and behaviours that fomented and perpetuated these violent structures. With the stability of tradition and the restraining influences of family, communal and institutional structures diminished, frameworks of cultural continuity eroded, and with aspirations for education and meaningful work denied to most children and youth, young people were increasingly vulnerable to the influence of emergent violent power struggles in the country. The spate of small arms that inundated Sierra Leone immediately prior to and throughout the conflict also greatly facilitated the transformation of highly impressionable youngsters into powerful combatants.

In the aftermath of conflict, children's lives and circumstances were once again dependent upon and deeply affected by socio-economic and

gendered forces and structures which shaped, both positively and negatively, the process of demilitarization and reintegration. The immeasur-
ably slow socio-economic recovery, the limitations of the DDR process,
lack of employment and educational opportunities, community rejection and the country's destroyed infrastructure invariably affected the
lives of the young people in their transition to civilian life.

Yet while structural forces were clearly critical to the making and
unmaking of the lives of child soldiers in this study, the data substantiate
the need to be cautious about discounting youth's capacity for reasoning
and independence of action. As some respondents attested, although they
were coerced into joining the RUF, many came to inflict the same ruthlessness that had been inflicted on them. In some cases, children's actions
assumed an increasingly voluntarist nature, with some developing a sense
of attachment, commitment and dedication to the RUF and its values.
However, what is also evident is that participants did not entirely succumb to the RUF's absolutist system of authority and violence. Some
reported publicly acquiescing to the demands of the RUF for the purpose
of survival, yet inwardly rejected its values and beliefs. Others bravely
resisted RUF authority and command, and while they did so, often
imperceptibly and in an ad hoc manner, they nonetheless engendered
precarious risks to their own safety.

While the accounts of children's lives and their experiences of victimization, participation and resistance during the heart of their captivity
are highly disturbing and demonstrate the transformative nature of the
RUF culture of violence on all aspects of the children's lives, their stories
and perspectives reveal a spirit of volition and a capacity for independence of action that counters a deterministic and commonly held depiction of children as having no capacity to resist or modify the
circumstances and forces imposed upon them. Indicative of Giddens'
notion of the 'dialectic of control', actors are never completely helpless
when subject to the power and control of others. As the participants
clearly demonstrated through their acts of wartime resistance, they
attempted to alter the balance of power and use the profoundly meagre
resources at their disposal to do so.

Children's actions were shaped and transformed by the social structures of Sierra Leonean society and the RUF and yet, over the course of
time, through their individual actions, they in turn helped to recreate,
reinforce and also challenge the aggressive power of the RUF. As
Giddens (1977) has proposed in his theory of structuration, the

structures of social systems, and the norms and values that reinforce them, are not separate from the agency of individuals, but are constantly enacted – and resisted – through myriad human actions. By the same token, while structures are the outcomes of action, in turn human action is bounded by historical and institutional conditionalities, and by unintended consequences. Reflecting Giddens' concept of the duality of structure, as child soldiers drew upon structures of violence (often for their very survival), they in turn reproduced, transformed and challenged them.

In the aftermath of the war, participants continued to demonstrate the capacity to make choices that would ultimately shape their post-conflict lives. For example, some children deliberately chose to avoid and ultimately reject DDR programming. Some girls chose life on the streets of Freetown in lieu of the dangers of DDR camps, and others made the decision to remain in RUF unions. In the face of stigma and ostracism, some participants actively concealed their former RUF status, and also constructed alternative forms of support and assistance through informal peer-support networks. They also opted to avoid areas of the country where they feared retaliation and further violence. Moreover, in contexts of dire poverty, social exclusion and marginalization, these young people attempted to create livelihoods and provide for themselves and their children. All of these examples highlight the participants' capacity to make decisions, and their ability to navigate and traverse the murky and sometimes disillusioning post-conflict context and the structural forces acting upon them.

In examining the process of unmaking, it becomes clear that children began to carve out their post-conflict identities under exceedingly dire and difficult circumstances and amid profound contradictions. Far from being destined to a post-conflict life of 'pathology', 'disorder', 'deviance' or as 'passive victims' or 'lost souls', the choices that participants made instead demonstrate their resounding agency, resilience, strength and self-efficacy.

But here, too, one must be cautious about being drawn too far down the path of rationalist conjecture. Growing up as dependents in patrimonial systems of authority and governance that were entrenched at all levels of society, and often wrenched from their home communities by rebel forces, child soldiers attached to the RUF were co-opted into a totalitarian social order that required absolute loyalty and obedience. The post-war structures and forces have been similarly constraining and limiting as Sierra Leonean society has made the uneasy transition from war to fragile peace.

Although this qualitative study does not allow for conclusive generalizations about the processes by which vast numbers of boys and girls took up arms on all sides of the conflict in Sierra Leone, the interview data do offer insights into complex and contradictory processes of militarization and reintegration. Clearly the mutually reinforcing duality of structure and agency underlay what happened to these young people and what they did, both during and following the conflict. The process of 'becoming', 'being' and eventually relinquishing one's status as an RUF child soldier was both enabled and constrained by the unique configurations of structural forces and the dynamics of the broader socio-historical context, as well as the young people's individual deliberations and independent choices. Ultimately, the stories of these child soldiers reinforce the argument that no matter how predominant and uniform are the structures of a particular social environment, even those that are horrific, in the literal and metaphorical process of 'picking up' and 'putting down' the gun, individuals will tend to cope with the influences of such structures in differentiated and individualized ways.

## Ambiguity, sweet sorrow and political action: The continued process of unmaking in post-conflict Sierra Leone

For the former child soldiers in this study, it is important to recognize that the journey out of violence did not have a clear 'ending', despite the formal establishment of 'peace'. The challenges that child soldiers faced thus continued long after the guns had fallen silent, long after the end of formal DDR programming, long after the TRC had published its final report, and well after international agencies had begun to pull out of the country and outside intervention had begun to fade. In fact, the ongoing journey out of the world of violence was evident during interviews with participants in 2008, and is likely to continue. Several factors were salient in the continued unmaking process, particularly the prolongation of the triad of victimization, participation and resistance/heroism and its impact on participants' identity construction, as well as the post-conflict disillusionment reportedly experienced by the participants. The seemingly unbounded and infinite process of unmaking thus represented a new, figurative and long-term 'battlefield' for these young people in post-conflict Sierra Leone. Yet despite the ongoing struggles, there is also important evidence of young people's increased political efficacy, opportunity and capacity to ensure their own survival. These post-conflict realities are explored below.

## *Living with ambiguity: The triad of victimization, participation and resistance*

The realities of victimization, participation and resistance, which consistently exemplified children's wartime experiences, continued to touch participants' post-war lives. In relation to victimization, former child soldiers were arguably subjected to various forms of 'secondary victimization' in the post-conflict period, as they continued to live in situations of profound adversity that was evident in the family and community rejection that they faced, as well as in the socio-economic and gendered marginalization. In relation to participation in violence, children disclosed engaging in acts of violence in the conflict's aftermath, whether in the private or public domains. Ongoing and persistent acts of courage were also evident as participants carved out their identities and lives under extremely difficult circumstances. In tandem with these realities, participants now had the time and space to reflect upon their wartime actions and experiences. These reflections garnered similar feelings of paradox: participants continued to report feelings of profound guilt and shame at their participation in violence, as well as anger at their own plight and victimization. They were also conscious of their skills and bravery that had helped them to survive the conflict. These participants explained their paradoxical feelings surrounding their post-conflict status and identities:

I see myself as a hero because I was able to go through all the difficulties and survive ... but I am also a victim because I was forced to join and I have suffered a lot ... but I also did horrible things. (Boy)

I see myself as a warrior because I was a brave and good fighter and I did it for more than three years ... I am a hero because I managed to survive so many times in combat ... I am a victim because I have two children and I'm finding it difficult to take care of them ... but I'm a survivor because I'm still able to withstand all the challenges. (Girl)

As evidenced in Chapter 5, during the conflict the paradox and ambiguity of their situations, and living within the triad of victimization, participation and resistance, had been deeply troubling and confusing to participants. Yet, as noted in Boothby, Crawford and Halperin (2006), it appears to have been even more disturbing in the war's aftermath and, in fact, one of the most challenging aspects of their post-conflict lives. As this girl noted:

I often think of the bad things that I did and I always pray and ask God for forgiveness ... I try to be a good person ... I don't know how to start over. (Girl)

It was in this tangled web of conflicting emotions and circumstances that children had to continually construct their post-conflict lives and identities. It represented a deeply personal and painstaking struggle.

Importantly, the confusion surrounding 'who they were' post-conflict (victims? war criminals? heroes?) was further reinforced by the conflicting perceptions of them by the individuals and structures that surrounded them. For example, in the post-conflict period the NGO community has tended to regard child soldiers predominantly as 'victims' in need of psycho-social support and assistance. Representing a similar outlook, the Special Court for Sierra Leone (SCSL) ultimately made the decision not to prosecute child soldiers. The former prosecutor for the SCSL, David Crane, publicly stated:

I am not interested in prosecuting children. I want to prosecute the people who forced thousands of children to commit unspeakable crimes. (Special Court for Sierra Leone 2002)

At the same time, however, in establishing the SCSL, the UN secretary-general and the UN Security Council allowed for the prosecution of children aged 15 and over, thereby propagating a view of child soldiers as 'perpetrators' and 'war criminals'. Many communities and individuals in Sierra Leone shared this view, actively rejecting them. Concurrently, the perception of child soldiers as 'survivors' and 'heroes' has also been noted in western media sources and discourses. These highly contradictory societal messages have done little to assist former child soldiers in constructing their post-conflict identities or in navigating their labyrinth of conflicting emotions.

## Post-conflict disillusionment

In the aftermath of conflict, there is often an expectation that with the end of protracted violence, people's lives and circumstances will inevitably improve. In the war's aftermath, however, many participants found themselves in a grim world of boredom, poverty and disenchantment (Denov and Maclure 2007). In these circumstances, there was a natural inclination among some boys and girls to regard 'peace' as disappointing, in many ways just as dispiriting as the period of war:

Yes, I feel depressed most of the time. I sometimes feel there is no hope for me because of the horrible things I have done. I just think of ending my life. (Girl)

I am depressed, I have a child and am pregnant but there is nobody to support me. (Girl)

I feel tormented and I sometimes cry … I live in the street … [P]eople don't treat me with respect … I have no family and no future. (Girl)

Some participants turned to drug use in order to cope. As this girl explained:

To cope, I take drugs: either cocaine or brown-brown [crack]. [When I take the drugs] I feel relieved and I don't think of any problems, no bad memories of the war, and no sadness. (Girl)

Others, under immense pressure to support themselves and their families, reported engaging in violent behaviour as a way to express their frustration and anger, often at those closest to them:

Sometimes, I just feel so angry and I want to beat my two children. (Girl)

Yes, I am angry and I often grow angrier. I [find myself] getting into trouble with my family. (Girl)

I weep at times – especially if am isolated. Sometimes, I become very aggressive to my husband and he beats me. (Girl)

As explored in Chapters 4 and 5, the conflict may in some instances have provided participants with opportunities, limited power and rewards. Yet many female and male participants came to associate the post-war period in Sierra Leone with a sense of powerlessness. With unmet expectations, particularly within the realms of education and employment, children's sense of frustration deepened. It was thus not entirely surprising that some of the participants appeared to yearn for the excitement and sense of self-importance that they had experienced as fighters during the war. Many thus recounted their wartime experiences with a sense of pride, accomplishment and even nostalgia:

I miss the power that I had during the war. (Boy)

With the rebels, we ate the best food, we had access to money, and any other property within our controlled territory. Civilians were working for us – we were highly respected. Now I have nothing. (Girl)

The taxi driver who came to me for paid sex and then refused to pay me and beat me wouldn't have even come near me if it were in those days during the war when we [the RUF] had power. I was better protected and I had better access to food and shelter with the rebels. (Girl)

The aftermath of war thus continued to bring about concurrent individual feelings of guilt, shame, boredom, powerlessness, anger, pride and nostalgia, as well as the necessity to contend with the conflicting experiences of victimization, participation and resistance/heroism. Importantly, however, these feelings have been juxtaposed with intense sentiments of happiness and relief that the war is over, along with participants' subservient and painful roles within the RUF. This joy accompanied by the many devastating individual and structural challenges illustrate the 'sweet sorrow' associated with the post-conflict period.

These post-conflict realities reveal that while the participants were no longer associated with the RUF, they were arguably experiencing a new and figurative battlefield. However, this battlefield existed within themselves as they confronted and struggled to come to terms with their wartime actions, inactions, identities, allegiances and the meaning that these factors held for them and their future in Sierra Leone. The internal battle that participants were engaged in was not clear in its form, nor did it occur at a particular moment in time, but it was instead ever-present and ever-changing, altering and influenced by the structures and forces that surrounded them, and alongside their own individual deliberations and reflections.

### Responding to individual and structural constraints: Political efficacy and collective action

In spite of important structural barriers and personal disillusionment, there are also examples of former child soldiers challenging the status quo, forging new opportunities for themselves through political activism and collective action. In particular, Sierra Leone's new motorbike taxi-riders provide a telling example of young people who are finding alternative means to contribute to their own reintegration, actively carving out their livelihoods, creating new niches in the job market and organizing politically. In Sierra Leone, motorbike taxis are increasingly replacing the four-wheeled conventional taxi. Conventional taxis, which almost completely disappeared after the war in provincial towns because vehicles were being burned or ambushed, tend to be owned by 'big men', who recruit a driver. Motorbikes have become an important alternative as they are less expensive to buy and can be acquired on credit from Guinean suppliers at a payback rate of one million leones per month for 6 months (Richards et al. 2004). Although largely unknown to Sierra Leone prior to the war, the phenomenon of motorbike taxis has emerged as one of the most visible post-conflict changes. Peters (2007b) explains the advantages and disadvantages:

The advantages are that these motor bike taxis literally criss-cross the towns in search of passengers and even on the back streets it is only a few minutes before a taxi arrives. It then takes you straight to the preferred destination, without detours to hunt or deliver other passengers, or losing time in traffic jams. The disadvantages are that costs are two to three times higher than a car taxi, you get wet when it is raining (although many passengers somehow manage to keep an umbrella above their head during their journey) and it is less safe, since no helmets are (yet) provided for the passengers ... Nevertheless the motor taxis have become an institution in Kenema, Bo, Koidu and Makeni. (Peters 2007b, p. 14)

Significantly, ex-combatants make up most of the motorbike riders. In fact, three-quarters of the three hundred motorbike riders in Makeni were combatants during the war, most of whom were associated with the RUF (Peters 2007b). In contrast, in Bo and Kenema, former CDF fighters are in the majority as riders (Peters 2007b). Typically, riders do not own their own bikes, but rent bikes for a fee from motorbike owners.[1] Richards et al. (2004, p. 35) note that some of the bike owners appear to be ex-combatant commanders who rent the bikes to riders who were formerly under their command.

What is important to recognize is that former combatant riders have carved out a high-demand niche that does not compete with existing trades such as tailoring or carpentry. Moreover, riders have organized

---

[1] Regional differences are important here. In Bo and Kenema a businessman normally provides the bike and the rider leases the bike. After a period of time, the rider becomes the owner of the bike. In Makeni, however, the riders only rent bikes from the owners and do not become the eventual owners of the bikes.

themselves into powerful unions in each region where riders are prominent, working to support fellow riders. These unions coordinate the activities of riders, assist them should they have an accident, and aid in events such as weddings, naming ceremonies and funerals (Search for Common Ground 2006). Perhaps most significantly, the unions 'avoid big men as political patrons believing that these men manipulated them to fight the war' (Richards et al. 2004, p. 36). In this sense, riders are challenging traditional authority structures in Sierra Leone: 'The unions not only look after the interests of sick or injured riders, resolve disputes between riders and customers and generally interest themselves in health, safety and innovation, but they are also explicit about the need to take on and challenge the prewar patrimonial order' (Peters 2007b, p. 19).

The phenomenon of former child soldiers turned bike riders is, without question, innovative and highlights the youths' collective and constructive responses to the post-war context. Nonetheless, the riders face many challenges. In particular are the difficulties confronting traditional authority structures, as well as stereotypical views of ex-combatants. The most serious conflicts occur between motorbike riders and the police. As it is common knowledge that most riders are ex-combatants, riders report feeling targeted, and accuse the police of unwarranted arrests, tickets and extortion. Recent reports suggest that police are using the failure to wear helmets[2] as a way to extort money from both riders and passengers (Massaquoi 2008). Officers allegedly request bribes of 30,000 leones (approximately US$8) or riders risk being taken to the police station and subsequently charged in court. If convicted, many are forced to pay fines of up to 150,000 leones (approximately US$40). On 7 November 2005, a violent confrontation occurred between Kenema riders and the police, triggered by the murder of two bike riders (Search for Common Ground 2006). Alongside altercations with police, traffic wardens accuse riders of violating traffic rules and driving dangerously. In turn, riders report that traffic wardens favour well-connected riders in the community and are

---

[2] Many passengers and riders refuse to wear helmets due to a fear of contracting tuberculosis from multi-owner second-hand helmets (Richards et al. 2004).

unnecessarily rough during arrests. Finally, passengers describe riders as 'dirty, poorly dressed, dangerous and irresponsible' (Search for Common Ground 2006, pp. 1–2). In turn, riders assert that their appearance is due to poverty and road conditions, and criticize passengers for unjustly assuming that, as ex-combatants, they are killers (Search for Common Ground 2006).

What is clear, however, is that despite ongoing tensions, these youth are responding with organized dissent, trade unions and strikes, rather than with guns. As an example, in February 2003 due to ongoing police harassment of riders for bribes and fines, and the eventual arrest of thirty-two riders, the Bo association went on strike (supported by women traders, who are among the key clients of riders). Through court action and the hiring of a commercial lawyer in Freetown to represent them, the Bo association succeeded in having fines reduced by an average of 40 per cent (Richards et al. 2004). Demonstrating the collective action and political efficacy of the riders' unions, Peters (2007b) notes that the associations are 'fighting a "war" for [their] young members, but not any more through force of arms, but through the classic instruments of trade unionism. Job interests, strikes and the laws of contract have become the weapon of choice, not forced recruitment and summary executions' (p. 19). The associations also act as a point of solidarity, promoting conciliatory practices across military groups as both CDF and RUF fighters work as bike riders and are integrated within the associations. As Peters (2007b) notes, the bike riders' association is an example of post-war organization around 'shared labour interests rather than ethnicity' or former military affiliation.

While the collective action of the bike riders represents hope, ingenuity and innovation, the issue of gender within the context of the riders needs to be addressed. In discussions of the bike riders, few have commented on the issue of gender. Only Richards et al. (2004) briefly note that in response to President Kabbah's 50:50 gender initiative, the Bo association recruited forty-five unemployed young women to learn to ride. Regardless, riders appear to be almost exclusively male (Conciliation Resources 2006). While further research is needed on the lack of female riders (is this by choice or by exclusion?), the invisibility of former girl and women soldiers within this initiative points to their continued absence in positive steps to promote long-term reintegration.

## Looking ahead: The needs of former child soldiers and the integration of structure and agency

When former child soldiers in this study were asked during focus group discussions what kinds of policies and programmes they would like to see in the future in order to facilitate their long-term reintegration, they articulated the following themes: community acceptance and forgiveness, opportunities and support to attend school, access to gainful employment, access to health care and specifically reproductive health care, child care assistance, the surgical removal of brandings, psychological counselling and support, family tracing and reunification programmes, and recreational activities. Indeed, local, national and international organizations have been working hard to meet these needs. Yet they represent a tall order for an impoverished, war-torn country that cannot easily transform the effects of history and the predominance of political and economic forces that have undermined the well-being of much of its population. Meeting these needs is likewise a major undertaking for an international community that is prone to 'donor fatigue'. Arguably, the post-war period also represents a 'new battlefield' to contend with for those seeking to assist child soldiers in the long-term process of unmaking.

There is clearly no straightforward set of policies or procedures that can address the psycho-social needs of war-affected young people in Sierra Leone. Nevertheless, from a conceptual perspective, the interconnected duality of structure and agency provides insights and direction for the management of the new figurative battlefields that exist for both the individual child soldiers, and the institutions and governments that aim to support them.

For all who are concerned about the plight of former child soldiers in Sierra Leone, and elsewhere in sub-Saharan Africa, the pressing challenge is to transform social environments that for too long have persistently marginalized and exploited vast numbers of children and youth. For this to have any chance of being achieved, there is a need for transparent democratic governance, substantial resource investments, coordinated interventions of government and non-government organizations, coalition building among a range of institutional actors and the emergence of a vibrant civil society. While progress has been extremely slow within the structural realm, Sierra Leone is moving through a transition from peacebuilding to development (Kemokai 2007). The country held national elections in 2002 and local government was reintroduced in 2004 after a period of 30 years. The Sierra Leonean government has been working towards institutional reforms, policy formulation and capacity building of its institutions with the goal of good governance and democracy. For youth, many legal, policy and institutional commitments have been introduced, particularly in relation to youth employment and education. For example, the Ministry of Education, Youth and Sport has been created to manage the general affairs of youth and within this ministry, a specific secretariat for youth employment has been established. This ministry has produced a Youth Policy, which has placed an emphasis on youth education and employment, including enterprise development, and entrepreneurship. The creation of the Local Government Act in 2004 now allows young people over the age of 18 to vote and be voted for in local government elections. Alongside the creation of the Poverty Reduction Strategy Paper, the government has established a Peacebuilding Commission, both of which address the issue of youth employment and education. In October 2006, Vice-President Solomon Berewa launched the Youth Employment Scheme, designed to address the short-, medium- and long-term job creation plan for youth in a sustainable manner, targeting thousands of jobs for youth nationwide (*Awareness Times* 2007). In 2008, a collaboration between the World Food Programme, the United Nations Development Programme and Sierra Leone's Ministry of Education, Youth and Sport was announced to implement a Food for Work programme. Under the programme, an estimated 4,000 people, representing 20,000 beneficiaries, were to participate in Food for Work activities, from April to December 2008. Efforts were to be made to encourage the participation of women, individuals from female-headed households and ex-combatants. The programme aimed to assist in reducing food gaps of vulnerable households and mitigate and reduce migration to urban areas, particularly by youth and ex-combatants (United Nations Development Programme 2008c).

Until the recent introduction of the Gender Bills,[3] which became law in 2007, both general and customary law offered little protection for women and girls. Under customary law, a husband had the right to

---

[3] The bills consisted of a) the Domestic Violence Act; b) the Devolution of Estates Act; and c) the Registration of Customary Marriage and Divorce Act.

'reasonably chastise his wife by physical force' and marital rape was not recognized under either customary or general law in Sierra Leone (Human Rights Watch 2003b). The newly enacted legal framework now outlaws domestic violence, recognizes women's right to inheritance and property, and the registration of customary marriages.

These are a few examples of some positive initiatives. Nonetheless, profound challenges remain. Kemokai (2007) maintains that the government does not have the capacity to fully implement many of the above-noted policies and programmes for youth or to monitor these programmes to ensure that those targeted are receiving maximum benefits. Indeed, such government programmes are largely donor driven and many of the funds come not through the government, but through UN agencies such as UNDP, and bilateral organizations such as the UK Department for International Development (DFID), which in turn finance programmes through NGOs.

There have also been growing fears that the culture of deference, authoritarianism, elitism and patronage is returning to Sierra Leone's system of governance (Hanlon 2005). In 2003, the International Crisis Group (ICG 2003) reported that the government's 'performance has been disappointing and complacency appears to have set in ... [T]here are consistent signs that donor dependence and the old political ways are returning' (p. 1). The ICG (2004) further reported that 'a consensus between donors and the political elite may entirely miss the realities of ordinary people' (p. 24). Concerned about the feasibility of structural reform in Sierra Leone, the World Bank (2003) has noted that many civil servants continue to have salaries that are close to or below the poverty threshold: 'public service pay is too low to attract, motivate and retain key staff needed to improve performance and lead reform' (p. 16).

Endemic corruption also continues to be a problem at all levels. Within the education system, reports of 'ghost' teachers on school payrolls, fictitious organizations collecting Ministry of Education, Youth and Sport vouchers, and various forms of kickbacks related to the allocation of contracts and promotions have been noted (Kpaka and Klemm 2005). There is also evidence that teachers are demanding bribes and favours in exchange for school enrolment and exams (Hanlon 2005). In 2004, the ICG (2003) wrote that 'the judicial system ... has shown itself unwilling or unable to go after corrupt officials' and accused donors and diplomats of 'turning a blind eye to local corruption and exercising influence through coalitions with old power elites while marginalizing those truly interested in reform' (pp. 8, 24). Similarly, members of the Anti-Corruption Commission (ACC) complained of government interference in late 2001. The Anti-Corruption Act of 2000 provides no penalties for refusing to comply with the ACC and its recommendations. Requests from the ACC are frequently ignored by government ministries and officials (Freeman 2008). In early 2002, the ACC indicted three of the five national election commissioners, but the Kabbah government refused to prosecute them (MacJohnson 2004). Demonstrating the overall constraints and limitations of the ACC, Freeman (2008) notes that by 2004 only two out of forty cases that were sent to the General Attorney's Office for prosecution had been concluded. There is also evidence that the government has been punishing its critics: three journalists who wrote about alleged government corruption were jailed in October 2004 and May 2005 for 'seditious libel' (Hanlon 2005, p. 465). Ultimately, the poor continue to suffer directly from corruption. The toll of poverty is exacerbated by extra payments demanded by local officials for health and education services (Freeman 2008).

Within the realms of women's rights, while women in Sierra Leone are demanding that their voices be heard and that their gender-based interests be included in the national constitution and on the new democratic agenda, this has not been fully realized because of 'cultural impediments, illiteracy and other political structures that tend to lower the status of women. Local customs and ignorance of their rights are also an obstacle to women's participation in the democratic process' (Joka Bangura 2007). Sharkey (2008) notes that the hegemony of patriarchy continues to be embedded in public and private discourse and that violence against women and girls remains commonplace. Up to 67 per cent of urban Sierra Leonean women were victims of domestic violence in 2008 (IRIN 2009). Moreover, many chiefs and traditional rulers may be unaware of the newly enacted laws designed to protect women and girls or unwilling to abide by them. As this Sierra Leonean lawyer noted: '[C]ourts [that are] operated by chiefs and traditional rulers ... do not even know that the gender bill exists. And even if they are aware, they will see it as a form of Western ideologies so they will not implement it' (Mossman 2008, pp. 87–8). Another area of concern has been the paramount chief system. As noted in Chapter 2, this local government system, where chiefs traditionally handled dispute resolution and tax collection, is viewed by many as an important cause of the war as a result of the corruption and systematic alienation of youth (Hanlon 2005; Richards 2005). This system, largely destroyed during the war with the death of many chiefs, was reconstructed by a DFID-funded programme (the Paramount Chiefs Restoration Programme). Elections to fill sixty-three vacancies were held in late 2002 and early 2003 whereby taxpayers (mostly men) elect councillors who then elect the paramount chiefs, who hold the position for life (Hanlon 2005). Richards (2005) notes that the reinstatement of the chiefdom system represents a reconstruction of the historical model of forced labour in the countryside that led to the war in the first place. Abuses of power, including exploitative punishments through local courts, high fines and seizure of property, were common in the past, and there is little evidence that this will change under the customary law of the system (Freeman 2008). Moreover, customary laws continue to allow human rights abuses, particularly in relation to women and young people. The Forced Labour Ordinance of 1932 continues to be listed on statute books, which allows chiefs and their extended families to force youth and outsiders to work for them. The final assessment of the government–donor post-war National Recovery Strategy points to the 'need to redress the bias of customary law and social system at the village and chiefdom levels which protect the "influential" at the expense of the poor and vulnerable' (cited in Hanlon 2005, p. 462). While the chieftaincy as an institution continues to be valued by some, and many people do not want to see it abolished, they do, however, want reform (Jackson 2006). Yet, according to Malan and Meek (2003), chiefs in the diamond mining areas are using the 0.75 per cent diamond tax they receive for personal gain instead of its intended use for the benefit of the community. Fanthorpe (2003) maintains that chiefs are using aid money for personal enrichment and to reward political supporters. Zack-Williams (cited in Hanlon 2005) similarly argues that Britain has chosen to rebuild a discredited feudal tradition, delaying the development of grassroots democracy. Ultimately, the reinstatement of the paramount chiefs will create 'new platforms for the old politics, and that the rural poor will be locked, as before, into a desperate scramble for elite patronage' (Fanthorpe 2005, p. 47).

Other structures remain problematic. Sierra Leone's judiciary is still plagued by extortion and bribery among court officials, has insufficient staff, and hundreds of accused individuals are detained without trial for participants' narratives have uncovered that despite the horrors of armed conflict, in the midst of state breakdown and in the absence of legitimate and formal support, children are able to find creative ways to defend and protect themselves and ultimately attempt to bring about change by themselves and for themselves. While children's acts of agency and resistance can be perceived as 'small victories' in light of the circumstances of ongoing victimization, terror and marginalization, the creative ways that the children coped with the surrounding chaos, insecurity, marginalization and exclusion reveal their capacity as successful negotiators and agents in the history of armed conflict and its aftermath.

Children's intrinsic capacity as agents of change has important implications for current post-conflict policies and programmes that are being developed for children in general. If, as the narratives of the research participants consistently indicated, many children were able to demonstrate a capacity for wilfulness and collective agency during and following the war (sometimes with tragic consequences), then it would seem imperative that current strategies of social assistance adopt approaches that aim to redress youth marginalization and subservience by tapping into children's agency and resilience. Substantial efforts need to continue in the areas specified by children, including the provision of educational and employment opportunities, income-generating skills training, health care, child care assistance, family tracing and reunification, counselling and community sensitization, as well as in cultural and recreational activities such as music, theatre and dance, which provide children with opportunities for cultural expression. Yet there is also a need to recognize the agency and ability of children to negotiate their lives and the world around them and to utilize this knowledge by involving former child soldiers in all aspects of policy and programme development, implementation and evaluation, and to engage youth as peacebuilders, peer educators, positive leaders and advocates. Who better to identify and respond to their post-conflict needs than the children themselves? As these participants noted:

Girls and boys should be involved in developing programs because they know where their interests lie. (Girl)

You know that during the war our lives were not valued. Our lives were put at great risk. We engaged in many things without fully appreciating the risks that they had even for our future. Besides, we had no rights because we were

protracted periods of time (Human Rights Watch 2007b). Tl
salaries for magistrates and judges increase the appeal of corri
Importantly, the backlog of cases in the judicial system leads
estimated 70 per cent of the population having access only
paramount chief courts, thereby bestowing the chiefs with even
power (Freeman 2008).

Pointing to a growing fear that history will repeat itself,
(2005) has suggested that not enough is being done to red
grievances that triggered the war in 1991: 'the same old men a
in power and women and young men are sidelined from the
process' (p. 471). Ultimately, formal structures of inequality,
discrimination and state failure, which never entirely disappea
creeping back into place. As UN Secretary-General Kofi Annan
in April 2005: 'Many of the key human rights issues that l
resulted from the Sierra Leone conflict still persist ... Lastii
cannot be achieved without addressing the significant politi
nomic, and social marginalization of the youth in Sierra Leoi
in Hanlon 2005, p. 470). As we have seen, structural consi
have a critical impact on the lives of these young people. The l
process of unmaking is thus substantially dependent on the
*transformation* of existing structures that have historically pe
inequalities. However, this is clearly a daunting task and a cor
challenge for a country consistently ranked last on the UN
Development Index and still struggling to emerge from the
effects of colonization, international plunder and civil war.

As is evident, however, structural considerations represen
part of the equation. The other critical part of the equation –
agency – also appears to remain problematic. Kemokai (
suggested that in its policy development and implement
Sierra Leonean government has not sufficiently utilized c
young people, but instead has viewed them as passive re
policies and programmes. Moreover, current policies hav
differentiate the lives and realities of young people livin
areas from those in rural ones, and overlooks essential fact
gender, level of education and (dis)ability.

While the wartime and post-war accounts of the young p
lighted in this study are deeply disturbing, in the face of gr
inevitable harm and unimaginable cruelty, both during an
armed conflict, children made complex and compelling c

children, our rights were just swept aside. So these are some of the things that should be reversed now that the war is over. (Boy)

Given participants' conflict experiences and the myriad demands placed on them to survive and cope under extreme circumstances, in the post-war context most respondents indicated that they felt a greater sense of maturity, independence and ability to take care of themselves, particularly when faced with difficult situations. These emerging leadership skills and burgeoning sense of independence, as evidenced in the example of the motorbike riders, should be progressively nurtured. Moreover, programmes of reintegration and social renewal in areas such as health, civic and land rights, education and employment must be expressly attuned to gender differentiation and the ongoing marginalization of girls and women. Instead of focusing solely on girls' vulnerability and victimization, it is essential to also direct our attention to their self-efficacy, resilience and skills. In addition, given their significant presence and multiple roles within the armed group, girls' experiences and perspectives should be considered as central and indispensable to understanding analyses of the war and not regarded as peripheral, or unwittingly or wittingly rendered invisible. To this extent, and reflecting a more rights-based approach, policies and programmes for former girl soldiers should be developed in a way that heeds their voices and encourages a stronger female role in public decision-making. If interventions enable girls to exercise their demonstrable capacity for independence of thought and action, then they are likely to enhance the prospects of greater numbers of war-affected girls assuming more public roles in a society that is struggling to substitute violent conflict with a social and institutional framework of peace and good governance.

However, as with structural reforms, prioritizing the rights and needs of boys and girls and involving them in decision-making is a formidably difficult task. Despite the tenets of the UN Convention on the Rights of the Child, which advocate for the active participation of children and youth in decision-making that affects their lives, war-affected children in numerous countries around the world, particularly girls, have largely been rendered voiceless and invisible in the conceptualization and implementation of programmes designed to meet their needs (McEvoy-Levy 2001). Also, giving young people a more powerful societal voice may, in some contexts, counter traditional social norms. In many societies, including Sierra Leone, traditional cultural practices may accord automatic respect, power and status to older males, while simultaneously discriminating against women and girls in both law and in custom, whether in the realms of social life, education, politics or economics (Denov 2007). In contexts where marginalization, exploitation and outright physical abuse of girls, boys and women have acquired a deep-seated cultural ethic, it is questionable whether new policies and principles aimed at empowerment, particularly of females, can generate a realignment of prevailing power structures. Indeed, planned social change, particularly when it entails a fundamental challenge to relations between men and women, boys and girls at all levels of private and public life, is invariably a slow process that requires comprehensive strategies of mass mobilization and actions that are highly political in nature. Moreover, within contexts of profound poverty and widespread social problems, as is often the reality of post-conflict countries, it is easy to see how the unique needs and circumstances of youth, and particularly girls, can take a back seat to seemingly more pressing and urgent socio-economic priorities. Yet given the turbulent life histories of innumerable war-affected children, to ignore or undermine their perspectives and needs, and their right to actively participate in post-war societal reconstruction and renewal, is to risk a continuation of disparity, instability and violence. As this participant noted:

I tell you, young people are staging strikes and organizing demonstrations in various parts of the country because what they fought and struggled for has not been realized ... For me it is the false promises ... the lies. (Boy)

Within situations of continued poverty and exclusion, with few viable alternatives, there is a realistic fear that children may return to their militarized lives as soldiers and commanders, perpetuating the cycle of violence and disrupting the country's fragile state of 'peace'. In fact, Human Rights Watch (2005) has identified a migrant population of young West African fighters – what they term 'regional warriors' – who, travelling back and forth across the borders of Liberia, Sierra Leone, Guinea and Côte d'Ivoire, view war as mainly an economic opportunity and the best option for economic survival. As former child soldiers struggling to support themselves within the war-shattered economy at home, they have been lured by recruiters back to the frontlines – this time to a neighbouring war (Ismail 2002). The accounts of these regional warriors illuminate a significant link between economic deprivation and the continuing cycle of violence and war crimes throughout the region. The regional warriors identify crippling poverty and hopelessness as the key factors motivating them to risk death in subsequent conflicts.

While it is often former boy soldiers who are typically viewed as 'security risks' in post-conflict situations, the reality of female anger and violence cannot be ignored. In response to mounting post-conflict frustration and disillusionment, some girls in this study reported engaging in violent behaviour. Although girls have not traditionally been perceived as presenting the same potential threat as disaffected young men, girls' growing dissatisfaction and frustration, as well as their potential for continued aggression in the private and public spheres in the aftermath of civil war, was evident. Within the climate of uncertainty and continued economic stagnation in many post-war contexts, many former girl soldiers are raising a new generation of children whose experiences are likely to inure them to violence. As a response to ongoing marginalization, outbursts of aggression reveal girls' capacity for agency and resistance. However, when expressed in violent form it likely exacerbates their alienation from the communities into which they must be successfully reintegrated if the prospect of long-term peacebuilding is ever to be realized. Failing to provide for the needs of these girls and their children after the war is extremely short sighted.

Moreover, the failure to recognize the ambiguous post-conflict status of child soldiers and the interconnectedness of victimization, participation and resistance experiences of *both* boys and girls will lead to programming that fails to meet the needs of young people. There has been an ongoing call for DDR programming to include *all* war-affected children, not just those associated with armed groups, so as to avoid 'privileging' former child soldiers, and preventing subsequent isolation, jealousy and the perception of rewarding those who engaged in wartime violence (Chrobok and Akutu 2008; UNICEF 2007). While this is an important and highly credible suggestion, given the anxiety and confusion brought forth by participation in violence and its multiple meanings, post-conflict programming must be made available that specifically deals with the after-effects and implications of participation in violence. Children who engaged in violence must be provided with a safe space to articulate and voice their conflicting feelings and concerns.

Although it is critical to consider the potential for children to be lured back into a world of violence, there is an accompanying danger that in presenting such risks, without also presenting counter-realities, misconceptions of war-affected youth as inherently 'pathological', 'warped' and 'disorderly' will continue to be propagated. Indeed, it is equally important to highlight the ways in which children have created and continue to create, under great adversity, peaceful and alternative lives for themselves with immense ingenuity and creativity. As Argenti (2002) has written:

The remarkable thing to consider is not why some of Africa's youth have embraced violence, but why *so few* of them have. The great majority – even amongst those subjected to military violence themselves – are proving to be extremely skilled and inventive in responding to the successive crises piled upon them by local communities, national governments and the adverse effects of free market capitalism ... [I]t is young people who are increasingly taking the helm and, against all odds, peacefully constructing alternative social orders ... Despite the disillusionment and criminalisation of the young ... the fact should also be underlined that young people do not simply reproduce state violence ... but rather find ways of appropriating it and subverting it. (Argenti 2002, pp. 151, 146; emphasis in original)

As the example of the motorbike taxi-riders demonstrates, the post-war period in Sierra Leone has seen an upsurge in self-organized social activism among young people (World Bank 2007a). It is said that social networks and institutions are strongest in those parts of the country that were hardest hit by the war (Bellows and Edward 2006). Youth have established business cooperatives and groups aimed at the development of a chiefdom, section or district, as well as occupational bodies including bike riders' or tape sellers' associations. In the Kono district alone, one NGO study counted 141 youth groups with a membership of over 17,000 people (Peters 2006). It is precisely this type of activism and engagement that can not only promote individual leadership skills, self-esteem, knowledge and experience that enables young people to assume greater control over their lives and bring about positive and sustainable change to their situations, but also can contribute to broader nation-building.

This book is based largely upon data collected between 2003 and 2004. Life in Sierra Leone has, of course, altered and changed since that time. I had the opportunity to follow up with several of the participants in 2008 and to explore how their lives were unfolding. Of the small number of participants that I was able to interview several years later, a few had been able to remain in school and two were attending university. One was working as a journalist for a local radio station, while another had been approached to fight as a mercenary in another country and was considering the offer. Most others were eking out a marginal living through odd jobs, selling or petty trading. I sadly learned of the death of three participants. All of those interviewed in 2008 reported living with horrific memories of wartime violence that continued to haunt them up to three times per week. For the girls, the memories of rape and the shame that it brought forth was reportedly worse than in 2004. They explained that at the time of our interviews in 2003 and 2004, they had not fully understood the implications of the rape for their future. As they grew more mature, the implications and shame associated with the rape became more apparent and more disconcerting. All those interviewed in 2008 reportedly continued to make great efforts to hide their former RUF status out of fear of discrimination and retaliation. Several reported that community members continued to treat them in hostile ways as a result of their former RUF affiliation. Others, however, believed that, with time, the stigma of their RUF affiliation would eventually diminish, although they articulated that they would still never openly reveal their former association with the rebels.

Importantly, the young people's passages in and out of violence, and the painstaking struggles that accompany them, are likely to persist. It is without question, however, that the ways in which these journeys take shape and the outcomes of the new and figurative battlefields will ultimately depend greatly on factors that are inevitably tied to both structure and agency. Ultimately, all forms of coalition building and collaboratively planned interventions must heed the lessons of the juxtaposition of structure and agency in children's lives. Structural influences cannot be isolated and analysed without reference to individuals and the shared meanings through which individuals frame events. If reforms of social and economic structures are to enhance the welfare of war-affected young people, youth from all walks of life must be engaged directly in the deliberations and decisions that affect their social development. Equally important, substantive attention must be directed towards fostering radical structural reforms that can facilitate young people's capacity to make judicious choices and to act in peaceful and constructive ways that are beneficial to themselves and to their communities. These young men and women are not destined to a life of crime or violence. However, if they are not provided with meaningful opportunities, violence and crime may represent an alternative source of survival. As one homeless participant living in the slums of Freetown noted: '[I]t is simply not possible to survive without stealing.'

Given the limited scope of this qualitative inquiry, it is crucial to reiterate that the participants' experiences and narratives cannot be generalized beyond their own immediate realities, or be extended to contexts beyond Sierra Leone. However, while the intricate details surrounding the militarization and reintegration of this cohort of child soldiers are undoubtedly unique, the overall process of making and unmaking, and its link to structure and agency, may offer important insights for societies struggling to overcome the effects of internecine warfare. More specifically, regardless of the context, historical and structural forces are likely to shape and form the relations, actions and dynamics of the militarization and demilitarization of the young. Also infused in the process of making and unmaking are the actions of individual actors who appear to produce, reproduce and alter broader structures in their everyday activities. To effectively understand and respond to the plight of child soldiers across the globe, both during and following conflict, the realities of structure and agency must therefore be heeded.

However, the ultimate fates of child soldiers do not lie *only* within the structures and actions within the contexts and countries in which they are found. Indeed, children's complex journeys in and out of violence do not exist in a vacuum, but are intimately connected to broader worldwide structures and actions. As global citizens, we must therefore acknowledge the ways in which our individual actions, inactions and omissions, as well as those of our structures of government, work to produce, reproduce and alter the existing structures and realities that inevitably contribute to and affect the realities of child soldiers around the world. If the practice of recruiting children as soldiers is to be curbed and eventually eradicated, this is essential. This represents a significant battlefield for us all and for which we must take responsibility.

# References

Abdullah, I. 1998. 'Bush path to destruction: The origin and character of the Revolutionary United Front/Sierra Leone'. *Journal of Modern African Studies* 36(2): 203–35.

—— 2002. 'Youth culture and rebellion: Understanding Sierra Leone's wasted decade'. *Critical Arts* 16(2): 19–32.

—— 2004. 'Bush path to destruction: The origin and character of the Revolutionary United Front (RUF/SL)'. In *Between Democracy and Terror: The Sierra Leone Civil War*, ed. I. Abdullah. Dakar, Senegal: Codresia.

—— 2005. '"I am a rebel": Youth culture and violence in Sierra Leone'. In *Makers and Breakers: Children and Youth in Postcolonial Africa*, eds. A. Honwana and F. de Boeck. Trenton, NJ: Africa World Press.

Abdullah, I., Y. Bangura, C. Blake, L. Gberie, L. Johnson, K. Kallon, S. Kemokai, P. Muana, I. Rashid and A. Zack-Williams. 1997. 'Lumpen youth culture and political violence: Sierra Leoneans debate the RUF and the civil war'. *Africa Development* 22(3/4): 171–214.

Abdullah, I. and I. Rashid. 2004. 'Smallest victims; youngest killers: Juvenile combatants in Sierra Leone's civil war'. In *Between Democracy and Terror: The Sierra Leone Civil War*, ed. I. Abdullah. Oxford, UK: UNISA Press.

Abraham, A. 1997. 'War and transition to peace: A study of state conspiracy in perpetuating armed conflict'. *Africa Development* 22(3/4):103–16.

—— 2004. 'State complicity as a factor in perpetuating the Sierra Leone civil war'. In *Between Democracy and Terror: The Sierra Leone Civil War*, ed. I. Abdullah. Dakar, Senegal: Codresia.

Adelman, M. 2003. 'The military, militarism and the militarization of domestic violence'. *Violence Against Women* 9(9): 1118–52.

Agence France-Presse. 1995. 'Boutros-Ghali calls for democracy in Sierra Leone ahead of trip'. 24 November.

Alberts, S. 2006. 'Teen is committed to killing, US claims'. 11 January. *The Montreal Gazette*, p. A17.

Alderson, P. 2000. 'Children as researchers: The effects of participation rights on research methodology'. In *Research with Children: Perspectives and Practices*, eds. P. Christensen and A. James. New York: Falmer Press.

Amowitz, L. L., C. Reis, K. Lyons, B. Vann, B. Mansaray, A. Akinsulure-Smith, L. Taylor and V. Iacopino. 2002. 'Prevalence of war-related sexual violence and other human rights abuses among internally displaced persons in Sierra Leone'. *Journal of the American Medical Association* 287(4): 513–21.

Aning, K. and A. McIntyre. 2004. 'From youth rebellion to child abduction: The anatomy of recruitment in Sierra Leone'. In *Invisible Stakeholders: The Impact of Children on War*, ed. A. McIntyre. Pretoria: Institute for Security Studies.

Annan, J. and C. Blattman. 2006. 'The psychological resilience of youth'. *Research Brief 2, Survey of War Affected Youth, Uganda.* Retrieved 4 June 2007 from www.sway-uganda.org/SWAY.RB2.pdf

Argenti, N. 2002. 'Youth in Africa: A major resource for change'. In *Young Africa: Realising the Rights of Children and Youth*, eds. A. de Waal and N. Argenti. Trenton, NJ: Africa World Press.

Ariès, P. 1962. *Centuries of Childhood*. London: Jonathan Cape.

Atanga, L. 2003. *Tackling Small Arms in Central Africa*. Bonn: Bonn International Centre for Conversion.

*Awareness Times*. 2007. 'Youth Employment Scheme on course in Sierra Leone by Youth Employment Scheme'. 14 March. Retrieved 26 October 2008 from http://news.sl/drwebsite/publish/article_20054975.shtml

Bandura, A. 1999. 'Moral disengagement in the perpetration of inhumanities'. *Personality and Social Psychology Review* 3: 193–209.

Bangura, Y. 1997. 'Understanding the political and cultural dynamics of the Sierra Leone war: A critique of Paul Richards' *Fighting for the Rainforest*'. *Africa Development* 22(3/4): 117–48.

  2004. 'The political and cultural dynamics of the Sierra Leone war'. In *Between Democracy and Terror: The Sierra Leone Civil War*, ed. I. Abdullah. Oxford, UK: UNISA Press.

Barker, J. and F. Smith. 2001. 'Power, positionality and practicality: Carrying out fieldwork with children'. *Ethics, Place and Environment* 4(2): 142–7.

BBC News. 2002. 'Sierra Leone's "flames of peace"'. Retrieved 25 July 2008 from http://news.bbc.co.uk/2/hi/africa/1767600.stm

  2003. 'Sierra Leone rebel leader dies'. 30 July. Retrieved 13 October 2008 from http://news.bbc.co.uk/2/hi/africa/3109521.stm

  2007. 'Child soldiers "are a time bomb"'. 5 February. Retrieved 4 June 2007 from http://news.bbc.co.uk/1/hi/world/europe/6330503.stm

Becker, H. 1970. *Sociological Work*. Chicago: Aldine.

Becker, J. 2004. *Children as Weapons of War*. New York: Human Rights Watch.

Bellows, J. and M. Edward. 2006. 'War and institutions: New evidence from Sierra Leone'. *American Economic Review* 96(2): 394–9.

Bennell, P., J. Harding and S. Rogers-Wright. 2004. *PRSP Education Sector Review, Sierra Leone*. Prepared for the PRSP Education Sub-Sector Working Group, Freetown, Sierra Leone.

Berman, B. 1998. 'Ethnicity, patronage and the African state: The politics of uncivil nationalism'. *African Affairs* 97: 315–41.

—— 2000. 'The relevance of narrative research with children who witness war and children who witness woman abuse'. *Journal of Aggression, Maltreatment and Trauma* 3(1): 107–25.

Betancourt, T. S. 2008. 'Child soldiers: Reintegration, pathways to recovery and reflections from the field'. *Journal of Developmental and Behavioral Pediatrics* 29(2): 138–41.

Betancourt, T. S., and K. T. Khan (2008). 'The mental health of children affected by armed conflict: Protective processes and pathways to resilience'. *International Review of Psychiatry* 20(3): 317–28.

Betancourt, T. S., S. Simmons, I. Borisova, S. Brewer, U. Iweala and M. de la Soudiere. 2008. 'High hopes, grim reality: Reintegration and the education of former child soldiers in Sierra Leone'. *Comparative Education Review* 52(4): 565–84.

Bhavnani, K.-K. 1993. 'Tracing the contours: Feminist research and feminist objectivity'. *Women's Studies International Forum* 16(2): 95–104.

Boothby, N. 2006. 'What happens when child soldiers grow up? The Mozambique case study'. *Intervention: International Journal of Mental Health, Psychosocial Work and Counselling in Areas of Armed Conflict* 4(3): 244–59.

Boothby, N., Crawford, J. and J. Halperin. 2006. 'Mozambique child soldier life outcome study: Lessons learned in rehabitation and reintegration efforts'. *Global Public Health* 1(1): 87–107.

Bouta, T. 2005. *Gender and Disarmament, Demobilization and Reintegration: Building Blocks for Dutch Policy*. Netherlands: Clingendael Conflict Research Unit.

Boyden, J. 2004. 'Anthropology under fire: Ethics, researchers and children in war'. In *Children and Youth on the Front Line: Ethnography, Armed Conflict, and Displacement*, eds. J. Boyden and J. de Berry. New York: Berghahn Books.

Boyden, J. and J. de Berry (eds.). 2004. *Children and Youth on the Front Line: Ethnography, Armed Conflict, and Displacement*. New York: Berghahn Books.

Boyden, J. and D. Levinson. 2000. 'Children as economic and social actors in the development process'. Working Paper 1. Stockholm: Expert Group on Developmental Issues.

Brett, R. and I. Specht. 2004. *Young Soldiers: Why They Choose to Fight*. London: Lynne Rienner Publishers.

Brocklehurst, H. 2006. *Who's Afraid of Children: Children, Conflict and International Relations*. Aldershot, UK: Ashgate.

Bryant, C. and D. Jary (eds.). 1991. *Giddens' Theory of Structuration: A Critical Appreciation*. London: Routledge.

Bundu, A. 2001. *Democracy by Force? A Study of International Military Intervention in the Conflict in Sierra Leone from 1991–2000*. London: Universal Publishers.

Burman, E. 1994. 'Innocents abroad: Western fantasies of childhood and the iconography of emergencies'. *Disasters* 18(3): 238–53.

Cain, K. 1999. 'The rape of Dinah: Human rights, civil war in Liberia and evil triumphant'. *Human Rights Quarterly* 21: 265–307.

Canadian Broadcasting Corporation. 2008. 'Publisher admits errors in memoir of child soldier'. 21 April. Retrieved 2 February 2009 from http://www.cbc.ca/arts/books/story/2008/04/21/memoir-child-soldier.html

Caputo, V. 2001. 'Telling stories from the field: Children and the politics of ethnographic representation'. *Anthropologica* 43(2): 179–89.

Cardoza, T. 2002. 'These unfortunate children: Sons and daughters of the regiment in revolutionary and Napoleonic France'. In *Children and War: A Historical Anthology*, ed. J. Marten. New York: New York University Press.

Carment, D., J. Gazo and S. Prest. 2007. 'Risk assessment and state failure'. *Global Society* 21(1): 47–69.

Cervenka, Z. 1987. 'The effects of militarization of Africa on human rights'. *Africa Today* 1–2: 69–84.

Chrobok, V. 2005. *Demobilizing and Reintegrating Afghanistan's Young Soldiers*. Bonn: Bonn International Centre for Conversion.

Chrobok, V. and A. Akutu. 2008. *Returning Home: Children's Perspectives on Reintegration*. London: Coalition to Stop the Use of Child Soldiers.

Clapham, C. 2003. *Sierra Leone: The Political Economy of Internal Conflict*. The Hague: Netherlands Institute of International Relations, Conflict Research Unit.

Coalition to Stop the Use of Child Soldiers. 2001. *Global Report*. London: Coalition to Stop the Use of Child Soldiers.

    2004. *Global Report*. London: Coalition to Stop the Use of Child Soldiers.

    2008. *Global Report*. London: Coalition to Stop the Use of Child Soldiers.

Cohen, I. 1989. *Structuration Theory: Anthony Giddens and the Constitution of Social Life*. New York: St Martin's Press.

    2001. *States of Denial: Knowing about Atrocities and Suffering*. London: Polity Press.

Collmer, S. 2004. 'Child soldiers: an integral element in new, irregular wars?' *Connections: The Quarterly Journal* 3(3): 1–11.

Conciliation Resources. 2006. 'Peace is not just the absence of the gun'. Retrieved 18 February 2009 from www.c-r.org/about/documents/CR_review_2006_West_Africa.pdf

Coulter, C. 2008. 'Female fighters in the Sierra Leone war: Challenging the assumptions?' *Feminist Review* 88: 54–73.

Coulter, C., M. Persson and M. Utas. 2008. *Young Female Fighters in African Wars: Conflict and Its Consequences*. NAI Policy Dialogue. Sweden: Nordiska Afrikainstitutet.

Craib, I. 1992. *Anthony Giddens*. London: Routledge.

Crelinsten, R. 1995. 'In their own words: The world of the torturer'. In *The Politics of Pain: Torturers and their Masters*, eds. R. Crelinsten and A. Schmid. Oxford, UK: Westview Press.

   2003. 'The world of torture: A constructed reality'. *Theoretical Criminology* 7(3): 293–318.

Decker, S. and B. Van Winkle. 1996. *Life in the Gang: Family, Friends, and Violence*. Cambridge: Cambridge University Press.

Denov, M. 2006. 'Wartime sexual violence: Assessing a human security response to war-affected girls in Sierra Leone'. *Security Dialogue* 37(3): 319–42.

   2007. *Is the Culture Always Right? The Dangers of Reproducing Gender Stereotypes and Inequalities in Psycho-Social Interventions for War-Affected Children*. Retrieved 13 October 2008 from /www.child-soldiers.org/psycho-social/Gender_stereotypes_and_inequalities_2007.pdf

   2008. 'Girl soldiers and human rights: Lessons from Angola, Mozambique, Sierra Leone, and northern Uganda'. *International Journal of Human Rights* 12(5): 811–33.

Denov, M. and C. Gervais. 2007. 'Negotiating (in)security: Agency, resistance and the experiences of girls formerly associated with Sierra Leone's Revolutionary United Front'. *Signs: Journal of Women in Culture and Society* 32(4): 885–910.

Denov, M. and R. Maclure. 2006. 'Engaging the voices of girls in the aftermath of Sierra Leone's conflict: Experiences and perspectives in a culture of violence'. *Anthropologica* 48(1): 73–85.

   2007. 'Turnings and epiphanies: Militarization, life histories and the making and unmaking of two child soldiers in Sierra Leone'. *Journal of Youth Studies* 10(2): 243–61.

Dinan, K. A. 2002. 'Migrant Thai women subjected to slavery-like abuses in Japan'. *Violence Against Women* 8(9): 1113–39.

Dodge, C. P. and M. Raundalen. 1991. *Reaching Children in War: Sudan, Uganda and Mozambique*. Uppsala, Sweden: Scandinavian Institute of African Studies.

Downe, P. J. 2001. 'Playing with names: How children create identities of self in anthropological research'. *Anthropologica* 43(2): 165–77.

Duffield, M. R. 2001. *Global Governance and the New Wars: The Merging of Development and Security*. London: Zed Books.

Ellis, S. 2003. Young Soldiers and the Significance of Initiation: Some Notes from Liberia. Unpublished manuscript.

Endleman, S. 2001. 'Arms for the poor: Small arms and light weapons in interstate and intrastate conflict'. *Humanity and Society* 25(3–4): 288–98.

England, K. 1994. 'Getting personal: Reflexivity, positionality, and feminist research'. *Professional Geographer* 46(1): 80–9.

Enloe, C. 2000. *Maneuvers: The International Politics of Militarizing Women's Lives*. Berkeley, CA, and London: University of California Press.

Erikson, E. H. 1963. *Childhood and Society*. New York: Norton.

Fanthorpe, R. 2001. 'Neither citizen nor subject? "Lumpen" agency and the legacy of native administration in Sierra Leone'. *African Affairs* 100: 363–86.

2003. 'Humanitarian aid in post-war Sierra Leone: The politics of moral economy'. In *Power, livelihoods and conflict*, HPG Report 13. London: Overseas Development Institute.

2005. 'On the limits of liberal peace: Chiefs and democratic decentralization in post-war Sierra Leone'. *African Affairs* 105(418): 27–49.

Farah, D. 2001. 'They fought for nothing and that's what they got'. 1 September. *Washington Post*, p. C1.

Farr, V. 2002. *Gendering Demilitarization as a Peacebuilding Tool*. Bonn: Bonn International Centre for Conversion.

Farrell, J. P. 1999. 'Changing conceptions of equality of education: Forty years of comparative evidence'. In *Comparative Education: The Dialectic of the Global and the Local*, eds. R. F. Arnove and C. A. Torres. Lanham, MD: Rowman and Littlefield.

Feldman, A. 2002. 'X-children and the militarisation of everyday life: Comparative comments on the politics of youth, victimage, and violence in transitional societies'. *International Journal of Social Welfare* 11: 286–99.

Ferme, M. 2001. *The Underneath of Things: Violence, History, and the Everyday in Sierra Leone*. Berkeley: University of California Press.

Ferme, M. and D. Hoffman. 2004. 'Hunter militias and the international human rights discourse in Sierra Leone and beyond'. *Africa Today* 50(4): 73–95.

Foucault, M. 1980. *Power/Knowledge: Selected Interviews and Other Writings, 1972–1977*. New York: Pantheon Books.

Fox, M.-J. 2004. 'Girl soldiers: Human security and gendered insecurity'. *Security Dialogue* 35(4): 465–79.

Freedson, J. 2002. 'The impact of conflict on children – the role of small arms'. *Disarmament Forum* 3: 37–44.

Freeman, C. 2008. 'The failures of post-conflict reconstruction in Sierra Leone and the threat to peace'. Retrieved 16 February 2009 from www.beyondintractability.org/case_studies/reconstruction_sierra_leone.jsp?nid=6811

Galanter, M. 1989. *Cults: Faith, Healing, and Coercion*. Oxford: Oxford University Press.

Gberie, L. 2005. *A Dirty War in West Africa: The RUF and the Destruction of Sierra Leone*. London: Hurst and Company.

Geyer, M. 1989. 'The militarization of Europe, 1914–1945'. In *The Militarization of the Western World*, ed. J. Gillis. New Brunswick, NJ: Rutgers University Press.

Giddens, A. 1976. *New Rules of Sociological Method*. London: Macmillan.
 1977. *Studies in Social and Political Theory*. London: Hutchinson.
 1979. *Central Problems in Social Theory*. London: Macmillan.
 1984. *The Constitution of Society*. Cambridge, UK: Polity Press.

Ginifer, J. 2003. 'Prioritising reintegration'. In *Sierra Leone: Building the Road to Recovery*, eds. M. Malan, S. Meek, T. Thusi, J. Ginifer and P. Coker. Pretoria: Institute for Security Studies.

Goffman, E. 1961. *Asylums*. Garden City, NY: Doubleday Anchor Books.

Goldstein, J. 2001. *War and Gender*. Cambridge: Cambridge University Press.

Government of Sierra Leone. 2003. 'Sierra Leone national youth policy'. Retrieved 8 September 2009 from www.daco-sl.org/encyclopedia/4_strat/4_2/National_Youth_Policy.pdf
 2005. Poverty Reduction Strategy Paper.

Grbich, C. 2007. *Qualitative Data Analysis: An Introduction*. London: Sage.

Green, E., W. Mitchell and R. Bunton. 2000. 'Conceptualizing risk and danger: An analysis of young people's perceptions of risk'. *Journal of Youth Studies* 3: 109–26.

Hanlon, J. 2005. 'Is the international community helping to recreate the preconditions for war in Sierra Leone?' *The Round Table* 94(381): 459–72.

Hansen, A., J. Nenon, J. Wolf and M. Sommers. 2002. *Final Evaluation of the Office of Transition Initiatives' Program in Sierra Leone, Final Report*. Washington, DC: USAID.

Haritos-Fatouros, M. 2003. *The Psychological Origins of Institutionalized Torture*. London and New York: Routledge.

Harris, G. 2006. 'The military as a resource for peacebuilding: Time for consideration?' *Conflict, Security and Development* 6(2): 241–52.

Hay, C. 1995. 'Structure and agency'. In *Theory and Method in Political Science*, eds. D. Marsh and G. Stoker. New York: St Martin's Press.

Held, D. and J. Thompson. 1989. *Social Theory of Modern Societies: Anthony Giddens and his Critics*. Cambridge: Cambridge University Press.

Helmus, T., C. Russell and W. Glenn. 2004. *Steeling the Mind: Combat Stress Reactions and their Implications for Urban Warfare*. Santa Monica, CA: Rand Arroyo Center.

Hiroto, D. and M. Seligman. 1975. 'Generality of learned helplessness in man'. *Journal of Personality and Social Psychology* 13: 311–27.

Hirsch, J. 2001. *Sierra Leone: Diamonds and the Struggle for Democracy*. London: Lynne Rienner Publishers.

Hogg, C. 2006. *Sri Lanka: The Liberation Tigers of Tamil Eelam (LTTE) and Child Recruitment*. London: Coalition to Stop the Use of Child Soldiers.

Honwana, A. 1998. 'Okusiakala ondalo yokalye: Let us light a new fire. Local Knowledge in the Post-War Healing and Reintegration of War-Affected Children in Angola'. Retrieved 14 October 2008 from www.forcedmigration.org/psychosocial/inventory/pwg001

2006. *Child Soldiers in Africa*. Philadelphia: University of Pennsylvania Press.

2008. 'Children's involvement in war: Historical and social contexts'. *Journal of the History of Childhood and Youth* 1(1): 139–49.

Honwana, A. and F. de Boeck (eds.). 2005. *Makers and Breakers: Children and Youth in Postcolonial Africa*. Trenton, NJ: Africa World Press.

Horn, R. 2001. 'Little lords of the jungle'. 29 January. *Time Magazine*. Vol. 157, No. 4: 52.

Howard, M. 2008. 'Captured videos show "al-Quaida children" training to kidnap and assassinate, says US'. 7 February. *The Guardian*, Retrieved 13 November 2008 from www.guardian.co.uk/world/2008/feb/07/alqaida.iraq

Human Rights Watch. 2003a. *Child Soldier Use 2003: A Briefing of the 4th UN Security Council Open Debate on Children and Armed Conflict – Rwanda*. New York: Human Rights Watch. Retrieved 28 October 2008 from www.hrw.org/reports/2004/childsoldiers0104/14.htm

2003b. *We'll Kill You If You Cry: Sexual Violence in the Sierra Leone Conflict*. New York: Human Rights Watch.

2003c. *World Report: Sierra Leone*. New York: Human Rights Watch. Retrieved 6 November 2007 from www.hrw.org/wr2k3/africa10.html

2005. *Youth, Poverty and Blood: The Lethal Legacy of West Africa's Regional Warriors*. Vol. 17, No. 53(A). New York: Human Rights Watch. Retrieved 9 February 2008 from www.hrw.org/reports/2005/westafrica0405/westafrica0405text.pdf

2006. *Trying Charles Taylor in the Hague: Making Justice Available to the Most Affected*. New York: Human Rights Watch. Retrieved 13 October 2008 from www.hrw.org/backgrounder/ij/ij0606/ij0606.pdf

2007a. *Sold to Be Soldiers: The Recruitment and Use of Child Soldiers in Burma.* New York: Human Rights Watch.

2007b. 'Sierra Leone: New leader must combat injustice, corruption'. New York: Human Rights Watch. Retrieved 17 February 2009 from www.hrw.org/en/news/2007/11/12/sierra-leone-new-leader-must-combat-injustice-corruption

Humphreys, M. and J. Weinstein. 2007. 'Demobilization and reintegration'. *Journal of Conflict Resolution* 51(4): 531–67.

Ibañez, A. 2001. 'El Salvador: War and untold stories: Women guerrillas'. In *Victims, Perpetrators or Actors? Gender, Armed Conflict and Political Violence*, eds. C. Moser and F. Clark. London: Zed Books.

Integrated Regional Information Networks (IRIN). 2008a. 'Sierra Leone: Still last on human development index'. 18 December.

2008b. 'Sierra Leone: Maternity hospital is "last resort"'. 12 March.

2009. 'Sierra Leone: Sexual violence defies new law'. Retrieved 7 September 2009 from www.irinnews.org/report.aspx?ReportId=85511

International Crisis Group (ICG). 2003. 'Sierra Leone: The state of security and governance'. *Africa Report* 67.

2004. 'Liberia and Sierra Leone: Rebuilding failed states' *Africa Report* 87.

Ismail, O. 2002. 'Liberia's child combatants: Paying the price of neglect'. *Conflict, Security and Development* 2(2): 125–34.

Jackson, P. 2006. 'Reshuffling an old deck of cards? The politics of local government reform in Sierra Leone'. *African Affairs* 106(422): 95–111.

James, A. and A. Prout. 1990. *Constructing and Deconstructing Childhood.* London: Falmer Press.

Jayamah, D. 2004. 'Partners in Arms: LTTE Women Fighters and the Changing Face of the Sri Lankan Civil War'. Unpublished manuscript.

Joka Bangura, F. 2007. 'Political and economic empowerment of Sierra Leone women'. 6 December. *Awareness Times*, from news.sl/drwebsite/publish/article_20057125.shtml

Kagawa, F. 2005. 'Emergency education: A critical review of the field'. *Comparative Education* 41(4): 487–503.

Kaldor, M. 1999. *New and Old Wars : Organized Violence in a Global Era.* Cambridge, UK: Polity Press.

Kalyvas, S. 2001. '"New" and "old" civil wars: A valid distinction?' *World Politics* 54: 99–118.

Kanagaratnam, P., M. Raundalen and A. E. Asbjornsen. 2005. 'Ideological commitment and posttraumatic stress in former Tamil child soldiers'. *Scandinavian Journal of Psychology* 46(6): 511–20.

Kandeh, J. 1999. 'Ransoming the state: Elite origins of subaltern terror in Sierra Leone'. *Review of African Political Economy* 81: 349–66.

2004. 'Unmaking the second republic: Democracy on trial'. In *Between Democracy and Terror: The Sierra Leone Civil War*, ed. I Abdullah. Dakar, Senegal: Codresia.

Kaplan, R. 1994. 'The coming anarchy'. February. *Atlantic Monthly*.

Kater, M. 2004. *Hitler Youth*. Cambridge, MA: Harvard University Press.

Kay, H., V. Cree, K. Tisdall and J. Wallace. 2002. 'At the edge: Negotiating boundaries in research with children and young people'. *Online Journal: Forum: Qualitative Social Research* 4(2).

Keairns, L. 2003. *The Voice of Girl Children Soldiers*. New York: Quaker United Nations Office.

Keen, D. 1997. 'A rational kind of madness'. *Oxford Development Studies* 25(1): 67–75.

2000. 'War and peace: What's the difference?' *International Peacekeeping* 7(4): 1–22.

2005. *Conflict and Collusion in Sierra Leone*. New York: Palgrave.

Kelman, H. 1995. 'The social context of torture: Policy process and authority structure'. In *The Politics of Pain: Torturers and their Masters*, eds. R. Crelinsten and A. Schmid. Boulder, CO: Westview Press.

Kemokai, A. 2007. 'The role of young people in local governance and accountability particularly regarding their education and employment in Sierra Leone'. Report for the Young Men's Christian Association, Sierra Leone.

Kemper, Y. 2005. *Youth in War to Peace Transitions*. Berlin: Berghof Research Center for Constructive Conflict Management.

Klare, M. 1999. 'The Kalashnikov age'. *Bulletin of the Atomic Scientists* 55(1): 18–22.

Kostelny, K. 2006. 'A culture-based integrative approach: Helping war-affected children'. In *A World Turned Upside Down: Social Ecological Approaches to Children in War Zones*, eds. N. Boothby, A. Strang and M. Wessells. Bloomfield, CT: Kumarian Press.

Kpaka, S. and J. Klemm. 2005. 'Sierra Leone expenditure tracking: Detecting leakages at primary school'. In *Stealing the Future: Corruption in the Classroom. Ten Real World Experiences*, eds. B. Meier and M. Griffin. Berlin: Transparency International.

Kpundeh, S. 2004. 'Corruption and political insurgency in Sierra Leone'. In *Between Democracy and Terror: The Sierra Leone Civil War*, ed. I. Abdullah. Dakar, Senegal: Codresia.

Kuterovac-Jagodic, G. and K. Kontac. 2002. 'Normalization: A key to children's recovery'. In *Children and Disasters: A Practical Guide to Healing and Recovery*, eds. W. N. Zubenko and J. A. Capozzoli. New York: Oxford University Press.

Kuttab, D. 1988. 'Profile of the stonethrowers'. *Journal of Palestinian Studies* 17(3): 14–23.

Layder, D. 1994. *Understanding Social Theory*. London: Sage.

Lee, R. and C. Renzetti (eds.). 1993. *Researching Sensitive Topics*. London: Sage.

Little, K. 1965. 'The political function of the Poro'. *Africa* 35(4): 349–65.

Luscombe, B. 2007. 'Pop culture finds lost boys'. *Time Magazine*. Available at www.time.com/time/magazine/article/0,9171,1584807,00.html

Lyons, T. 2004. *Guns and Guerilla Girls: Women in the Zimbabwean Liberation Struggle*. Asmara, Eritrea: Africa World Press.

Machel, G. 1996. *The Impact of War on Children*. New York: United Nations.

Maclure, R. and M. Denov. 2006. '"I didn't want to die so I joined them': Structuration and the process of becoming boy soldiers in Sierra Leone'. *Terrorism and Political Violence* 18(1): 119–35.

2009. 'Reconstruction versus transformation: Post-war education and the struggle for gender parity in Sierra Leone'. *International Journal of Educational Development* 29: 612–20.

MacJohnson, R. 2004. 'Spotlight falls on corruption in Sierra Leone'. 6 May. South African Press Association.

Macmillan, L. 2009. 'The child soldier in north–south relations'. *International Political Sociology* 3: 36–52.

MacMullin, C. and M. Loughry. 2004. 'Investigating psychosocial adjustment of former child soldiers in Sierra Leone and Uganda'. *Journal of Refugee Studies* 17(4): 460–72.

Malan, M. and S. Meek. 2003. 'Extension of government authority and national recovery'. In M. Malan, S. Meek, T. Thusi, J. Ginifer and P. Coker. 2003. *Sierra Leone: Building the Road to Recovery*. Pretoria: Institute for Security Studies.

Malan, M., S. Meek, T. Thusi, J. Ginifer and P. Coker. 2003. *Sierra Leone: Building the Road to Recovery*. Pretoria: Institute for Security Studies.

Marlowe, D. 2001. *Psychological and Psychosocial Consequences of Combat and Deployment with Special Emphasis on the Gulf War*. Santa Monica, CA: RAND.

Marten, J. (ed.) 2002. *Children and War: A Historical Anthology*. New York: New York University Press.

2004. *Children for the Union: The War Spirit on the Northern Home Front*. Chicago: Ivan R. Dee.

Massaquoi, M. 2008. 'Sierra Leone: Police wage war on Okada riders'. Retrieved 18 February 2009 from http://allafrica.com/stories/200811200960.html

Mauthner, M. 1997. 'Methodological aspects of collecting data from children: Lessons from three research projects'. *Children and Society* 11: 16–28.

Mawson, A. 2004. 'Children, impunity and justice: Some dilemmas from northern Uganda'. In *Children and Youth on the Front Line: Ethnography, Armed Conflict and Displacement*, eds. J. Boyden and J. de Berry. New York: Berghahn Books.

Maxted, J. 2003. 'Children and armed conflict in Africa'. *Social Identities* 9(1): 51–72.

Mazurana, D. and K. Carlson. 2004. *From Combat to Community: Women and Girls of Sierra Leone*. Women Waging Peace.

Mazurana, D., S. McKay, K. Carlson and J. Kasper. 2002. 'Girls in fighting forces and groups: Their recruitment, participation, demobilization and reintegration'. *Peace and Conflict: Journal of Peace Psychology* 8(2): 97–123.

McAdams, D. 2001. 'The psychology of life stories'. *Review of General Psychology* 5(2): 100–22.

McEvoy-Levy, S. 2001. 'Youth as social and political agents: Issues in post-settlement peace building'. Kroc Institute Occasional Paper 21.

McIntyre, A. 2003. 'African children in armed conflict: Bridging rights and reality'. *Commonwealth Youth and Development* 1(2): 5–21.

McKay, S. 2004. 'Reconstructing fragile lives: Girls' social reintegration in northern Uganda and Sierra Leone'. *Gender and Development* 12(3): 19–30.

  2005. 'Girls as "weapons of terror"'. *Studies in Conflict and Terrorism*, 28(5): 385–97.

  2006. 'The inversion of girlhood: Girl combatants during and after armed conflict'. In *A World Turned Upside Down: The Social Ecologies of Children in Armed Conflict* (pp. 89–109), eds. N. Boothby, M. Wessells and A. Strang. Bloomfield, CT: Kumarian Press.

McKay, S. and D. Mazurana. 2004. *Where Are the Girls? Girls in Fighting Forces in Northern Uganda, Sierra Leone, and Mozambique: Their Lives During and After War*. Montreal, Canada: International Centre for Human Rights and Democratic Development.

Médecins Sans Frontières. 2006. *Access to Healthcare in Post-Conflict Sierra Leone*. Amsterdam: Médecins Sans Frontières.

Mehari, S. 2006. *Heart of Fire*. London: Profile Books. (Originally published in German in 2004.)

Mendel, M. 1995. *The Male Survivor: The Impact of Sexual Abuse*. London: Sage.

Miles, M.B. and A.M. Huberman. 1994. *Qualitative Data Analysis: An Expanded Sourcebook*. 2nd edn. Thousand Oaks, CA: Sage.

Miller, D., D. Ladouceur and Z. Dougal. 2006. *From Research to Road Map: Learning from the Arms for Development Initiative in Sierra Leone*. Geneva: United Nations Institute for Disarmament Research.

Ministry of Education, Science and Technology. 2003. *National Report on the Development of Education in Sierra Leone for 2003*. Freetown: Government of Sierra Leone.

  2007. *Sierra Leone Education Sector Plan: A Road Map for a Better Future, 2007–2015*. Freetown: Government of Sierra Leone.

Mishna, F., B. Antle and C. Regehr. 2004. 'Tapping the perspectives of children: Emerging ethical issues in qualitative research'. *Qualitative Social Work* 3(4): 449–68.

Mkandawire, T. 2002. 'The terrible toll of post-colonial rebel movements in Africa: Towards an explanation of the violence against the peasantry'. *Journal of Modern Adolescent Studies* 40(2): 181–215.

Molloy, D. 2004. *The DDR Process in Sierra Leone: An Overview and Lessons Learned*. Freetown: United Nations Mission in Sierra Leone.

Moore, K., C. Squire and F. MacBailey. 2003. *Sierra Leone National Recovery Strategy Assessment, Final Report*. Freetown: United Nations Development Programme/Government of Sierra Leone.

Morrow, V. and M. Richards. 1996. 'The ethics of social research with children: An overview'. *Children and Society* 10(2): 90–105.

Mossman, L. 2008. *Gender Equality in Post-Conflict Sierra Leone*. Unpublished Master's thesis, Carleton University.

Muana, P. 1997. 'The Kamajoi militia: Civil war, internal displacement and the politics of counter-insurgency'. *Africa Development* 22(3/4): 77–100.

Muggah, R. (ed.). 2006. *No Refuge: The Crisis of Refugee Militarization in Africa*. London: Zed Books.

Munford, R. and J. Sanders. 2004. 'Recruiting diverse groups of young people to research: Agency and empowerment in the consent process'. *Qualitative Social Work* 3(4): 469–82.

Murphy, W. 2003. 'Military patrimonialism and child soldier clientalism in the Liberian and Sierra Leonean civil wars'. *African Studies Review* 46(2): 61–87.

Mutua, K. and B. Blue Swadener. 2004. 'Introduction'. In *DecolonizingResearch in Cross-Cultural Contexts*, eds. K. Mutua and B. Blue Swadener. Albany: State University of New York Press.

National Committee for Disarmament, Demobilization and Reintegration (NCDDR). 2004. 'Final reports'. Available at www.daco-sl.org/encyclopedia/5_gov/5_3ncddr.htm

*New York Times*. 2006. 'Armies of children'. 12 October.

Newman, E. 2004. 'The "new wars" debate: A historical perspective is needed'. *Security Dialogue* 35(2): 173–89.

*Newsweek*. 1995. 'Special report: Boy soldiers'. 7 August.

2000. 'Terror twins'. 7 February. Vol. 135, Iss. 6: 42–3.

Nordstrom, C. 1997. *Girls and Warzones: Troubling Questions*. Uppsala, Sweden: Life and Peace Institute.

Otunnu, O. 2000. 'Innocent victims: Protecting children in times of armed conflict'. In *United Nations 2000*. London: Agenda Publishing.

Park, A. 2006. '"Other inhumane acts": Forced marriage, girl soldiers and the Special Court for Sierra Leone'. *SocioLegal Studies* 15(3): 315–37.

Pavlos, A. 1982. *The Cult Experience*. Westport, CT: Greenwood Press.

Peters, K. 2004. *Re-examining Voluntarism: Youth Combatants in Sierra Leone*. Retrieved 12 November 2008 from www.iss.co.za/pubs/Monographs/No100/Contents.html

2006. *Footpaths to Reintegration*. Unpublished PhD thesis, Wageningen University.

2007a. 'Reintegration support for young ex-combatants: A right or a privilege?' *International Migration* 45(5): 35–59.

2007b. 'From weapons to wheels: Young Sierra Leonean ex-combatants become motorbike taxi-riders'. *Journal of Peace, Conflict and Development* 10: 1–23.

Peters, K. and P. Richards. 1998. 'Why we fight: Voices of youth combatants in Sierra Leone'. *Africa* 68(2): 183–209.

Physicians for Human Rights. 2002. *War-Related Sexual Violence in Sierra Leone: A Population-Based Assessment*. Boston: Physicians for Human Rights.

Pombeni, M., E. Kirchler and A. Palmonari. 1990. 'Identification with peers as a strategy to muddle through the troubles of the adolescent years'. *Journal of Adolescence* 13: 351–69.

Post, J., E. Sprinzak and L. Denny. 2003. 'The terrorists in their own words: Interviews with 35 incarcerated Middle Eastern terrorists'. *Terrorism and Political Violence* 15(1): 171–84.

Rashid, I. 1997. 'Subaltern reactions: Lumpen, students, and the left'. *Africa Development* 22(3/4): 19–44.

Regan, P. 1994. 'War toys, war movies, and the militarization of the United States, 1900–85'. *Journal of Peace Research*, 31(1): 45–58.

Rempel, G. 1989. *Hitler's Children: The Hitler Youth and the SS*. Chapel Hill: University of North Carolina Press.

Reno, W. 1995. *Corruption and State Politics in Sierra Leone*. Cambridge: Cambridge University Press.

Revolutionary United Front. 1995. 'RUF Anthem'. *Footpaths to Democracy: Toward a New Sierra Leone*.

Richards, P. 1996. *Fighting for the Rainforest: War, Youth and Resources in Sierra Leone*. Oxford, UK: James Currey.

2003. 'The political economy of internal conflict in Sierra Leone'. Working Paper 21. Netherlands Institute of International Relations Clingendael, Conflict Research Unit.

2005. 'To fight or to farm? Agrarian dimensions of the Mano River conflicts (Liberia and Sierra Leone)'. *African Affairs* 104(417): 571–90.

Richards, P., K. Bah and J. Vincent. 2004. *Social Capital and Survival: Prospects for Community Driven Development in Post-Conflict Sierra Leone*. Washington, DC: World Bank.

Rosen, D. 2005. *Armies of the Young: Child Soldiers in War and Terrorism.* New Brunswick, NJ: Rutgers University Press.

2009. 'The child soldier in literature or how Johnny Tremain Became Johnny Mad Dog'. In *Restaging War in the Western World: Noncombatant Experiences*, eds. M. Abbenhuis and S. Buttsworth. New York: Palgrave MacMillan.

Rotberg, R. I. 2002. 'Failed states in a world of terror'. *Foreign Affairs* 81(4): 127–40.

2003. *Failed States, Collapsed States, Weak States: Causes and Indicators.* Retrieved 13 November 2008 from www.wilsoncenter.org/topics/docs/statefailureandstateweaknessinatimeofterror.pdf

Rudd, P. and K. Evans. 1998. 'Structure and agency in youth transitions: Student experiences of vocational further education'. *Journal of Youth Studies* 1: 39–62.

Schabas, R. 2004. 'A synergistic relationship: The Sierra Leone Truth and Reconciliation Commission and the Special Court for Sierra Leone'. In *Truth Commissions and Courts*, eds. W. Schabas and S. Darcy. London: Kluwer Academic Publishers.

Scheyvens, R. and H. Leslie. 2000. 'Gender, ethics and empowerment: Dilemmas of development fieldwork'. *Women's Studies International Forum* 23(1): 119–30.

Schmid, T. and R. Jones. 1991. 'Suspended identity: Identity transformation in a maximum security prison'. *Symbolic Interaction* 14(4): 415–32.

Schmidt, R. 2007. *No Girls Allowed? Recruitment and Gender in Colombian Armed Groups.* Unpublished Master's thesis, Carleton University.

Schroven, A. 2008. *Women After War: Gender Mainstreaming and the Social Construction of Identity in Contemporary Sierra Leone.* Berlin: LIT Verlag Berlin-Hamburg-Münster.

Schuler, C. 1999. 'Special report from Sierra Leone'. 15 September. *National Post*, p. A14.

Search for Common Ground. 2006. 'Key findings from bike riders in Sierra Leone'. Retrieved 18 February 2009 from www.sfcg.org/Programmes/sierra/pdf/bike.pdf

Sela-Shayovitz, R. 2007. 'Suicide bombers in Israel: Their motivations, characteristics, and prior activity in terrorist organizations'. *International Journal of Conflict and Violence* 1(2): 160–8.

Shahar, S. 1990. *Children in the Middle Ages.* New York: Routledge.

Sharkey, D. 2008. *Education, Violence and Resilience in War-Affected Girls in Sierra Leone: An Ecological Case Study.* Unpublished PhD dissertation, University of Ottawa.

Shaw, R. 2002. *Memories of the Slave Trade.* Chicago: University of Chicago Press.

Shepler, S. 2003. 'Educated in war: The rehabilitation of child soldiers in Sierra Leone'. In *Conflict Resolution and Peace Education in Africa*, ed. E. Uwazie. New York: Lexington Books.

—— 2004. *The Social and Cultural Context of Child Soldiering in Sierra Leone*. Oslo: PRIO.

—— 2005. 'The rites of the child: Global discourses of youth and reintegrating child soldiers in Sierra Leone'. *Journal of Human Rights* 4: 197–211.

Sideris, T. 2002. 'Rape in war and peace: Social context, gender, power and identity'. In *The Aftermath: Women in Post-Conflict Transformation*, eds. S. Meintjes, A. Pillay and M. Turshen. New York: Zed Books.

Sieber, J. 1993. 'The ethics and politics of sensitive research'. In *Researching Sensitive Topics*, eds. R. Lee and C. Renzetti. London: Sage.

Sierra Leone Truth and Reconciliation Commission. 2004. *Witness to Truth: Report of the Sierra Leone Truth and Reconciliation Commission*. Available at www.trcsierraleone.org/drwebsite/publish/index.shtml

Silberfein, M. 2004. 'The geopolitics of conflict and diamonds in Sierra Leone'. *Geopolitics* 9(1): 213–41.

Singer, P. W. 2003. *Corporate Warriors: The Rise of the Privatized Military Industry*. Ithaca, NY: Cornell University Press.

—— 2005a. 'Child soldiers: The new faces of war'. Retrieved 25 April 2007 from www.brookings.edu/articles/2005/winter_islamicworld_singer.aspx

—— 2005b. *Children at War*. New York: Pantheon Books.

—— 2006. 'The new children of terror'. In *The Making of a Terrorist*, ed. J. Forest. Westport, CT: Praeger Security International.

Sirajsait, M. 2004. 'Have Palestinian children forfeited their rights?' *Journal of Comparative Family Studies* 35(2): 211–28.

Skinner, E. 1999. 'Child soldiers in Africa: A disaster for future families'. *International Journal on World Peace* 16(2): 7–22.

Small Arms Survey. 2007. *Guns and the City*. Geneva: Small Arms Survey.

—— 2009. *Shadows of War*. Cambridge: Cambridge University Press.

Smillie, I., L. Gberie and R. Hazleton. 2000. *The Heart of the Matter. Sierra Leone, Diamonds, and Human Security*. Ottawa: Partnership Africa Canada.

Snow, D. 1996. *Uncivil Wars: International Security and the New Internal Conflicts*. London: Lynne Rienner Publishers.

Solomon, Z. 1993. *Combat Stress Reaction: The Enduring Toll of War*. New York: Plenum Press.

Spear, J. 2002. 'Disarmament and demobilization'. In *Ending Civil Wars: The Implementation of Peace Agreements*, eds. S. Stedman, D. Rothchild and E. Cousens. Boulder, CO: Lynne Rienner Publishers.

Special Court for Sierra Leone. 2002. 'Special Court Prosecutor says he will not prosecute children'. Press release, 2 November. Retrieved 13 October 2008 from www.sc-sl.org/Press/prosecutor-110202.pdf

2008b. 'Appeals Chamber overturns convictions, Civil Defence Forces leaders'. Outreach and Public Affairs Office, press release. Retrieved 13 October 2008 from www.sc-sl.org/Press/pressrelease-052808.pdf

Specker, L. 2008. *Reintegration Phase of DDR Processes*. The Hague: Netherlands Institute of International Relations.

Stacey, J. 1991. 'Can there be a feminist ethnography?' *Women's Studies International Forum* 11: 21–7.

Stark, L. 2006. 'Cleansing the wounds of war: An examination of traditional healing, psychosocial health and reintegration in Sierra Leone'. *Intervention* 4(3): 206–18.

Stasiulis, D. 1993. '"Authentic voice": Anti-racist politics in Canadian feminist publishing and literary production'. In *Feminism and the Politics of Difference*, eds. A. Yeatman and S. Gunew. Sydney: Allen and Unwin.

Statistics Sierra Leone. 2005. *Sierra Leone Integrated Household Survey 2003–2004*. Freetown: Statistics Sierra Leone.

Staub, E. 1989. *The Roots of Evil: The Origins of Genocide and Other Group Violence*. New York: Cambridge University Press.

Stavrou, V. 2004. *Breaking the Silence: Girls Abducted During Armed Conflict in Angola*. Report for the Canadian International Development Agency.

Stohl, R. 2002a. 'Children in conflict: Assessing the optional protocol'. *Conflict, Security and Development*, 2(2): 135–40.

2002b. 'Targeting children: Small arms and children in conflict'. *The Brown Journal of World Affairs* 9(1): 281–92.

Sykes, G. and D. Matza. 1957. 'Techniques of neutralization: A theory of delinquency'. *American Sociological Review* 22(6): 664–70.

Thapar-Bjorkert, S. and M. Henry. 2004. 'Reassessing the research relationship: Location, position and power in fieldwork accounts'. *International Journal of Social Research Methodology* 7(5): 363–81.

The Fund for Peace. 2007. *The Failed States Index 2007*. Retrieved 26 May 2008 from www.foreignpolicy.com/story/cms.php?story_id=3865&page=7

The Hindu News Update Service. 2008. 'LTTE got new method of child recruitment, Lanka tells UN'. 25 February.

*The Independent*. 1993. 'Liberian boy soldiers leave a swathe of ruin'. 27 March. 2007. 'From child soldier to poster boy'. 22 January.

*The Los Angeles Times*. 1999. 18 October. p. 18A–11.

*The Montreal Gazette*. 1999. 'Drug crazed child soldiers kill like unfeeling robots'. 9 August.

*The Ottawa Citizen*. 1998. 13 May. p. A15.

*The San Francisco Chronicle*. 2007. 'Once a drugged child soldier, Beah reclaims his soul'. 27 February.

Thomas, N. and C. O'Kane. 1998. 'The ethics of participatory research with children'. *Children and Society* 12(5): 336–48.

Thorpe, C. 2002. 'Statement at the UN Special Session on Children'. New York: United Nations.

Tidwell, A. 2004. 'Conflict, peace, and education: A tangled web'. *Conflict Resolution Quarterly* 21(4): 463–70.

Troyer, K. 2005. 'The mental health needs of child soldiers in Uganda: A case study of structural violence'. *The Applied Anthropologist* 25(2): 135–46.

Twagiramariya, C. and M. Turshen 1998. '"Favours" to give and "consenting" victims: The sexual politics of survival in Rwanda'. In *What Women Do in Wartime: Gender and Conflict in Africa*, eds. M. Turshen and C. Twagiramariya. London: Zed Books.

Twum-Danso, A. 2003. *Africa's Young Soldiers: The Co-Option of Childhood*. Retrieved 9 February 2008 from www.iss.co.za/Pubs/Monographs/No82/Content.html

Ukeje, C. 2003. 'Sierra Leone: The long descent into civil war'. In *Civil Wars, Child Soldiers, and Post-Conflict Peace Building in West Africa*, ed. A. Sesay. African Strategic and Peace Research Group.

Ungar, M. and E. Teram. 2000. 'Drifting toward mental health: High-risk adolescents and the process of empowerment'. *Youth and Society* 32: 228–52.

UNICEF. 2001. 'Small arms and children: UNICEF fact sheet'. Available at www.un.org/Depts/dda/CAB/smallarms/presskit/sheet5.htm

2004. *From Conflict to Hope: Children in Sierra Leone's Disarmament, Demobilization and Reintegration Programme*. New York: UNICEF.

2005. *The Disarmament, Demobilisation and Reintegration of Children Associated with the Fighting Forces: Lessons Learned in Sierra Leone 1998–2002*. Dakar: UNICEF.

2007. 'The Paris Principles. Principles and guidelines on children associated with armed forces or armed groups'. February. Retrieved 8 September 2009 from www.unhcr.org/refworld/docid/465198442.html

2008. *State of the World's Children*. New York: UNICEF.

UNICEF Sierra Leone. 2005. *Education Programme*. Retrieved 14 October 2008 from www.dac-sl.org//encyclopedia/4_part/4_2/icef_edu_may05.pdf

United Nations. 1999. *Small Arms*. Geneva: United Nations Publications.

2005. *Sierra Leone – UNAMSIL – Background*. Retrieved 13 December 2007 from www.un.org/Depts/dpko/missions/unamsil/background.html

2006. *Integrated Disarmament, Demobilization and Reintegration Standards*. Retrieved 15 October 2008 from www.unddr.org/iddrs/framework.php

2007. 'Ten years on, Machel Review cites continued abuse against children in conflicts'. UN press release, 17 October. Retrieved 13 October 2008 from www.un.org/children/conflict/pr/2007–10–17167.html

United Nations Commission on Human Security. 2003. *Human Security Now: Protecting and Empowering People*. New York: United Nations Commission on Human Security.

United Nations Development Programme. 2008a. *Human Development Index Rankings. Statistical Update 2008/2009*. Retrieved 24 February 2009 from www.hdr.undp.org/en/statistics/

2008b. *Draft Country Programme Document for Sierra Leone 2008–2010*. Retrieved 15 October 2008 from www.undp.org/africa/programmedocs/ sierra%20leone%20CPD%20-%202008–2010%20_english.pdf

2008c. 'UNDP and World Food Programme conclude US$1M youth employment agreement'. Retrieved 26 October 2008 from www.sl. undp.org/4_media/Newsroom/undp_wfp_1m_project_youth.htm

United Nations News Centre. 2008. 'Strong link between child soldiers and small arms trade, UN experts say'. 15 July.

United Nations Security Council. 2007. *Report of the UN Secretary General on Children and Armed Conflict in Myanmar*. S/2007/666. 16 November. Retrieved 11 February 2008 from www.child-soldiers. org/regions/country?id=146

US Department of State. 2008. *Sierra Leone: Country Reports on Human Rights Practices 2007*. Retrieved 22 October 2008 from www.state.gov/ g/drl/rls/hrrpt/2007/100503.htm

Usher, G. 1991. 'Children of Palestine'. *Race and Class* 32(4): 1–18.

Utas, M. 2003. *Sweet Battlefields: Youth and the Liberian Civil War*. Unpublished PhD thesis, Uppsala University.

2004. 'Fluid research fields: Studying excombatant youth in the aftermath of the Liberian civil war'. In *Children and Youth on the Front Line: Ethnography, Armed Conflict, and Displacement*, eds. J. Boyden and J. de Berry. New York: Berghahn Books.

2005a. 'Agency of victims: Young women in the Liberian civil war'. In *Makers and Breakers: Children and Youth in Postcolonial Africa*, eds. A. Honwana and F. de Boeck. Trenton, NJ: African World Press.

2005b. 'Victimcy, girlfriending, soldiering: Tactic agency in a young woman's social navigation of the Liberian war zone'. *Anthropological Quarterly* 78(2): 403–30.

Utas, M. and M. Jorgel. 2008. 'The west side boys: Military navigation in the Sierra Leone civil war'. *Journal of Modern African Studies* 46(3): 487–511.

Van de Voorde, C. 2005. 'Sri Lankan terrorism: Assessing and responding to the threats of the Liberation Tamil Tigers of Eelam (LTTE)'. *Policy Practice and Research* 6(2): 181–99.

Van Gurp, G. 2009. 'Asset-based needs assessment: Paki Masebong and Gbongaleiken chiefdoms Northern Province, Sierra Leone'. Unpublished report.

Veale, A. 2003. *From Child Soldier to Ex-Fighter. Female Fighters: Demobilisation and Reintegration in Ethiopia*. Pretoria: Institute for Security Studies.

Warchild UK. 2006. *I Am Not Trash: A Call to Action from Child Soldiers*. Retrieved 9 February 2008 from www.crin.org/docs/I%20Am%20Not%20Trash.pdf

Wasswa, H. 1997. 'Uganda's children have been warped by war'. 20 December. *Kingston Whig Standard*, p. 16.

Watchlist on Children and Armed Conflict. 2008. *No Safety, No Escape: Children and the Escalating Armed Conflict in Sri Lanka*. New York: Watchlist on Children and Armed Conflict.

Watkins, M. H. 1943. 'The West African "bush" school'. *American Journal of Sociology* 48(6): 666–75.

Watson, A. 2006. 'Children and international relations: A new site of knowledge?' *Review of International Studies* 32: 237–50.

Weissberg, M. 2003. 'Conceptualizing human security'. *Swords and Ploughshares: A Journal of International Affairs* 13(1): 3–11.

Wessells, M. 2006. *Child Soldiers: From Violence to Protection*. Cambridge, MA: Harvard University Press.

West, H. 2004. 'Girls with guns: Narrating the experience of war of FRELIMO's "female detachment"'. In *Children and Youth on the Front Line: Ethnography, Armed Conflict, and Displacement*, eds. J. Boyden and J. de Berry. New York: Berghahn Books.

Williamson, J. 2006. 'The disarmament, demobilization and reintegration of child soldiers: Social and psychological transformation in Sierra Leone'. *Intervention* 4(3): 185–205.

Women's Commission for Refugee Women and Children. 2002. *Precious Resources: Adolescents in the Reconstruction of Sierra Leone*. New York: Women's Commission on Refugee Women and Children.

2008. *Country at a Crossroads: Challenges Facing Young People in Sierra Leone Six Years After the War*. New York: Women's Commission for Refugee Women and Children.

Wong, L. 1998. 'The ethics of rapport: Institutional safeguards, resistance and betrayal'. *Qualitative Inquiry* 4(2): 178–99.

World Bank. 2003. *Sierra Leone – Strategic Options for Public Sector Reform*. Washington, DC: World Bank.

2006. *World Development Report 2007, Development for the Next Generation*. Washington, DC: World Bank.

2007a. *Education in Sierra Leone: Present Challenges, Future Opportunities*. Washington, DC: World Bank.

2007b. *Sierra Leone: Youth and Employment*. Environmentally and Socially Sustainable Development Unit, West Africa.

Zack-Williams, A. 1999. 'Sierra Leone: The political economy of civil war 1991–98'. *Third World Quarterly* 20(1): 143–62.

# Index